CARE IN THE COMMUNITY: THE FIRST STEPS

This book is dedicated to all those people who will be resettled under the Care in the Community initiative.

Care in the Community: the First Steps

JUDY RENSHAW
ROGER HAMPSON
CORINNE THOMASON
ROBIN DARTON
KEN JUDGE
MARTIN KNAPP

Gower

Published by
Gower Publishing Company Limited
Gower House
Croft Road
Aldershot
Hants GU11 3HR
England

Gower Publishing Company
Old Post Road
Brookfield
Vermont 05036
USA

British Library Cataloguing in Publication Data

Care in the community: the first steps.
  I.Great Britain. Community health
  services.Great Britain.Department of
  Health and Social Security.Care in the
  community
  I.Renshaw,J.,1954-
  362.1'0425

Library of Congress Cataloguing-in-Publication Data
Care in the community: the first steps / J. Renshaw .. [et al.]
      p.   cm
  Bibliography:p.
  Includes indexes.
  ISBN 0-566-05737-9: $43.00 (U.S.)
  1.Social service--Great Britain--Case studies. 2.Mentally
handicapped--Care--Great Britain--Case studies. 3.Aged--Care-
-Great Britain--Case studies. 4.Community health services--
--Great Britain--Case studies. I. Renshaw, J. (Judy), 1954-
  HV245.C27 1988
  361.8'0941--dc19   88-25210
  Reprinted 1991

ISBN 0 566 05737 9

Typeset by Saxon Printing Limited, Derby.
Printed and bound in Great Britain by
Athenaeum Press Limited, Newcastle-upon-Tyne

Contents

Tables and figures

Preface

Few books appear with as many as six authors. Nobody would rationally contemplate involving five other people in the writing of a volume which includes both policy commentary and insight into practice, combines broad generalisation with minute detail, ranges from theory to empirical evidence, and — in the process — endeavours to distil the very varied experiences of 28 demonstration projects. Few writers would want to send their draft manuscript to 28 liaison officers to be pulled apart, and then to do it again with an amended version. And rarely is a book describing a research project published before the project has ended. The six of us named on the cover committed all these 'crimes'. We did so because the 28 demonstration projects funded under the government's Care in the Community initiative offer a wealth of valuable information on the resettlement of long-stay hospital residents in the community. That information is all the more valuable now that the emphasis on community care has spread nationwide, and given the speed with which many regional health authorities are planning to run down their long-stay hospitals.

The idea for the book germinated in mid-1985. At the time the research team comprised Ken Judge, Roger Hampson, Judy Renshaw, Corinne Thomason and Robin Darton. Ken moved from the Personal Social Services Research Unit to be the founding director of the King's Fund Institute and I took over management of the team in January 1986. Since that date all six of us have been involved in the writing and rewriting of this book. Overall, of course, some have been involved

1

more than others, whether it be through intensive fieldwork activity, planning and administration, data preparation and analysis, project management, writing or whatever.

A great many other people have contributed to the shape of the final product. Absolving them from all blame, we gratefully thank the avid readers in each of the 28 projects who corrected our many errors of omission and commission. Some of them clung tenaciously to their suggested amendments until we were able to dissuade them or until we took them on board. Usually it was the latter. Among those changes was our switch in terminology from 'mental handicap' to 'learning difficulty'. The latter term may not be free of all the criticisms levelled at the former, but it is less pejorative. A number of people at the Department of Health and Social Security made very detailed comments on our various drafts. We particularly thank Cyril Stone, Brian McGinnis, Peter Webb, Peter Wiles, Hazel Canter and Jenny Griffin for their encouragement and advice.

Of course, the monitoring and evaluative frameworks which surround the demonstration projects were greatly influenced by their basis in the PSSRU. Probably every Unit member has had some influence on our thinking and writing at some time or another. Our especial thanks are extended to Jane Dennett for fastidious copy-editing attention and preparation of discs for the publisher, to Paul Cambridge and Caroline Allen for corrections to the final copy, and to Rebecca Robson for secretarial support. Appropriately the manuscript for this book went to the publishers at about the same time that Rebecca headed for the maternity ward. Between them, the book and Rebecca seem to have dominated the PSSRU Care in the Community team's work for two and a half years — one as eventual output, the other as essential input. We wish them both well!

This book is dedicated to all of those people making the move from hospital under the auspices of the Care in the Community initiative.

Martin Knapp
PSSRU
September 1987

1. Introduction: the Care in the Community initiative

In 1983 the Department of Health and Social Security (DHSS) issued the *Care in the Community* circular. This was intended to help people unnecessarily kept in hospital to live in alternative settings in the community, where this is more appropriate for them. To this end the circular described further incentives — over and above those introduced during 1976 and 1977 — to encourage a transfer of responsibility from health authorities to local authorities and other organisations. Among other things, the circular recommended that a number of pilot or demonstration projects be established to investigate ways of moving long-stay patients out of hospital (DHSS, 1983a). Twenty-eight projects have each been centrally funded for three years — 13 in the first round which began in April 1984, and 15 in the second which commenced a year later. Most of the projects represent models of care for people with mental illness or learning difficulties, and elderly or elderly mentally infirm people. Together these pilot projects expect to provide services which will enable about 900 hospital patients to move into the community.

The projects

A total sum of about £19 million was added to joint finance funds over five years to support the programme of pilot projects.

The programme was intended to launch the initiative, explore and evaluate different approaches to moving people and resources into

3

community care, and build up experience which may then be disseminated. Projects were designed to identify and meet the needs of long-stay hospital patients who can be moved into the community. Those needs had to be specified and assessed in advance, and the wishes of patients and their families taken into account. Up to 100 per cent funding could be requested for capital or revenue expenditure or both. Revenue support was made available for each project selected for a period of three years on the understanding that the project would continue with local funding after that time if it was successful.

The projects deal with a variety of services catering for those who need different degrees of support and care. This includes residential care and day care provision, and support services for their families. Projects range in size from those which will involve nearly 100 clients, to those which cater for less than a dozen. The large projects all intend to make broad structural changes to the nature of the total service offered locally to the client group concerned. All projects are expected to take into consideration the wishes of clients and their families, where appropriate. Individual care plans should be made for everyone discharged from long-stay hospitals. These facets of pilot projects will be discussed in some detail in this book. The 28 projects are introduced and briefly described below.

Eleven projects are for adults with learning difficulties. In the *Bolton* project 80 people are leaving several large hospitals in the north-west to live in ordinary houses or with families in the Metropolitan Borough of Bolton. Day care is provided by the project in settings such as a farm or a college of further education and a variety of professional services are also employed.

In *Calderdale* 32 people in Fielden and Stansfield View Hospitals will move to a hostel and shared homes, and attend day care units, training centres or adult education classes. A resource centre will make advice and support available to carers, friends and relatives. The scheme will contribute to the programme of hospital closures.

Seventeen people from St Lawrence's Hospital, Caterham will move to community care in their home area of *Camden*. Four community groups will be set up, each based on a group house where the residents will have tenancy rights. The project involves a local voluntary organisation and a housing association.

The *Derby* scheme intends to move 40 people from Aston Hall and Makeney Hospitals into their own homes in the city of Derby. Support services and professional back-up are being provided and people will also make use of ordinary community facilities wherever possible.

In *Islington* eight people with learning difficulties will move from various hospitals into special flats. Support will be provided in a flexible manner, depending on the needs of clients at any time.

4

The Dis-Co project in *Kidderminster* will help 33 people in Lea and Lea Castle Hospitals to move into houses, hostels and group homes in various parts of the country. A training house will be a half-way step for some. Day care instructors will help to provide day placements and some work opportunities for clients.

The *Liverpool* project provides three group homes for 12 people from Olive Mount Hospital, with staff support. It is run by Mencap and Liverpool Housing Trust.

The *Maidstone* project will facilitate the movement of 50 people from Lenham and Leybourne Grange Hospitals into a range of facilities in the Maidstone district. The project provides training and support for clients and aims to promote self-advocacy and individual decision-making as far as possible.

Forty-five people in *Somerset* hospitals will move to core-and-cluster developments in Yeovil and Bridgwater. They will move to group homes after a period of rehabilitation in the training houses, which will also develop into resource centres for both clients and staff. The project is part of a broader, county-wide strategy of similar developments.

Ten people in *Torbay* have moved from Hawkmoor Hospital to a supported hostel in Newton Abbot. It is run by a voluntary agency, the Parkview Society.

The *Warwick* project will help approximately 40 people to move from large hospitals to core-and-cluster accommodation in the county. There are other similar local developments which will offer opportunities to compare experiences and progress.

One project is for children with learning difficulties. Three children have moved from Ida Darwin Hospital, *Cambridge* to an ordinary house in a residential area. Foster parents have been recruited, with additional staff to provide organised support and relief. The children will continue to attend a special school unit.

Eight projects are for people with mental illnesses. The *Brent* project provides rehabilitation training, housing and support for 60 people from Shenley Hospital in their home area. A variety of accommodation is available to suit individual needs, such as hostels, group homes and adult foster care. A resource centre provides an administrative base for staff and a setting for day-time and evening activities.

In *Buckinghamshire*, plans have been made for 100 people to move from St John's Hospital, Aylesbury to a range of supported accommodation. A day centre and professional support will also be provided.

In *Chichester*, 30 people will move from Graylingwell Hospital to a core-and-cluster scheme in Bognor Regis. Rehabilitation in the hospital is also an important part of the project.

The *Greenwich* project will provide supported ordinary housing for 16 people from Bexley Hospital. The staff team spend several months getting to know individuals and preparing them for the transfer.

The MIND project in *Waltham Forest* will provide ordinary housing for 18 people from Claybury Hospital. An extended process of getting to know individuals and preparing them is an important feature. Staff support and an on-call system are provided in the community, together with a day-time resource centre.

In *Warrington* 16 people left Winwick Hospital after a preparation programme, and moved into a hostel in the town. The project is run by a voluntary organisation — Warrington Community Care — but retains close links with the hospital and back-up services. A nearby day centre is provided by an associated voluntary organisation.

The *West Berkshire* project plans to provide community care for 50 people currently in Fairmile Hospital. It also aims to co-ordinate the existing services provided by health, social services and voluntary organisations in the Reading area. New facilities will include a hostel, a day centre and group homes.

Forty people will move to a range of placements in *West Lancashire* from Ormskirk General and Winwick Hospitals. A rehabilitation officer and team of support staff will help to find the most appropriate accommodation and day care services for individuals.

Three projects are for elderly people who are physically frail. In *Coventry* 17 very dependent patients in hospital will move into a sheltered housing development with enhanced staffing. Seventeen other places, funded by the local authority, will be available for less dependent people referred from the community. A range of support services and day care will be provided.

The *Darlington* project aims to move 62 people from hospital back to their own homes. An intensive home care support scheme is provided which uses trained assistants and volunteers. The care is co-ordinated by specialist case managers who have control of individual budgets and decide on the most suitable package of care.

In the *Winchester* project two sheltered housing schemes in Winchester and Andover each have five special flats for very dependent people from St Paul's and St John's Hospitals respectively. Extra staff support is provided for the occupants of these flats in addition to the warden and domiciliary services available to all.

Four projects are for elderly mentally infirm people. A residential home will be provided by Age Concern in *Camberwell* to enable 30 people to move from Cane Hill Hospital. A psychogeriatric support team will be available.

In *Hillingdon* 40 special places will be provided in five residential homes for elderly people. Extra staff will be available for these places.

The *St Helens* project will provide 20 places in a purpose-built home for people from Rainhill Hospital. The project will contribute to the run-down of the hospital. Day care will also be provided.

In *West Cumbria* 18 people from various hospitals are being accommodated in a home at Whitehaven. The home is highly staffed, and techniques of reality orientation and reminiscence therapy are provided for residents.

One project is for people with physical handicaps. Three long-stay hospital patients with severe physical handicaps will move to homes of their own in *Glossop*. A purpose-built unit comprises four self-contained flats, one of which is used as a base for care staff and volunteers providing around-the-clock support.

Further details about each project and the services which it provides are shown in the matrix which follows.

The first steps

The Personal Social Services Research Unit (PSSRU) at the University of Kent at Canterbury was commissioned to promote the Care in the Community initiative and to monitor and evaluate the pilot projects. *Care in the Community: The First Steps* describes the initiative and traces the early development of the projects. It documents how the projects have met the challenge of successfully engineering a transition from hospital to community care.

In Chapter 2 we briefly outline the policy background to community care over a number of decades. The rise and fall of the institutions are considered, together with some of the concurrent events and trends which have influenced developments over this period. A comprehensive analysis of policy is not attempted, but it is important to place current developments in their historical context. We then describe the Care in the Community initiative which emerged after a series of attempts to promote community services and improve collaboration between the various agencies involved. In Chapter 3 the role of the PSSRU is explained. We tell the story of the pilot programme, the selection of demonstration projects and the somewhat unusual involvement of a university-based research unit in its development. Chapter 4 takes a slightly broader look at current policies for people with learning difficulties and mental illnesses, and elderly people. The policies are outlined for each client group and features of pilot projects are described where they illustrate particular policy elements.

Matrix of projects

PROJECTS FOR PEOPLE WITH LEARNING DIFFICULTIES

Project	Total funding awarded	Initiated/led by	Hospitals of origin	Capital developments	Type of housing	Type of day care	Assessment and individual care planning	Type of staffing	Staff training	Management arrangements	Voluntary sector involvement
BOLTON Started in 1984. To move 80 clients	£1,700,000	SSD/NHS	Brockhall, Calderstones, Royal Albert, Newchurch, Swinton	£128,000 for land and buildings for rural training scheme	Range – adapted housing with staffed support, sheltered accommodation, family placements, other independent accommodation	Rural training scheme, education support tutors, other employment opportunities	IPP and key workers, principal care workers	Core support team, home core teams, education support tutors, rural training instructors, CMHN, SW, OT, PT etc.	Various workshops and courses staged. Induction course, Training Packs for care staff, professionals and managers	Project co-ordinators represent both authorities. Network co-ordination group	Volunteers to have a valuable role in resettlement process helping clients take full advantage of local community opportunities. Paid home care scheme
CALDERDALE Started in 1985. To move 32 clients	£1,027,992	SSD	Stansfield View, Fielden	£170,500 for purchase of hostel and equipping other homes and resource centre	Two 8-place houses, one 7-place, and 4- and 5-place houses adjacent	A resource centre. Use of local college of further education and ATC. Access to all community resources	Assessment by key workers, care plans chaired by social worker	All accommodation to have staffed support	Induction course 'Patterns for Living'. In-service training courses	Project committee, project co-ordinator, core team. Responsible to principal residential and day care manager (mental health and handicap)	Local volunteer bureau initiated through project, volunteers to befriend residents. Representation of Parents and Friends Association and MH Society.
CAMDEN Started in 1985. To move 17 clients	£529,220	SSD/CSMH	St Lawrence's	£153,070	Range – from small flats to houses via Housing Co-operative, Housing Association and Camden Housing Department	Access to all community resources. Special needs programmes to be created	Case reviews for first 3, others will have Individual Service Planning (ISP)	Team of project leaders and team of support workers	Attended various courses, conferences and seminars from training budget	Four team leaders to have operational responsibility, CSMH sub-group	Use of CSMH services and informal representation as CSMH is the project's managing agency
DERBY Started in 1984. To move 40 clients	£396,150	NHS/SSD	Aston Hall, Makeney	£52,000 for offices, equipment and alterations	Normal housing partly arranged through voluntary HAs	Total range available by use of existing services	IPPs, co-ordinators, operation in 4 different city sectors	Multidisciplinary teams, IPP co-ordinators, instructors, residential care staff	Training tailing off due to financial constraints. Some attendance at external courses.	Partnership Team reporting to JCPT. 2 sector groups. IPP co-ordinators	Residential facilities provided by Derby Mencap. No representation on the steering group but represented at Partnership and Local Development Group level, giving access to steering group
ISLINGTON Started in 1984. To move 8 clients.	£410,000	SSD	St Lawrence's, Leavesden, Queen Elizabeth	£135,000 for conversion and equipment	Shared or single flats in two houses provided by housing department	New day centre established, also uses ATC and educational facilities	Ad hoc, based on primary criterion of Islington origin. A new tailor-made assessment form is being introduced	Initially supported by residential social workers who may be withdrawn later. Support workers	3-week induction course and various in-service courses	Responsible to SSD	Good network of volunteer involvement in area and commitment to ensure voluntary participation in project. Plan to use volunteers to assist clients when attending adult education classes.

PROJECTS FOR PEOPLE WITH LEARNING DIFFICULTIES continued

Project	Total funding awarded	Initiated/led by	Hospitals of origin	Capital developments	Type of housing	Type of day care	Assessment and individual care planning	Type of staffing	Staff training	Management arrangements	Voluntary sector involvement
KIDDER-MINSTER Started in 1985. To move 33 clients	£470,562	SSD	Lea, Lea Castle	No capital developments	Using range of existing facilities and two health authority houses for assessment and training	Work experience, recreational schemes and variety of diversified day services. Instructors employed from ATCs	Via work of project resettlement team and hospital resettlement teams and day centre managers	Resettlement workers, part-time evaluation officer, training instructors, pre-discharge nurses	In-service training seminars, a range of workshops. Secondment to external conferences and courses – BIMH, etc.	Co-ordinating group of senior managers in health and social services. Project co-ordinator	Close working relationship with Mencap, yet no formal representation at present. Citizen advocacy scheme, separately funded
LIVERPOOL Started in 1984. To move 12 clients	£250,000	Mencap. LHT	Olive Mount	£6,000 for furniture	Three 4-place houses bought by Liverpool Housing Trust	ATCs and some further education facilities	Homes co-ordinator to get key worker scheme in operation	Houses have 24-hour staffing managed by a homes co-ordinator	Maketon evening classes. Input by dietician	Co-ordinating group of health, Mencap and LHT	Mencap and Liverpool Housing Trust have taken leadership of project. Volunteers will be used in addition to staff
MAIDSTONE Started in 1984. To move 50 clients	£712,000	SSD	Lenham, Leybourne Grange	£100,000 plus regional development capital	Adapted and staff support. Private and voluntary, family placement, shared living	Tailor-made to fit individual needs. Training workshops. Self advocacy, new resource centre, adult education, clubs, employment, SEC	IPP, weekly contracts, case managers and service co-ordination	Co-ordinator, evaluator, resource management teams, case management teams, CMHT, residential staff, part-time support workers	In-service training by joint tutor, plus external courses. Team workshops	Project co-ordinator. Joint advisory board	No formal links. Limited individual input
SOMERSET Started in 1985. To move 45 clients	£806,000	SSD	Sandhill Park, Norah Fry	£360,000 for two core and cluster houses	Core and cluster homes in Yeovil and Bridgwater	Three days per week at ATC or day centre	HALO, individual case review, hospital reviews, selection by hospital case review panels	24-hour support in core houses. Some support in clusters	In-house/in-service training programmes. Plans for joint training with HA. Specialist social service MH training officer	Responsibility with director SSD. Mental Handicap Action Team. Project Team. Joint Planning Team	No use made of voluntary sector yet. Considering working with Mencap for housing. Some limited volunteer input
TORBAY Started in 1984. To move 10 clients	£100,000	NHS	Hawkmoor	£125,000 for hostel	Hostel to be run by Parkview Society	Running of home, participation in general life of community if wished. ATC	Key worker called special friend with monthly IPP meetings	24-hour staffing	Implementation of staff training programme. Tap into joint MI/MH programme	Management Committee. JCPT	Almost exclusively run by voluntary sector. Not formally represented on planning committee

PROJECTS FOR PEOPLE WITH LEARNING DIFFICULTIES continued

Project	Total funding awarded	Initiated/led by	Hospitals of origin	Capital developments	Type of housing	Type of day care	Assessment and individual care planning	Type of staffing	Staff training	Management arrangements	Voluntary sector involvement
WARWICK Started in 1984. To move 44 clients	£524,000	SSD and Mencap	Chelmsley, Coleshill Hall, Weston, Abbeyfields	£530,327 including £125,000 local joint finance for purchase and adaptation of core and cluster houses	Core and cluster or hostel facilities managed by Mencap	SECs or more appropriate care as required	Local assessment form procedures adapted	Multidisciplinary selection and staffed homes staffed by Mencap employees	No project-specific strategy, King's Fund. SAUS, SSD 'living like other people' training courses. Local staff developed own packages; Open University 'Patterns for Living' material purchased	Management Committee Development Officer	Functionally the project is a partnership headed by local Mencap societies. Regional representatives of national voluntary groups also involved. Strategic planning groups locally, County level representation

PROJECTS FOR CHILDREN

Project	Total funding awarded	Initiated/led by	Hospitals of origin	Capital developments	Type of housing	Type of day care	Assessment and individual care planning	Type of staffing	Staff training	Management arrangements	Voluntary sector involvement
CAMBRIDGE-SHIRE Started in 1985. To move 3 clients	£36,000	NHS	Ida Darwin	£10,000 for setting-up costs, furniture and equipment for house	An ordinary house with four bedrooms	Children attend local special school	Case review forms built into IPP and case review locally	Professional foster parents	4 weeks induction. In-service training in response to encountered needs; plus evaluation sessions	Line manager, SSD, joint support group	Limited representation. Housing association house

PROJECTS FOR PEOPLE WITH PHYSICAL HANDICAP

Project	Total funding awarded	Initiated/led by	Hospitals of origin	Capital developments	Type of housing	Type of day care	Assessment and individual care planning	Type of staffing	Staff training	Management arrangements	Voluntary sector involvement
GLOSSOP Started in 1985. To move 3 clients	£147,000	SSD	Withington, Brockhall, Parkside	£115,000	Four flats, purpose-built, designed by Northern Counties Housing Association	Ordinary community opportunities in education, work and social areas	Active resident involvement in development of their care plans. Service co-ordinator will be case manager. Instructor will monitor care plans day to day	24-hour support from domiciliary staff, paid volunteers, warden on site	All staff and volunteers to train alongside nursing staff in hospital. On-going training in practical and theoretical aspects; co-ordinated by service co-ordinators	Multi-agency management group. Service co-ordinators and domiciliary staff employed by SSD	Planned involvement of voluntary sector, which is represented. CSVs will be used

PROJECTS FOR PEOPLE WITH MENTAL ILLNESS

Project	Total funding awarded	Initiated/led by	Hospitals of origin	Capital developments	Type of housing	Type of day care	Assessment and individual care planning	Type of staffing	Staff training	Management arrangements	Voluntary sector involvement
BRENT Started in 1984. To move 60 clients	£1,029,000	NHS/SSD	Shenley	£90,000 for renovation and possible purchase of group home facilities	Core and cluster principle – hostel, group homes, bed-sitters, adult home-finding, support to families	Core unit (resource centre) will provide 15 hours per day drop-in facility	Regular case reviews – multidisciplinary team	Use of all disciplines and voluntary sector, staffed and unstaffed provision	Four induction courses, various topics. Training seminars plus normal professional supervision	Management group representatives, NHS and SSD, rehabilitation co-ordinator, community project manager	Help from Brent Community Transport, Irish Advisory Service, Shape Ticket Scheme, Community Relations Council plus local church, ethnic groups. MIND members of management group
BUCKS Started in 1984. To move 65 clients	£994,000	NHS	St John's	£632,000 for hostel and day centre, £15,000 for conversion of 3 group homes	12-place hostel, supported lodgings, 3 group homes, other mainstream services	30-place day centre	Built into SSD/HA existing systems	Mainly use of staff in a group home/hostel and day centre with a contribution from social work staff	Variety of in-service training. Formal pilot-project training and joint training just begun.	JCPT sub-group for MI and project co-ordinator, joint funded	Voluntary sector input through Guideposts Trust bed sit development and TocH Friendship circles. Representation on JCPT sub-group and other planning and advisory groups.
CHICHESTER Started in 1984. To move 30 clients	£827,000	NHS	Graylingwell	£299,000 core house, £99,000 first cluster, £131,000 second cluster, £14,000 activity centre	Core house and two cluster houses	Day activity centre	Conducted by CRT. Some social services input via social worker member of CRT.	24-hour staffing and housekeeper in core house, visits from members of community rehab team in clusters. One project worker	Nursing courses on rehabilitation, violence, diploma in nursing, plus psychotherapy in the community, health and hygiene, social skills, first aid	Core and cluster project team – joint committee, community rehabilitation team.	Some fronting for developments and administration but no formal representation on HA planning group as there is none
GREENWICH Started in 1985. To move 16 clients	£510,860	SSD	Bexley	Purchase of project base. Conversion of HA property	Ordinary housing obtained by HA	Daytime activities from project base	Intense team work with identified individuals, self-selection	Varied degrees of staffed support as appropriate. Mainly 24-hour cover with visiting support	In-house training with some attendance at external courses. Induction period, ongoing team training, support group, external courses on various topics.	Advisory joint steering group. SSD overall managerial responsibility. Project leader co-ordinates.	None yet but MIND services and National Schizophrenia Fellowship have representation on steering group
WALTHAM FOREST Started in 1985. To move 18 clients	£364,600	MIND	Claybury	£226,500 for day facility. Housing scheme funded by East London HA	Unstaffed ordinary 2-3 bedroom flats and houses	Adapted shop-front community facility plus normal community facilities	Self-selection. Getting to know clients individually on wards and formal hospital assessments. Continuous review of normalisation philosophy.	Multidisciplinary team employed by MIND, on-call service evenings and weekends, portable 'phone system	Staff support meetings and personal external supervision	Project co-ordinator reports to a joint MIND, SSD, DHA committee	Managed by MIND Waltham Forest Company, limited by guarantee

PROJECTS FOR PEOPLE WITH MENTAL ILLNESS continued

Project	Total funding awarded	Initiated by	Hospitals of origin	Capital developments	Type of housing	Type of day care	Assessment and individual care planning	Type of staffing	Staff training	Management arrangements	Voluntary sector involvement
WARRINGTON Started in 1984. To move 16 clients	£504,000	Warrington Community Care	Winwick	£424,000 conversion	16-place staffed hostel	Day centre weekdays and Sundays, IT centre at hospital, other community resources	Each key-worker has responsibility for 4 clients. A care co-ordinator has overall responsibility for care plans	24-hour staffing	Formal induction course, placement in other agencies involved, on-the-job training	Care co-ordinator, Warrington Community Care – a voluntary organisation promoted by the North West Fellowship. The committee of representatives from NWF, Grosvenor HA, Warrington HA and SSD Treasurer	Managed by WCC. Care co-ordinator reports to committee of WCC and is responsible for creating and maintaining links with other agencies and community resources
WEST BERKSHIRE – THE READING PROJECT Started in 1985. To move 50 clients	£537,790	SSD	Fairmile	£307,500 for day facility and equipment	15-place staffed group home, staffed hostels, supported group homes, existing hostels and sheltered accommodation	New 35-place treatment unit. Other community resources	Assessment committee – principal psychologist, senior nurse and social worker accountable to monitoring committee	24-hour staffing in hostel, multidisciplinary teams and day treatment unit staff	On-site joint training planned, attendance at seminars and workshops, visits to other hospitals	Joint project management group, project manager responsible to SSD	Voluntary service organiser, MIND chairman represents all voluntary organisations. HA and Richmond Fellowship
WEST LANCASHIRE Started in 1985. To move 40 clients	£191,800	SSD	Ormskirk General and Winwick	£22,500 to furnish rented accommo-dation, for office equipment	Range – supported or independent flats, family placements, etc	Social club, leisure centre, educational and recreational schemes. Use of existing day centre	IPP workshop in late spring/early summer. Workshop in April. Rehab assessments in hospital with clients and other staff relating to IPP	Community team headed by rehabilitation officer, staff provide a caring service 8 a.m. -11 p.m.	Induction and familiarisation period for all staff. Individually tailored programmes	SSD director responsible to Lancashire Social Services Committee, joint steering group, community team	Plans to work closely with Richmond Fellowship and hopes to work closely with the voluntary Skelmersdale Day Centre, involving W Lancs MIND and NW Fellowship for Schizophrenia

PROJECTS FOR ELDERLY PEOPLE

Project	Total funding awarded	Initiated/led by	Hospitals of origin	Capital developments	Type of housing	Type of day care	Assessment and individual care planning	Type of staffing	Staff training	Management arrangements	Voluntary sector involvement
COVENTRY Started in 1985. To move 17 clients	£303,110	SSD	Gulson, High View, Walsgrave, Whitley	Coventry Housing Committee have met capital costs	34-place very sheltered housing development	Not yet fully operational 20-place day centre, 7-day week, 2 care staff, voluntary workers.	Multidisciplinary admissions panel, key worker system, 3 monthly case conferences, unit head monitors care plans	24-hour staffing – care staff and daytime nursing staff	3 day induction, monthly meetings, care assistant courses, observation days, on-the-job training, in-service training, CSS training as appropriate	SSD overall responsibility. Joint advisory panel. Officer-in-charge responsible to SSD	Little use. Centre planned for the future. No representation at present. Individual volunteer input.
DARLINGTON Started in 1985. To move 54 clients	£930,000	NHS/SSD	Darlington Memorial, Greenbank	£30,000 for aids and adaptations	Domiciliary support to families and clients in own homes. Ordinary housing and HA property	Access to community services not supplied by project	Multidisciplinary team. Individual care plans drawn up at assessment meetings. Regular reviews to modify plans, responsibility of service managers	Home care assistants provide a maximum of 9 hours per 2 clients per day	Home care assistants training. Assessing project management team training needs	Joint co-ordinating group. Project manager day-to-day responsibility. Service Manager networking re care plans	Housing associations provide accommodation for a few clients
WINCHESTER Started in 1984. To move 10 clients	£135,000	NHS	St Pauls, St Johns	£5,000 for minor capital expenditure	Two very sheltered housing schemes	A warden and access to normal community services	Hospital consultants, ward staff, project community nurse	24-hour on-call system, additional 4 hours care per day from care attendants	Training according to experience/need in situ in hospital and community	Winchester multi-agency steering group and Andover separate group convened to voluntary Housing Society	Hampshire Voluntary HA in Andover

PROJECTS FOR ELDERLY MENTALLY INFIRM PEOPLE

Project	Total funding awarded	Initiated/led by	Hospitals of origin	Capital developments	Type of housing	Type of day care	Assessment and individual care planning	Type of staffing	Staff training	Management arrangements	Voluntary sector involvement
CAMBERWELL Started in 1985. To move 30 clients	£1,206,341	Age Concern	Cane Hill	£1,206,341 for purchase and adaptation of property	Specialist residential home of 3 units of 10 places each, operational end 1988	Based on care plans, utilising volunteers, relatives and paid local people. Support and bereavement counselling for relatives	Multidisciplinary core team – selection. Individual care planning	Core team of health service staff to provide protection and support	Investigating training needs	Managed by Age Concern via a management subcommittee	Southwark Age Concern will manage home and provide access to services for residents
HILLINGDON Started in 1985. To move 40 clients	£753,000	SSD	St Bernards, Hillingdon, Harefield, Hayes Cottage, St Johns, Mount Vernon	£380,000 development of all old people's homes and creation of EMI units	5 special EMI units attached to existing OPHs	Social care to enable enjoyment of common domestic practices and experiences	Multidisciplinary discussion about selection. Multidisciplinary team to prepare care plans, monitor progress via a key worker review scheme	Additional staff to work in units and home care staff to help clients live at home	1 week induction course by SSD. Day placements for staff	Overall responsibility SSD and project co-ordinating group	Indirect support to informal carers, some voluntary involvement appropriate in certain situations
ST HELENS Started in 1985. To move 20 clients	£763,931	NHS	Rainhill	£339,430 to build and furnish home	30-place residential home. Building commenced March 1987, operational mid-1988	Clients to receive health care from the primary health care team as used in other local old people's homes	Multidisciplinary assessment and preparation of care plan with six-monthly reviews	Staffing will be based on the staffing levels of local authority homes of 50-55 places, reflecting greater levels of dependency	2 weeks induction training plus ongoing training. Training day, team building, reality orientation	Overall responsibility through the JCPT. Residential services officer responsible to JCPT and officer-in-charge responsible to RSO	More voluntary sector involvement anticipated, operational policy forthcoming
WEST CUMBRIA Started in 1984. To move 18 clients	£332,000	SSD	Garlands, West Cumberland, Workington Infirmary	£82,000 for conversion and equipment	18-place home, formerly half-way house for MI	24-hour reality orientation. Use of day centre, relatives, neighbours and friends.	Each client has a key worker and officer. Staff are case managers.	24-hour staffing – enhanced staffing	2 weeks induction to familiarise staff with philosophy of home. Individual training programmes on understanding dementia, reality orientation, reminiscence therapy and achievement of maximum client independence	SSD project co-ordinator, officer-in-charge	Not at present but possibly in the future. No representation

14

The remaining chapters examine specific features of the demonstration projects, some of the problems they face and some of the ways which have been found to overcome them. Chapter 5 takes a look at the management of the pilot projects, in particular the collaboration of different agencies to produce a community care package. Public relations have been important for all projects. They can make or break a new service development, particularly in the crucial area of local acceptance of people with a people with learning difficulties or mental illness. We consider public relations in Chapter 6.

In Chapter 7 case management is introduced. Case management programmes have developed in North America as a means of organising and co-ordinating services for people in need of long-term support. We describe the principles and some of the questions for practice which are raised. Chapter 8 continues the case management theme but focuses on the Care in the Community programme. It examines the ways in which projects have decided to organise the care of individual clients and some of the difficulties they have encountered.

In Chapter 9 the logistics of providing accommodation and other support services for people moving from hospital are discussed. This discussion is based on the experiences of the pilot projects as they began to get under way. We then turn, in Chapter 10, to a consideration of the economic and financial aspects of projects and community care services generally. We look at financial issues which surround work in this area and some of the principles which lie behind the assessment of service costs. This chapter introduces the costing methodology we are employing in our evaluation of the Care in the Community projects. We continue this theme in the next chapter, where we describe the activities of the PSSRU in monitoring and evaluation of the programme. Our research framework and its development from the theoretical 'production of welfare' model are presented in some detail. A second book will be published after the end of the initiative in 1988 and will describe the comprehensive results of the evaluation.

Finally, Chapter 12 points out some of the issues which have emerged from the pilot programme so far, which have either caused problems or which seem to be particularly noteworthy. We hope that documentation of issues in this way will provide some guidelines for others who attempt community care developments.

2. The genesis of Care in the Community

Community Care: The historical context

The care of elderly people, and people with a mental illness or learning difficulties, has overwhelmingly been in the community, by the community, for centuries. But during all of that time there have also been many varieties of institutional provision. Since the second world war there has been growing doubt as to the proper place of such care, building on what was even then a long tradition of advocacy of moving people out of institutions. As early as 1900 the Local Government Board recommended 'more homely' accommodation than the work-house (Walker, 1982). In the 1920s the Royal Commission on Lunacy and Mental Disorder promoted the appointment of almoners (medical social workers) to help keep families together. The Curtis Committee, whose proposals were formalised in the 1948 Children's Act, advocated the care of children in private homes or small groups rather than in large institutions.

Planned services — as opposed to informal community care — for people with mental illnesses and learning difficulties were for a long time dominated by the asylums and colonies established in the nineteenth century. Both society and the person with a mental illness or learning difficulties would, it was believed, be better off if the person could be removed to some isolated setting. Such a setting would afford protection from the evils of society and allow the person to lead a useful life. Society could avoid being swamped with 'defectives and idiots'. But a landmark in official attitudes was the Royal Commission on the law relating to mental illness and mental deficiency (1957), which is widely held to be the earliest reference to community care. Of course, comprehensive care includes the use of suitable hospitals where this is appropriate for particular individuals. The emphasis was no different from before; what was new was the concerted push to make it a reality by the introduction of new mechanisms to enable transition.

The term 'community care' has been much abused and over-used during the last 30 years. Its definition varies with the wishes of its user. It is sometimes taken to mean 'care outside of institutions' although the 1959 Mental Health Act refers only to 'local authority services'. Later the definition was expanded to mean obviating the need for institutions for some people by the provision of alternatives locally. As positive ideological arguments in favour of the concept developed, the term also incorporated positive moral connotations. It has recently begun to be understood to be more to do with the style of care than with its physical location. Community care in this sense is seen to be socially, morally and politically desirable.

On the other hand, community care has also picked up negative connotations over the years. Some have seen it as synonymous with public expenditure cuts and the decline of the welfare state. Concern over the burden on informal carers which community care involves has spawned an extensive literature. Community care thus might mean a lower standard of care, reduced state involvement and inadequate monitoring or regard for consequences. For many the term has become a political slogan, an ideal, a catchphrase. For the client, the day-to-day reality of community care may be a far cry from the ideological concept carried high by enthusiasts. Jones, Brown and Bradshaw state their view:

> To the politician, community care is a useful piece of rhetoric; to the sociologist it is a stick to beat institutional care with; to the civil servant it is a cheap alternative to institutional care which can be passed to the local authorities for action or inaction; to the visionary, it is a dream of the new society in which people really do care; to social services departments, it is a nightmare of heightened public expectations and inadequate resources to meet them. We are only beginning to find out what it means to the old, the chronic sick and the handicapped (Jones et al., 1978, p.114).

There has been much media coverage of patients 'dumped' on the streets with little regard for their needs. Whether true or not, such cases do not inspire confidence in the efficacy of community care or in the hope of ever translating the philosophy into practice. Its meaning was usefully broadened by Bayley (1973). He made the distinction between care *in* the community and care *by* the community, the latter implying the moral assumption of mutual responsibility. He was in favour of the latter, the former being in his view prone to many of the same faults as institutions. He advocated the organisation of a 'structure for coping' built up from statutory and voluntary services, and family, friends and neighbours.

The truth of the matter is probably that there is more agreement about the goals of community care than about what it means in practice. The day-to-day reality for many clients is a far cry from its admirable connotations in political banter, as Walker comments:

> Notwithstanding the expected gap between political rhetoric and reality in public policy, the division is remarkable for a policy which has for so long been officially considered to be central to the development of the health and personal social services, and which now occupies the centre stage in discussions about the future of these welfare services (1982, p.13).

Although official documents since the 1961 Hospital Plan have advocated a transition to community care, they have often been broad statements of intent with little direct guidance. A variety of factors, including funding differences between the health service and local authorities, have given the move little muscle in practice. The failure to implement community care, despite the continued interest in it, can only be understood in the context of trends in the development of policies for the care of the client groups concerned.

The institutional background

The system of care for chronically ill and disabled people was inherited from a period in which very different values were held. The Victorian era saw dramatic change and innovation. It also saw fear, strict moral codes and strong paternalistic views. The notion of asylum for vulnerable people became widespread:

> The old asylums had two particular virtues according to nineteenth-century thought; they provided care and treatment for the sick away from the stresses of everyday life and they neatly resolved the conflict between the need to care for such people (charitable and Christian) and the desirability of isolating them from the rest of society. In a sense, the old institutions were a salve to society's conscience (Kenny and Whitehead, 1973, p.170).

Institutions were assumed to be an appropriate way of providing for people with disabilities of many different kinds. Mental handicap (learning difficulties) and mental illness were often confused, but different establishments were developed for people with these conditions.

Caring for people in a segregated environment has itself served to reinforce myths about illness, made it something to be suspected and feared, and sustained its mystique.

'Mental subnormality' (as it was called) was also a source of fear and self-doubt. Connections were suspected between the prevalence of mental subnormality and the dramatic upheaval of industrialisation. Perhaps there were limits to the extent of mankind's ability to develop, and the prevalence of subnormality was an indication of a reverse trend. Tolerance of unusual behaviour seemed to decrease. Mechanic (1969) notes that 'industrial and technological change ... coupled with increasing urbanisation brought decreasing tolerance of bizarre and disruptive behaviour within the existing social structure' (p.54, quoted in Scull, 1977).

A combination of such factors, in the general guise of a paternalism which would not allow poor unfortunates to be left unaided, resulted in the emergence of the asylums. They were built on a grand scale, involving huge capital investment. People labelled ill, inadequate or subnormal were locked away from the public gaze and easily forgotten. The public's conscience was eased knowing something was being done for the incurables, and segregation also allowed society to forget the existence of people with mental illnesses and disabilities. Since asylums were founded there was a consistent pattern of year-on-year increases in demand. This persisted throughout the first half of the twentieth century.

Institutions began to fall from favour after the second world war. The whole health care and hospital system of the country was, of course, much reformed both by the war itself and by the various social changes thereafter. The war changed many long-stay hospitals. Those with wards which were used to house the injured lost some of the stigma of segregation by the mere entry of other categories of people. This was not enough to stem the growth of provision: the hospital population in England and Wales peaked at 148,000 in 1954, a rate of 33.45 per 10,000 people (Scull, 1977).

In the mid-1950s there was an abrupt reversal of the historical trend. Commentators place different weights on the factors involved. New ideas about the treatment of psychiatric illness were coupled with the introduction of psychotropic drugs which could mitigate the symptoms of schizophrenic illness. In 1971, Sir Keith Joseph, speaking in a House of Commons debate of the drug revolution, accorded this the merit of curing people with mental disorder, whereas others such as Scull (1977) and Wing and Brown (1970) argue strongly that new patterns of release were observable prior to drug introduction. They suggest that the tremendous change which took place was due largely to alterations in administrative policies. Certainly, many would argue that the new drugs helped the policy of early discharge at the very least by making it more credible. The 1959 Mental Health Act freed the majority of patients with mental illness and learning difficulties from legal detention. It also set out a major role for local authorities.

There were also, as ever, resource constraints on service development. The Victorian and Edwardian buildings were beginning to deteriorate. A massive programme of re-investment would have been needed to keep the system running as it was. Barbara Castle was later to say that the money required was not a question of a few million pounds, but a question of thousands of millions over many years.

In 1961 the Minister of Health set the scene for the future when he announced that the acute population of mental hospitals was to drop by half in the next 15 years and the long-stay population ultimately to dwindle to zero. A 1961 circular to regional hospital boards instructed them to ensure that no more money than was necessary was spent on the upgrading or reconditioning of mental hospitals which in ten to fifteen years were not going to be required.

The 1962 Hospital Plan was to be the cornerstone of community-orientated policies. The Plan based its proposals for mental illness services wholly on a paper by Tooth and Brooke (1961). The paper recognised that there were problems estimating future bed requirements and that other factors might affect their predictions, but as Martin remarks: 'There must be few statistical enquiries either before or since 1961, that have so rapidly and unquestioningly been accorded the status of foundation of a new national policy as was the not very sophisticated forecasting of Tooth and Brooke' (Martin, 1984, p.7).

Many others have criticised the paper by Tooth and Brooke, and the Hospital Plan it generated, for the rudimentary nature of the quantitative forecasting and for their casual optimism about the future (although, to be fair, Tooth and Brooke's central prediction — that the number of in-patients would fall to about 1.8 per 1000 by 1975 — proved precisely accurate). There has always, for example, been serious doubt as to whether the implications of reduction had ever been seriously evaluated: 'The intentions underlying social legislation and administrative change are often debatable and sometimes morally questionable, but the consequences of implementation may be quite at variance with anything the legislators or administrators had in mind' (ibid., p.10). However, despite doubt about the rationale behind the dramatic change in direction espoused in the Hospital Plan, there were other currents favourable to a move towards community care prevalent at the time.

From scandal to cost-effectiveness

From the 1950s onwards there are clearly identifiable trends in the development of the policy of community care: the 1960s saw the emergence of an anti-psychiatry movement and anti-institutional views, at about the same time as scandals occurred over specific cases of ill treatment and mismanagement; the 1970s were dominated by major administrative and organisational change and the 1980s were governed by recapitalisation strategies and the cost-effectiveness imperative.

At the beginning of the 1960s there was a general feeling that asylums had become anachronistic. Psychiatry, previously a rather isolated branch of medicine, welcomed the closer links with more prestigious specialties offered by the proposed integration of services in a general hospital setting. For some doctors it was a preferred course of action, which bestowed enhanced respectability and status. The new ability to control some psychiatric conditions with the use of drugs had also given the profession more power. Care of people with learning difficulties, however, was moving in a different direction; research was beginning to show the benefits of care in smaller residential units or in family settings. The emphasis in care for these people shifted away from the medical model towards one of learning and development.

The instruction to regional boards in 1961 to minimise spending on refurbishment and reconditioning meant that, over the next decade and beyond, the physical environment and structure of the hospital institutions fell further into decay. Other strands combined with the physical decay provided evidence of an 'irredeemably flawed' institutional system. Between 1959 and 1970 there was a series of major critical publications. These included Morris's *Put Away* (1969) and Townsend's *The Last Refuge* (1962). Particularly influential was Goffman's *Asylums* (1961) which introduced the idea of the 'total institution' and its effects on inmates. The general attack on psychiatric hospitals and other residential institutions was given a boost by the publication of *Sans Everything* by Robb (1967), a compilation of reports of cruel acts against geriatric patients. There followed an exposé in the *News of the World* of conditions at Ely Hospital in Cardiff and a spate of scandals about cruelty, squalor and neglect. The resultant sequence of inquiries led to the creation of the Hospital Advisory Service in 1969, with specific responsibility to visit and report on hospitals for people with a mental illness and learning difficulties.

In the late 1960s there had been a trend towards more intensive treatment in mental hospitals followed by rapid discharge. This resulted in a large increase in the number of psychiatrically disturbed people in the community. Local authorities had a statutory duty (under Section 28 of the National Health Service Act, 1946) to provide certain services, including some residential care and day services. In 1968 the Seebohm Committee reported (Cmnd 3703). It had been set up to review the organisation and responsibilities of the local authority personal social services in England and Wales and to consider what changes were

21

desirable to secure an effective family service. This was the precursor to a decade dominated by administrative and structural change, the spectre of management consultants, super-ministries and, above all, re-organisation.

The National Health Service (NHS) was re-organised in 1974. The new service did not provide well-integrated care for clients with long-term needs. The new social services departments (SSDs), established in 1971, were responsible for the social work functions of the old medical officers of health, but the health service was still responsible for health visits. Primary health care in the form of general practice retained a large measure of independence from the control of area health authorities through the establishment of family practitioner committees.

The services were also characterised by attempts to set priorities in a proper manner and an awareness of the limitation of resources. Both of these were highlighted in documents such as the consultative paper *Priorities for Health and Personal Social Services in England* (DHSS, 1976). Not unconnected was a preoccupation with planning: the same document allowed for the devolution of responsibility to local areas within a framework of national guidelines.

During this time the documents which still form the basis of provision for the main client groups were also produced. The White Paper *Better Services for the Mentally Handicapped* (Cmnd 4683, 1971) and the 1979 report of the Jay Committee (Cmnd 7468) both recommended development of community services and the run-down of hospitals. There has also been the Children's Initiative, focusing on moving children with learning difficulties out of hospital. The 1975 White Paper *Better Services for the Mentally Ill* (Cmnd 6233, 1975) lent strong support to prevention of mental illness, early recognition of problems, help for families, provision of suitable accommodation and housing, and social support. Education of the local community, which was to become more involved, was emphasised.

For elderly people, however, developments did not run in parallel with other services. Over 90 per cent of all elderly people have always been cared for in the community, but the demographic changes which have occurred over the last 20 years, combined with social changes, will impose an increasing burden on society. This phenomenon has been constantly addressed in a series of documents concerned with elderly people, such as *A Happier Old Age* (DHSS, 1978), *Care in Action* (DHSS, 1981c), *Growing Older* (Cmnd 8173, 1981) and *The Rising Tide* (Health Advisory Service, 1982). Each of these recognised the problem of meeting the increasing needs of growing numbers of elderly people in the community.

Official philosophy did not change in the 1980s. What did change (from 1979 on) was the style of government, which much affected the tone of public statements. The Conservative administration's social policy has been characterised by more than a degree of contradiction between intention and achievement: they firmly held an explicit belief in personal self-help, combined with an intention to reduce reliance on the state, and thus to cut public expenditure. In practice, largely but not solely because of unemployment, no previous government has ever had to directly support more people through the benefit systems. The result has been a considerable increase in public expenditure (Webb and Wistow, 1982). One effect of this dissonance has been that, whilst public policy-making has become gripped by the 'cost-effectiveness imperative' (Davies, 1980), the actual areas in which cost-effectiveness campaigns can even begin coherent targeting have been very limited. There has been something of a spotlight effect, with small discrete programmes being carefully monitored, whilst huge open-ended programmes utterly defy restraint. A system at cross-purposes is apparent where the two paths meet, for instance where unintended consequences of changes in the supplementary benefit regulations have a greater impact on the style of new developments in care than do well-planned but usually minor local or health authority initiatives.

The Royal Commission on the National Health Service reported in 1979. It suggested that community care policies had failed in a number of respects. *Care in Action*, a handbook of policies and priorities for the health and personal social services in England, was published in 1981. This document carried clearer guidance on the future of hospitals, suggesting closure plans phased over a ten-year period where hospitals could not provide a service reaching out into the community. Resources gained from closure were to be redeployed on the 'new pattern of health services'. The document identified four primary groups: elderly people, especially the very frail; people with a mental illness or learning difficulties; and people who are physically or sensorily handicapped. It also stressed the need for collaboration between health and social services.

Joint working and the birth of the Care in the Community initiative

The development of community services since the war has been paralleled by the development of central government thinking about the proper local organisational context for that development. 'Joint working' and 'joint planning' between health and social services began to be seen as necessary in the middle of the 1960s, and the emphasis on them has grown since (Wistow, 1982, 1983).

Joint finance was born out of a need for both practical and financial collaboration. The fundamental arrangement is a simple one: pressure on a number of different health service facilities could be relieved, and patients better cared for, if social services departments provided more appropriate facilities outside the health service. These services might even be cheaper into the bargain. But local authority budgets were also fully stretched, and it was therefore in everybody's interest for some portion of NHS money to be earmarked to pay for social services facilities. Many of those facilities were called 'community care'. The rhetoric of community care has been central to the debates which have surrounded joint finance and its administrative and service practice.

An obligation to collaborate was placed on health and local authorities by the 1974 National Health Service Reorganisation Act with the establishment of joint consultative committees (JCCs). The Act also redrew health service internal areas to match local government boundaries, without obvious regard for medical exigencies. Health and local authorities were to be allowed to furnish each other with a large range of goods and services, and this interchange was presented as an infrastructural base for the essential collaboration.

Moreover, the impetus within the health service to devolve to local authorities many functions which were not related to the care of acute patients waxed throughout the decade. This goal became a central tenet of the developing planning system for the NHS alongside a similarly burgeoning view that non-acute patients should anyway have a larger proportion of resources channelled towards them. There is an irony at the core of this. The strategy to devolve non-acute patients was acceptable to the medical view of life — since it concentrated medical activity on the acute services — but the acceptance of devolution meant, at least in principle, some hard planning for, and *financing of*, the non-acute groups. This of course was just the point as far as the non-medical planners were concerned, but the net effect, in principle, was to make use of the medical view of the world to re-organise the balance of health and social services expenditure away from a medical model.

There were clear reasons why local authorities were hardly likely to shoulder their new burden without hesitation. Community care cost money, and in certain ways care seemed to cost a local authority even more than it did the NHS, since the former paid loan charges on capital monies whilst the latter received allowance from central funds.

Other difficulties arose from the resistance of hospital staff, lack of agreement about which patients might be discharged, and the absence of consensus on models for services in the community. A further barrier was the weakness of arrangements established in 1974 for co-ordinating health and local authority planning (Wistow, 1983, p.34).

This stimulated the changes of 1976 and the introduction of joint finance; practical collaboration appeared to be hamstrung unless matched by arrangements for financial collaboration.

To encourage co-operation, various circulars in 1976 and 1977 set up the joint finance scheme, hand in hand with joint planning arrangements. Joint care planning teams (JCPTs) of senior personnel from the different agencies at area level were convened. Joint finance was the bribe, albeit at the tactical level, to promote strategic thinking about mutually beneficial joint objectives.

Although the fundamental concept of joint finance is simple, the history of the practice of joint finance is not without complexity, conflict and controversy. There is insufficient space here to discuss these in any depth, but a few points may be mentioned. First, joint finance has only been available for limited time periods in pursuit of limited objectives, and the receiving authorities have seen those limits as severe, distorting, and even dangerous. Local authorities had to provide continued support at a time of increasing financial stringency for schemes which were intended to benefit the health service as well as themselves (Wistow and Hardy, 1986).

In the DHSS's view, the main problem with joint finance was that, since eventually they would be left with the financial responsibility, local authorities had little incentive to ask for more projects. Consequently, the 1983 *Care in the Community* circular sought to overcome this disincentive by allowing health authorities to make annual payments financed out of hospital savings. (Most of the joint finance money goes to social services, although as the restraint on local authority expenditure has taken effect a growing proportion has been accounted for by transfers between health districts.) The period of partial financing by health authorities had been increased on a number of occasions. The new scheme meant that district health authorities could fund (out of their own money, not joint finance) the whole cost of transfer to community care where it was in the interests of patients.

Second, planning itself imposes costs on the agencies involved. Although 'take-up' of joint finance has been very good, the overall amount of money is presumably the same as *could* have been found for similar services via a different route. Such a scheme might well have been much cheaper administratively. The substantial time costs of joint finance negotiation provide little incentive for health authorities to involve social services departments in each and every stage of planning.

Third, joint finance has always been seen as part of a package which includes such major government aims as community care, preventive medicine and the priority groups strategy. These have had to become major aims precisely because, in the officially validated view, they were unpopular with powerful elements in the welfare, and particularly the medical, establishment. *The priority groups are called priority groups precisely because they have never been priority groups.* Many of the difficulties of joint finance have stemmed from broader difficulties of the policies which surround it.

There are two royal roads towards widespread community care. On the one hand present long-stay patients have to leave hospitals for alternative services outside. On the other hand, facilities have to be provided for people in the community, to stop them entering institutions in the first place, at least as long-stay patients. Needless to say, both strategies have to be pursued to reach the objective. Furthermore, there is little evidence that in the second half of the 1970s the DHSS, or anybody else, had any settled view on how to co-ordinate the strategies, although long-stay admissions to psychiatric hospitals have fallen considerably. There *is* much evidence that the arrangements as they then stood were very imperfect tools for the task. A main difficulty was one of administrative and economic logic.

The savings made at the margin of old inadequate institutions are likely to be much less than the costs of brand new community care even if it were the case that community care was cheaper when standardised for age, dependency and other factors. The joint finance scheme was designed to sidestep this by earmarking NHS money for the new community care, irrespective of whether that amount of money could be realised as savings in the original institution.

Furthermore, although the receiving agency may have an incentive for general co-operation with the original agency, it has no incentive for co-operation over any particular group of individuals. In the nature of the case, the receiving agency will want to spend the money on clients high on its own list of priorities, who may well be an entirely different set of people. This problem would be easily resolvable by a joint consultative committee where both sides had a veto on any plan they disliked, so long as all the money for a new project came through that JCC. All schemes would fit an equilibrium which involved the priorities of both agencies. But such was precisely not the case.

Joint finance was always partial, tapering and time-limited. The Department proposed in 1975 that joint finance should be made available as 'pump-priming' money to support up to 60 per cent of expenditure on schemes for a period of three years, after which the revenue from the health authority would taper out. This therefore favoured capital-intensive projects. After consultation with the local authorities, circulars were issued in 1976 and 1977 which enabled health authorities to meet the full cost of schemes for a period of seven years.

In relation to joint working, joint finance has had a positive, but only marginal, effect. Ferlie, Challis and Davies discuss the role of joint finance in the promotion of innovation in the care of the elderly, one of the main client groups affected.

> The introduction of joint finance can ... be justified in terms of producing limited and local improvements in service within the framework advanced with shifts away from continuing institutional care and towards earlier discharge, basic nursing care and multidisciplinary assessment. ... [The] evidence certainly does not support the more severe criticisms of the efficacy of joint finance. Indeed, these innovations were significantly more likely to display key indicators of good practice. However, there was no evidence of a systematic shift towards priority groups such as the elderly mentally infirm and the high bargaining costs associated with such innovation also have to be taken into consideration. Although best use is not always made of joint finance; nevertheless without such incentives there would probably be even less collaboration. An important question is whether the pattern of incentives and central inputs can be changed to promote such collaboration further and to develop the opportunities opened up by the joint finance initiative (Ferlie et al., 1985, pp.155–6).

The Comptroller and Auditor General's report on joint finance in seven area health authorities (1981/82) showed that most schemes had been instigated by local authorities, and had not been fully considered by the NHS as to the likely costs and benefits. The Public Accounts Committee also expressed some concern as to whether health authorities' approval and monitoring procedures were sufficient to ensure that NHS money was being efficiently spent in the interests of the health service (House of Commons Committee of Public Accounts, 1983). The DHSS, too, accepted that there was a need to improve the administration, documentation and financial control of joint finance. The *Care in the Community* consultative paper was issued in 1981 and the response to it confirmed overwhelming support for the concepts of joint planning and finance (DHSS, 1981a). As a result the government devised an additional new scheme directed at people currently in hospital and aimed at moving them out. This scheme was consolidated in the 1983 *Care in the Community* circular. The aim of the Care in the Community initiative is to help long-stay hospital patients unnecessarily kept in hospital to return to the community, where this will be best for them and is what they and their families prefer (DHSS, 1983a).

The basis for financial collaboration between district health authorities and local authorities was improved. DHAs are now able to make extended payments from their normal funds to help the move to community care although the arrangements for doing so vary from region to region. The qualifying conditions and time periods for joint finance itself have been extended in relation to projects for transfers from hospital to community care, and DHAs are now able to support education and housing for handicapped people.

Not surprisingly, these changes have not removed all of the difficulties and disincentives. Some of the problems of transferring funds to

27

local authorities, on the basis of rules devised by regional health authorities (RHAs), are described in Chapter 10. Many local authorities feel that they have been excluded from the formulation of policies which depend for success on their co-operation (Wistow and Hardy, 1986).

In addition, the new arrangements are not sufficient to encourage the diversion of persons with a mental illness or learning difficulties or elderly persons away from long-stay hospitals in the first place. Some local authorities and health districts have placed major reliance on social security payments — with all the long-term risks entailed — to fill the gap between payments based on hospital savings and the, usually higher, costs of community care. Joint finance money may also eventually become part of a local authority's base budget, and so liable for all the usual grant penalties.

Some recent statements

We should briefly mention the recent draft circular on joint planning and collaboration (DHSS, 1986a). This circular follows the publication of *Progress in Partnership* (DHSS, 1985) by a working group drawn from DHSS and health and local authority bodies. Its main proposals were:

1 Total resource planning: joint planning should embrace all the resources already available or planned including staff and finance, both capital and revenue, for the particular client group or service.
2 A strengthened role for JCCs, whose primary task in the longer term is to secure the production of genuinely joint strategic plans in relation to all main client groups.
3 Local joint planning teams with a balanced health and local authority membership should be established in place of separate health and local authority teams for services of common concern.
4 A strengthened monitoring role for regional health authorities.

But as the Audit Commission reports, 'In effect the draft circular is proposing the virtual amalgamation of health and local authority to all intents and purposes for the priority groups — but without changing the lines of responsibility and without changing the funding arrangements' (Audit Commission, 1986, p.106).

The report of the House of Commons Select Committee on the Social Services (1985) eschewed the temptation to offer any very precise definition of 'community care', but it strongly supported the philosophy of normalisation and emphasised the value of learning from international comparisons. One of the recurring themes of the report is that community services for patients with mental disabilities discharged from hospital are too frequently a mirage. The Committee feared that there was a real danger that British developments would mirror the US experience which 'warns powerfully against closing down one set of facilities, however imperfect, until there is a firmly established alternative set of facilities' (ibid., para. 18).

The government's response contains detailed replies to the 100-plus recommendations contained in the report of the Social Services Committee. Perhaps more important than these, however, is the spirited restatement of 'its commitment to the development of the integrated network of central policies and local services necessary for community care' (Cmnd 9674, 1985, p.2). Their conception of community care has been articulated in a way which serves as an indictment of those who imply that the principal objective of policy is to encourage economy as a goal in itself.

> Community care is a matter of marshalling resources, sharing responsibilities and combining skills to achieve good quality modern services to meet the actual needs of real people, in ways those people find acceptable and in places which encourage rather than prevent normal living ... This requires the better use of that large proportion of ... resources which is now locked up in the hospitals. A good quality community-orientated service may well be more expensive than a poor quality institutional one ... The aim is not to save money; but to use it responsibly (ibid., pp.1–2).

But practical achievement on the ground has been slow and uneven despite clearly stated central goals; the care that people receive is as much dependent on where they live as on what they need.

The Audit Commission report *Making a Reality of Community Care* (1986) has drawn attention to some fundamental obstacles which have shaped the slow and uneven progress towards community care:

- resource allocation;
- social security policy;
- organisational confusion; and
- inadequate staffing.

A number of problems arise in the funding of community care. First, there are few incentives within the NHS planning and resource allocation mechanisms to encourage the transfer of resources to social services departments and other agencies. Second, certain aspects of the local authority rate support grant system inhibit the expansion of social services. Third, an increasing proportion of joint finance (22 per cent in 1985–86) is used to fund unilateral health service developments. Finally, there is a severe shortage of bridging finance to cover the transitional costs of developing community services as old hospitals run down.

The unplanned explosion of social security payments to private residential and nursing homes has made a major impact on the financing of community care. Since April 1987, elderly and disabled people who fulfil the supplementary benefit criteria have been entitled to allowances of at least £130 per week (£147.50 in London) for residential care, but there is no test of need other than financial circumstances. As a result, the system has generated perverse economic incentives in favour of residential care which contrast sharply with the stringent conditions attached to allowances — such as attendance or invalid care — for people who remain in ordinary housing. Since the early 1980s, social security expenditure on residential care has grown at an exponential rate, reaching an estimated £500 million at the end of 1986 (Audit Commission, 1986).

Care in the community is a complex business. If services are to genuinely enhance the well-being of individuals and also to represent value for money then available resources have to be matched to identifiable needs in a very sophisticated way. The present pattern of services lacks cohesion and integration. There are both unnecessary duplication and yawning gaps. One of the main problems is caused by the fragmentation of responsibility and accountability across different agencies and tiers of government. Individual joint finance initiatives are rarely if ever linked to any form of multi-agency strategic planning.

Finally, perhaps the most important resources of all for the effective implementation of community care policies are the staff. 'Sound manpower planning and effective training are, therefore, essential. But unfortunately, both appear conspicuous by their absence' (Audit Commission, 1986).

The picture of community care development, of course, is not totally gloomy. There are a number of exciting innovations and experiments in different parts of the country. The Audit Commission report highlights successful schemes in Hampshire, Hastings, Hillingdon, Plymouth, Torbay and Wigan, but there are many others.

Generally, however, progress is very uneven and is likely to remain so unless dramatic changes in policy are introduced. A radical change in policy direction could include the designation of single-agency responsibility for particular client groups or unambiguous client-group budgets with purchase-of-service arrangements. Reform of the supplementary benefit regulations to facilitate better co-ordination with health and social services is also proposed. At the time of writing, the health and social care systems await the reports of Sir Roy Griffiths and Lady Gillian Wagner, on community care and residential care respectively. Action is awaited on the Firth Report on the social security funding of private and voluntary residential care (DHSS, 1987). By the end of the decade, the deliberations of these various people and the experiences registered in projects like those funded under the Care in the Community initiative may have profoundly altered the picture.

3.   The pilot projects and the role of the PSSRU

Animation and evaluation

One of the major reasons for the incorporation of a monitoring and evaluation exercise into the eventual Care in the Community pilot scheme was the concern expressed by both the Public Accounts Committee and the DHSS about the need to monitor the use of joint finance and to review the cost-effectiveness of community care.

The pilot projects are intended to demonstrate methods of developing community care services for former residents of long-stay hospitals, and to examine the processes and effects of such a move. They are to provide useful lessons to smooth the path of future enterprises in this field.

A somewhat surprising feature of health and social welfare in Britain is the relative lack of experimentation. Instead of using demonstration projects to prepare the way, radical changes have often been introduced universally and at short notice. The introduction of general management into the National Health Service following the Griffiths Report (DHSS, 1983c) is one of many examples which can be cited. The American Alain Enthoven expressed his surprise about the lack of experimentation in the health and social services.

> Bureaucratic forces in the NHS today drive for uniformity. Variation is equated with inequality and injustice. The idea of Districts trying something distinctly new and different, other than in response to orders from DHSS, is perceived as a threat to the Minister ... The NHS could

benefit greatly by the infusion of a spirit of experimentation, an appreciation of the value of variety. In order to develop and test the innovation in management and organization that will enable the NHS to do a better job, I suggest the NHS would benefit from making greater use of demonstration projects (Enthoven, 1985, p.27).

However, at the very time Enthoven was writing, some interesting developments were taking place. One of the least noticed social policy innovations of the Conservative government has been an increasing use of central initiatives of various kinds to stimulate innovation and change. Since 1982, no fewer than 13 initiatives have been launched by Ministers. These schemes vary considerably in their objectives and focus: the following list gives some indication of the range of interests covered: opportunities for volunteering; care in the community; getting children with learning difficulties out of hospital; drug misuse services; development of services for mental illness in old age; children under five; intermediate treatment; primary health care; helping the community to care; teenage smoking; AIDS; community mental health projects; and family planning and pregnancy counselling for young people.

But perhaps the most interesting feature to report is that many of them are being evaluated and it should be possible in due course to learn valuable general lessons about the processes of 'planning for change' in health and social welfare. The Social Services Committee of the House of Commons certainly took the view that the DHSS should be making every effort to learn general as well as specific lessons for policy and practice from the various projects. In its 1986 report, the Committee made a series of recommendations. For example, it stated that:

We recommend that the Department consolidates its experience of the initiatives currently underway and ... draw together the lessons learned from the launch of previous projects about their design, implementation, management and evaluation (House of Commons Social Services Committee, 1986).

The reply produced by the DHSS failed to respond in detail to this suggestion but it did state: 'The Government accepts the need to draw for the future on the lessons which are to be learned from the existing programme of central initiatives' (DHSS, 1986b).

It is in the context of these remarks that it seems essential to provide some account of the PSSRU's role in the evolution of the pilot project programme of the Care in the Community initiative. We will describe how the PSSRU set out to develop an information exchange and a monitoring system. But in doing so it will become clear that we also became key agents in the 'animation' of the initiative.

33

Animation is a term which is more familiar on the continent than in Britain, but at its simplest it refers to the process of co-ordination, development and support which enables an action programme to 'come alive'. It is crucial to the success of any major demonstration programme. One of the questions raised by the various central initiatives is how closely related the animation of the programme should be to its evaluation.

Launching the initiative

The Care in the Community initiative was launched in the spring of 1983. On 14 March 1983, the Minister of State for Health announced the intention to set up a programme of projects to explore ways of moving people from hospital into community care. Central financial support — top-sliced from the joint finance allocation — would be available in three tranches of three years each and totalling up to £15 million between 1983 and 1988. It was intended that the programme would be 'monitored and assessed' and the results made widely available.

The PSSRU involvement, however, had begun some months before the initiative was officially announced. During the autumn of 1982 officials within the DHSS were making arrangements for handling pilot project proposals. It was assumed that they would be received in three batches: (a) immediate submission in an advanced state of planning and only needing finance; (b) a further batch, to be submitted by the end of November 1983; and (c) a final batch, to be submitted by the end of November 1984.

It was expected, therefore, that the first proposals would arrive at the DHSS soon after the public announcement. For this reason the application process and the monitoring arrangements demanded urgent consideration. Thus it was that the PSSRU — as a DHSS-funded research unit — became involved.

Before describing the way in which the PSSRU contributed to the initiative as a whole, it might be enlightening to consider some of the influences which shaped the approach then and which have had a lasting effect. Perhaps the most important intellectual stimulus was the 'production of welfare' paradigm developed at the PSSRU (see, for example, Davies and Knapp, 1981), outlined in Chapter 11. Equally influential was an awareness of the crucial role played by case management in earlier projects, where resources were carefully matched to suit the varied needs of frail elderly people who might otherwise have been admitted to institutional care (Davies and Challis, 1986). The vital importance of individual care planning was reinforced by the findings of colleagues in other parts of the University about the need for 'key workers' in supporting the parents of children with learning difficulties (Pahl and Quine, 1984). Further important lessons had been learnt about the peculiarities of evaluating action-research projects by the ESPOIR team which had been responsible for the first EEC poverty programme (Room, 1983).

To return to the narrative, the PSSRU was initially invited by the DHSS to participate in two ways in the implementation of the programme of pilot projects. First, by developing ideas about the form of application by agencies for central funds. Second, by suggesting methods of monitoring the programme and exchanging information about them.

The application process was intended to provide information for two purposes: to help the Department decide whether or not it wished to support a particular project; and to provide a foundation for a common reporting framework for projects in order to monitor their progress. The application process took place in two stages: outline information at the preliminary stage was to be followed by a more detailed submission from shortlisted projects only. The detailed application form was drafted by the PSSRU. The choice of questions was influenced by both the Department's need for information on which to base its selection and by the PSSRU itself. The Unit had considerable experience of recent innovatory schemes for long-term care groups, developed by a variety of agencies, some of which were reported by Ferlie (1982; see also Ferlie, Challis and Davies, 1988). This knowledge was used in the application form in order to highlight certain features, such as project co-ordination and individual care planning.

On the monitoring front, our original intentions were to do two things. First, to establish an information exchange to identify, and disseminate widely, accounts of practices which enhance the effectiveness of care in the community. Second, to use routinely collected data, supplemented by some special collections, to make evaluative judgements about the performance of the projects. It was therefore assumed that all of the selected projects would agree to a common reporting framework, that key personnel would participate in regular information exchanges between all of the pilot projects; and that the researchers would be allowed access to more detailed information about clients and services where appropriate.

The information exchange was intended to provide support for project managers and workers who might otherwise become isolated within their own schemes. In this way new ideas could be introduced and problems more easily overcome. Previous experience at the PSSRU with the family of community care projects for elderly people (Challis and Davies, 1986) had shown that regular meetings of key workers could be enormously valuable in maintaining the momentum of project development. The exchange was also intended to provide ideas and information for groups outside the programme of pilot projects. Important features were the production of a newsletter with a wide distribution, organisation of regular seminars for project managers and key workers, and promotional activities such as seminar presentations.

The second objective was to undertake a set of more conventional monitoring and evaluation activities. The monitoring was to proceed at two levels. First, it was intended to make use of information routinely supplied by projects (including the initial application, annual reports of progress and data about client numbers and expenditure incurred). Second, it was hoped to obtain a more detailed account of the progress of clients in each project. This meant, at least, interviewing the case managers of clients about their progress and the resources they used. In addition, we hoped to make use of existing instrumentation to collect data about changes in client welfare.

From the beginning we recognised that achievement of these goals depended critically on the relationships established with the projects. Our ambition was to move the research framework as far as possible in the direction of the production of welfare model developed by the PSSRU. But it was not possible to be very prescriptive in the early stages because we did not know with whom we would be working or how much they might be able to help. In the event, we were able to adopt a reasonably sophisticated research design, and this is described in Chapter 11.

Getting started

On the basis of the proposals described above, in March 1983 the DHSS commissioned the PSSRU to undertake promotional and research activities in connection with the Care in the Community initiative. Two researchers and a secretary were appointed to work with an established member of the Unit.

While waiting for applications to arrive, members of the research team visited a number of progressive schemes for integrating former long-stay patients into local communities, some of which eventually became pilot projects. But it soon became apparent that the DHSS assumption about the existence of 'off the shelf' schemes waiting only for finance was false. By the end of June 1983 the team was encouraged to undertake some more promotional activities so as to identify and stimulate local activity. As a result the first issue of the Care in the Community newsletter was produced in the summer of 1983 in an attempt to advertise the initiative to the widest audience in as tempting a fashion as possible. We also decided to organise a series of regional seminars before the end of 1983 to further promote the initiative.

In October 1983, invitations were sent out to all regional and district health authority administrators and directors of social services in

Box 3.1
Care in the Community: criteria for pilot projects

1   First and foremost, proposals for projects should be for moving long-stay hospital patients into the community. In addition a reasonable spread of projects is looked for, both geographically and among client groups.

2   Projects should relate to identified long-stay patients to be transferred from hospital. Where community care places are funded, it will be advisable to determine in advance how the places will be filled as the original occupants vacate them. They could subsequently be filled by moving more long-stay patients from hospital and possibly also by people in the community in imminent need of hospital beds.

3   Projects should be designed to meet the specific needs of the hospital patients being transferred. They should provide for prior assessment of the needs of the people concerned and take their wishes and those of their families into account.

4   Projects must be recommended by the joint consultative committee and have the endorsement of all the statutory authorities concerned and their acceptance of responsibility for providing what complementary support services may be needed. There must be an undertaking that once support from centrally reserved funds ceases, a project will continue subject to the authorities being satisfied as to its effectiveness. In all other respects the guidance relating to projects for moving people out of hospital set out in this circular must be complied with.

5   Projects may provide both residential and other forms of care: for example, they might provide support services and day care to enable people with learning difficulties to move from hospital into ordinary housing, or provide a form of adult fostering. Projects for people with learning difficulties should not normally provide for both children and adults under the same roof.

6   For people with a mental illness a project should aim at helping those who do not need to be in hospital to find suitable residential accommodation, support and day care, according to their individual needs. The projects should address themselves to a variety of services catering for those who need different degrees of support and care. This would include residential and day care provision and support services for clients and their families. It should be planned jointly, involving health and local authority services and where appropriate voluntary organisations and should form part of a comprehensive district service.

7   Where residential provision of any care group is concerned, projects should preferably provide small homely units, though this need not exclude adaptations of existing local authority or voluntary home premises. However, siting should take account of the need to establish community links with access to the same health, education and social services, shops and transport as are normally available to other people living in the community.

8   A number of potentially relevant models of care already exist. Some are already well-established (e.g. staffed or unstaffed housing provision for the mentally handicapped). Others are in the experimental stage (e.g. Kent community care scheme for the elderly). Both tried and tested, and innovatory approaches might be adopted in the pilot projects. Plans for residential provision might usefully pay particular attention to avoiding institutionalisation, for example through units based on small-group living and emphasis on links with the local community, and variety and choice of activities. Support schemes linking very sheltered housing with packages of domiciliary care and involving housing associations and voluntary organisations providing the care element might be appropriate for some projects. These examples are purely illustrative of the wide scope for developing imaginative approaches to caring for people moving out of hospital.

England to attend the regional seminars. These had three main objectives: to clarify any remaining doubts about the meaning of the circular and the allocation of funds; to outline the role of the PSSRU and what information would be expected from projects for monitoring and evaluation; and to gain an overall impression of local reactions to the circular, the projects it had catalysed, and also to discover which embryo plans should be encouraged.

A series of five regional seminars were well attended by health and local authority representatives, both members and officers. They gave the DHSS officials an opportunity to explain fully the details of the Care in the Community programme, and to discuss individual projects with representatives. By now the DHSS was being inundated with outline proposals. No submissions had been received early enough for a 1983/84 start, but by Christmas 1983 applications for about 110 projects had arrived.

The programme of pilot projects had therefore been reduced to two rounds. The immediate task was the selection of the first group. This involved various divisions within the Department — including client group teams and regional representatives such as the social work service — considering the applications in the light of criteria specified in the original circular (see Box 3.1) and forwarding their comments to the appropriate section. A shortlist gradually took shape. The PSSRU visited all of these projects to assist with the completion of the application forms and to pass on additional information. Some local managers, no doubt, used these sessions to deduce from PSSRU the features that DHSS might be looking for and may have shaped their plans accordingly. A number of meetings were also organised by client group teams at the DHSS to clarify and modify certain aspects of project proposals; the PSSRU also participated in these meetings. One, largely unintended (at least initially), consequence of what may have been a slightly unconventional process could have been the selection of projects somewhat moulded by an emerging consensus of what a good project would look like, in terms of its management, general feasibility and innovatory practices.

At least one of the projects selected by DHSS, the Maidstone scheme for people with learning difficulties, was in important respects intended to be a replication for the client group of the community care scheme for elderly people, developed jointly by the PSSRU and Kent Social Services Department (Challis and Davies, 1986; Davies and Challis, 1986). The research unit's influence was sometimes seen in applications, particularly in relation to the second round of projects, when some broad principles of project management had had time to emerge. PSSRU did not refrain from making strong suggestions, for instance about the usefulness of project co-ordinators. But we should point out

Box 3.2
PSSRU assumptions

1 There exist feasible cost-effective solutions outside hospital for long-term patients.

Whether or not it is possible to use realisable savings from closing hospital beds to establish viable community facilities for long-term care groups varies considerably with local circumstances. But even where spending has to increase, perhaps because the previous level of care was very poor, it is essential to ensure that such expenditure is cost-effective, by which we mean that the observable benefits to clients justify the greater expense. This judgement is ultimately ethical and social, but nevertheless relatively uncontentious at the moment: there is widespread agreement, which we share, that increased benefits to clients can be obtained at an acceptable price. But this clearly does not preclude the possibility that some community care facilities could make better use of the resources at their disposal than others.

Our interest in the cost-effectiveness of Care in the Community projects, therefore, is twofold. On the one hand, we need to establish that services provided for discharged patients are cost-effective as compared with hospital provision. On the other hand, it is likely that there will be a set of possible discharge strategies all of which, compared with hospital, are cost-effective. In these circumstances, the service intervention strategy – the choice of technique – will have considerable implications for the relative 'value for money' of different options. A primary concern of ours will be to investigate the differential cost-effectiveness of the various ways of promoting community care.

2 To implement these solutions involves substantial transaction costs of a political and organisational kind.

The Care in the Community initiative arose in the first place because of dissatisfaction amongst policy-makers at the speed at which existing joint working arrangements were affecting the move to community care which has been (in one guise or another) an explicit aim of national policy for quite some time. We share the assumption of the promoters of the initiative that this delay has been largely centred on the difficulty of putting together effective coalitions at the local level of health authority, medical, and local authority personnel armed with sufficient financial and political muscle.

This is not to suggest a dearth of people capable of taking the lead in different localities. But they are often constrained by an absence of evidence about the financial viability of implementing their proposals. It is essential that this straitjacket on local entrepreneurship be removed. One of DHSS's aspirations of the programme of pilot projects is that they will demonstrate how different strategies can be carried through without undue strain on local authority or health service budgets. A premium is placed on the search for imaginative ways of making use of different kinds of resources – real savings from hospitals, the skills and expertise of community and voluntary associations, social security payments, and the critical brokerage role that can be placed by RHAs –so as to inspire confidence in potential local innovators.

box 3.2 continues next page

Box 3.2
PSSRU assumptions

3 We share certain widespread assumptions about the technology of intervention.

We think it almost inconceivable that a project could properly assess the needs of clients and tailor services to meet those needs without a key worker or case manager taking a close interest in each individual. We regard this case-management function as being of critical importance. The major elements in it are multidisciplinary asessment and individual planning under the aegis of key workers, who implement care plans on the basis of need judgements and are enabled to mobilise resources to match those needs. Needless to say, one of the major benefits to be garnered from such an approach is the emphasis it places on peer-group review and the flexibility, imagination and experience of the individual workers involved.

4 We hold largely to the production of welfare perspective.

The production of welfare perspective is the major analogy developed by the PSSRU for the intellectual organisation of causal arguments about production relations in social care. In essence, individual, social and physical characteristics and resources combine to determine the degree of success achieved by the social care agency in the pursuit of its policy objectives. There is nothing about the production of welfare approach that encourages the researcher to perceive complex human relationships as simple and mechanistic: on the contrary, the approach's subtlety and complexity are its main strength. It demands the imaginative modelling of observed links between individual welfare outcomes and clients' characteristics, care inputs and measures of environment, process and organisation.

5 Questions of individual rights and procedural justice are central to the valuation of 'community care'.

Where projects are genuinely about moving people into the community (rather than about providing a kind of alternative long-term institutional care) then issues of procedural justice, civil rights and autonomy are raised which may well both in reality and in rhetoric be important to project workers, administrators, pressure groups, clients and ourselves. At the core of these issues is the notion that the very fact of movement into the 'community' in itself constitutes a valuable change in a person's circumstances. This notion is of course related to arguments in political theory about individual freedom, and the benefit to third parties of living in the kind of society which wishes to promote personal liberty within caring communities is obvious enough. We are concerned to match this rhetoric with the reality of project practice.

6 One of our obligations is to feed back information to projects about their achievement of their own goals.

Part at least of our own evaluation must be an assessment of the extent to which projects have attained the goals they set themselves: this is the natural baseline for any statement of the success or failure of a project. Insofar as it is possible, the more we can feed such information back to projects on a continuing basis the better, not least because co-operation in the research task is more likely to be forthcoming if the information can be reworked as a prompt managerial input.

that only very slight influence has been attempted or achieved on service delivery itself, which of course has always been the responsibility of the respective authorities.

It is also important to emphasise that the PSSRU did not select the projects to be funded. (Indeed, had we done so, we might well have selected a rather different set of projects.) At a later stage, when we became more involved, we could not avoid making some assumptions based on our own values, and these were advertised in one of the Care in the Community newsletters (see Box 3.2).

A notable feature of the selection process was its somewhat protracted nature. The extensive consultations which were necessary, both within the DHSS and with the projects, meant that formal notification of funding was delayed until late April 1984. This caused continuing difficulties for some of the projects which had based their plans on a full three years' implementation time. Some projects were delayed for many months because they were unable to recruit staff until formal approval had been obtained. Yet despite the late notification — and its knock-on effects — the DHSS continued to insist that central funding would cease on 31 March 1987, that is three years after the notional start date. Some of the projects protested, in vain, about this decision.

The delay also caused some minor problems for the PSSRU, since we were anxious to finalise the research framework, although the precise details have continued to change throughout the life of the programme. Research of this kind is a necessarily dynamic process in which the different parties involved have to be consulted extensively before plans can be finalised and later implemented. A seminar for representatives of the successful projects was held at the beginning of April 1984. This was a critical meeting for the future of the evaluation, although we had been forced to second-guess what the DHSS decisions would be. As it turned out, we were not far wrong, but representatives of one or two projects which were not funded had been invited and we failed to invite some which were. Nevertheless, the meeting was very useful. It helped to shape certain elements of the research design and, importantly, began to forge a sense of identity across the pilot projects, shared with the research team. Subsequently it has been possible to spread knowledge about project development more widely through the medium of the Care in the Community newsletter.

Thirteen projects were funded in this first round. Together they aimed to help 478 people make the move from long-stay hospital into the community. 'Community' in this context could include a period of residence — perhaps for many years — in a residential care facility or similar establishment. The initiative was most certainly not targeted at the 'easy to move' clients in hospital. Many projects set out to develop and support community-based services for a very dependent clientele. (We return to this in Chapters 4, 8, 10 and 12.) The projects were briefly introduced in Chapter 1, and are more fully discussed throughout the remainder of this book. Table 3.1 lists the 13 first-round projects, their client group foci and target numbers, and their progress in moving people into the community by the end of the central funding period. Each of these projects will continue beyond this period and most will eventually achieve their target numbers. Some of the factors which help to explain the speed with which projects were able to move hospital patients are discussed in Chapter 12. It must be emphasised, however, that the speed with which projects are able to help clients move from hospital into community settings is only one of a number of objectives.

Table 3.1
First round pilot projects

Project	Client group	Clients moved to community	
		Target number	At 31.3.87*
Bolton	Learning difficulties	80	47
Brent	Mental illness	60	40
Buckinghamshire	Mental illness	65	37
Chichester	Mental illness	30	10
Derby	Learning difficulties	40	28
Islington	Learning difficulties	8	0
Liverpool	Learning difficulties	12	14
Maidstone	Learning difficulties	50	27
Torbay	Learning difficulties	10	10
Warrington	Mental illness	16	17
Warwickshire	Learning difficulties	44	25
West Cumbria	Elderly mentally infirm	18	18
Winchester	Elderly	10	10

* In some cases the number of clients moved exceeds the number of available places. This arises because of 'replacements' for those clients who died, or returned to hospital, or moved on to other community settings.

The second stage: 1984–85

There was greater confidence that the second round of project applications would be timely and numerous and would contain some suitable schemes. Another series of three seminars, covering similar ground to those of the previous autumn, was attended by some hundreds of senior administrators. Those participants who seriously intended to make applications were then invited to a two-day workshop at Kent University, where they were advised in much more detail about what was most likely to attract the different client group divisions at DHSS. It was particularly important to ensure that no misunderstandings arose; that as far as possible the applications answered all of the relevant questions posed by the Department and that aspirant authorities recognised the research implications of being chosen as demonstration projects.

At the same time, some important decisions were being taken about some of the monitoring procedures. These procedures also feed into the 'process' side of the evaluation, which is described later. Soon after the first round of projects had been selected we drafted a *project description* for each scheme which served a number of purposes. First, it provided an opportunity to clarify important details about the scheme with the relevant project managers, the drafts produced by the PSSRU being modified locally so that the final product was a joint statement. Second, since the documents provided a comprehensive set of descriptions which outlined objectives, *modus operandi*, management, local evaluation criteria and so on, they have been used as important benchmarks against which to assess progress. In this respect, the projects have been required to produce annual reports for the DHSS which, in addition to accounting for centrally-financed expenditure, detail progress in achieving objectives and outline any changes in managerial or operational aspects of the project.

In the autumn of 1984 the role of the PSSRU in connection with the Care in the Community initiative was reviewed by the DHSS. Consideration was given to the developmental, promotional and research work undertaken by the PSSRU, plans for the future and the associated resource requirements. The research strategy at that time was outlined; the latest version is set out in Chapter 11. We were still working somewhat in the dark since the second round of projects had not been chosen. Hard choices about priorities — both in terms of data-gathering activities and analysis — would have to be taken once the shape of the second round became clear, and these would almost certainly need to be kept under regular review thereafter. The Department agreed, among other things, to continue the PSSRU involvement until the end of 1988.

The next task for the DHSS was to select a second round of schemes. A shortlist of applicants was drawn up before Christmas 1984. Each one

43

was visited by a representative of the PSSRU to clarify and discuss certain aspects of the proposals.

The second set of 15 schemes was approved in February 1985. This time the DHSS set down more explicit requirements of the projects. In addition, all projects were asked to make reasonable arrangements for the PSSRU team to have access to staff and clients for research purposes. They were also requested to prepare a joint statement of operational strategy in the form of a project description with the PSSRU. These second-round projects are listed in Table 3.2, with an indication of progress towards target numbers of moves in the first two years of the three-year funding period.

Table 3.2.
Second round pilot projects

Project	Client group	Clients moved to community	
		Target number	At 31.3.87*
Calderdale	Learning difficulties	32	7
Camberwell	Elderly mentally infirm	30	0
Cambridge	Very disabled children	3	3
Camden	Learning difficulties	17	3
Coventry	Elderly	17	16
Darlington	Elderly	54	66
Glossop	Physical handicap	3	2
Greenwich	Mental illness	16	5
Hillingdon	Elderly mentally infirm	40	32
Kidderminster	Learning difficulties	33	9
St Helens	Elderly mentally infirm	20	0
Somerset	Learning difficulties	45	14
Waltham Forest	Mental illness	18	10
West Berkshire	Mental illness	50	2
West Lancashire	Mental illness	40	4

* In some cases the number of clients moved exceeds the number of available places. This arises because of 'replacements' for those clients who died, or returned to hospital, or moved on to other community settings.

General observations

Since its DHSS funding began the PSSRU research team has been putting into effect the evaluation, monitoring and promotional activities agreed with the Department and the projects. Documents have been collected, research instruments have been distributed and completed, and a series of workshops have been held in different parts of the country. Much of this material has been used in the chapters which follow. Further lessons for future policy development must await the final report for which the more detailed analyses will be available. Nevertheless, there are certain general observations about the programme of pilot projects which it is appropriate to make at this time. These points are of two kinds. Some of them simply summarise important elements of the PSSRU approach. Others reflect general lessons from the Care in the Community initiative which may have relevance to other demonstration programmes.

1 A research team with extensive data collection aspirations and limited resources must rely on the active collaboration of local project personnel. The best way to engender the necessary enthusiasm is to develop instrumentation which, wherever possible, contributes to operational as well as research objectives.

2 A major part of the brief from DHSS has been to promote the initiative. This has been interpreted widely, by more than just advertising the existence and scope of the programme, and disseminating news about its progress. The PSSRU's activities have also 'animated' the initiative and helped to develop individual schemes, aiming to encourage quality and compatibility with the requirements of the circular. This work was on behalf of the DHSS, but at arm's length in the sense that it was always made diplomatically clear to local administrators that our view of what was likely to prove acceptable to fundors might not be shared by the DHSS. On the other hand, we were able to report back frankly to the Department about the probable value to them of investing their time in attempts to bring different projects up to scratch.

3 All the selected projects — and some which were not successful — were visited by us at some point in the selection process. These visits almost certainly had some influence on local project development, also established an atmosphere in which projects could see themselves as part of a larger national programme, and of course helped to lay the foundations of the research aspects of the programme. In addition, for some of the projects, these visits enabled us to provide encouragement and assistance to local efforts to obtain additional resources for a more focused evaluation.

4 Since the PSSRU first became involved with the Care in the Community initiative there have been changes in membership of the

research team, although without any discontinuity in activity or major changes of direction. Such continuity is crucial to the success of any research enterprise of this kind. The location of the Care in the Community research effort in a well-established DHSS-sponsored research unit has provided an environment in which consistent intellectual and managerial support is readily available. Agencies responsible for commissioning longer-term research projects — of five or more years — could well take heed of this lesson.

Finally, it is perhaps appropriate to note here a degree of disquiet about the criteria of eligibility of the schemes used to promote the Care in the Community initiative and one or two aspects of their selection.

First, we think that pilot projects which aim to demonstrate anything within a short period of time should not depend too heavily on building new premises, which can often lead to long delays in getting started. Most of the 28 pilot projects are not reliant on major capital investment, but some of those which are will be unlikely to produce results within the allotted time-scale. The Camberwell project, for example, involves capital investment of £1.25 million to provide a facility which will not be available for some years. For *demonstration purposes* this is a waste of scarce finance. In contrast, the Warrington project was able to complete a £400,000 conversion and move clients (after a preparation programme) in 18 months. Nevertheless, a general view — which we pick up again in later chapters — is that major capital investment has been a significant delaying factor, important though it is from other perspectives.

Second, it has become clear in retrospect that the definition of 'long-stay' hospital patients is problematic, particularly for elderly people and to a lesser extent for people with mental illness. (The DHSS would not commit itself to a particular definition of 'long-stay' and the practical manifestation of the term has sometimes been the subject of local negotiation.) It might have been more useful, for demonstration purposes, to restrict the Care in the Community initiative to people with a mental illness or learning difficulties who had been in hospital care for a given number of years. As it was, there was increasing pressure for all the priority groups to be represented in the programme. This resulted in some token schemes for children with learning difficulties, physically disabled people and elderly people being supported. These are proving invaluable to the clients concerned, but their demonstration potential is limited.

Third, the emphasis on the geographical spread of projects (in this and other central initiatives) confuses two distinct objectives. It is possible, though unlikely, that spreading central finance across different regions provides some form of encouragement to areas which are not very progressive. On the other hand, if the aim of a demonstration programme is to support innovative schemes from which broad lessons can be learnt then geographical considerations should not figure in the allocative criteria.

4. Central government policies and the pilot projects

The second chapter has shown the development of concern and policy for the so-called 'Cinderella groups' from the late 1960s through the 1971 and 1975 white papers, the emergence of joint finance and the consultative papers in the early 1980s, followed by recent statements from bodies such as the Audit Commission. It has described the general background to the Care in the Community initiative. This was followed by the story of the pilot programme from its early days and the role of the PSSRU. In this chapter the focus will be narrowed: how do the 28 pilot projects relate to the agreed national policy for each of the client groups concerned? 'National policy' in this context means, with some reservations, the avowed policy of the Department of Health and Social Security.

Clearly, whereas the second chapter was largely concerned with community care across the client groups, this chapter will in the main examine the client groups separately.

Policies and projects for people with learning difficulties

National policies for people with learning difficulties have been developed along broadly similar lines by successive governments; present policies are in essence still based on the principles outlined in the White Paper, *Better Services for the Mentally Handicapped* (Cmnd 4683, 1971). The overall aims are to develop co-ordinated health and social services in each locality, and to pass over much of the responsibility for people with learning difficulties from health to local authorities, but within a framework in which joint planning and working between such authorities is seen as crucial.

The White Paper spelt out what these aims should mean in practice, both for those living in the community — either with their families or in more formal care — and for those in the hospital sector. Some of the goals which it described were very general in intent (though none the less important for that): to 'prevent mental handicap if possible' and to mitigate its effects, for instance, and to 'prevent unnecessary segregation', especially of children, from other people of similar age and from the general life of the local community. Other goals were arguably more specific, but still ambitious and yet to be fulfilled: to 'provide an adequate range of residential services for mentally handicapped people in every area', for instance.

But there were three key elements in the paper which have remained central for some years now, though perhaps with accelerating real effect, and are the main principles behind what might be termed the 'new consensus' on the care of people with learning difficulties.

First, there was an emphasis on limiting intervention by the health services to those people who genuinely have clear medical or nursing needs: learning difficulty or disability is no longer to be seen as in itself a 'health' problem. The 1980 review of services decided in broad outline that every DHA would need to have at least one small health service unit, remits to vary from place to place as appropriate (DHSS, 1980). Here as elsewhere the National Development Team has been a key provoker and handmaiden of governmental wishes. The authorities have also felt able to be firmer about the needs of children with learning difficulties in particular (as opposed to adults) to be kept away from NHS facilities as much as possible, or moved from them as soon as practicable.

Second, although caution has always to be exercised with terms such as 'normalisation', and although government has certainly never aligned itself with any particular factional sense of the term, there is a constant assumption that it is desirable that people with learning difficulties should live in more ordinary accommodation than some of them had done previously (although large numbers of course have always lived with their families). In a similar vein it is felt that their contacts with family and friends in ordinary settings should be maximised, that the range of occupations thought fitting for them should be increased, and the opportunities to be so occupied actually provided. The philosophical base for all service provision for people with learning difficulties is increasingly understood to be one which recognises their rights as citizens to live a fuller life.

49

Third, to be seen in virtually every specific new policy development after 1971, large or small, is an absolute acceptance that services will only be deliverable properly to these clients if they are 'integrated', 'joint' and 'co-ordinated'. At the general level this involves phrases such as: 'Joint planning between health and local social services authorities, and close involvement of voluntary bodies and other agencies such as education and housing authorities, are essential' (DHSS, 1981c, para. 5.12). However, it also involves broad commitments, such as to the community mental handicap team as a useful element in the care for these people; less on the basis of evidence (though there may eventually be such) than because the notion fits with the prevailing set of principles.

As we have already seen, all these elements re-emerged in the *Care in the Community* circular in 1983, specifically applied to the limited problem of the movement out of hospital of long-stay patients.

Eleven of the 28 pilot projects funded under the circular are for people with learning difficulties, and another is for very handicapped children from the Ida Darwin Hospital outside Cambridge. The latter is for only three children, and four of the others are for less than 20 people. There are therefore seven reasonably large projects for people with learning difficulties. That is not to say that there are no lessons to be learned from the small scale. We will consider the largest project, Somerset, in greater detail below, but first we shall see how the other projects match up with national policy.

Formal or national policy has little relevance to many of the most important aspects of projects. Maidstone's attempt to replicate the community care scheme developed elsewhere in Kent for elderly people, or Bolton's rural training scheme, scarcely follow from any national model of care (though they do not contradict a national model, or fail to embody nationally valued principles). But at the same time, people with learning difficulties are for a number of reasons simply easier to have a policy for than people with a mental illness or those who are old. The client group is very much smaller, it is easier to identify and define, and there has been for some time (however slow it may have been in getting off the ground) a strong degree of consensus around the major planks of the policy and the delivery changes required.

This can clearly be seen if we match up pilot projects generally against the three key elements of national policy outlined above. In the first place, all the projects by definition are moving clients away from hospital care towards care in the community provided largely by non-health agencies. Much more to the point, the care they move to is identifiably a social services' (or voluntary) *style* of care, and much more so than is sometimes the case for other client groups.

50

In the second place, whilst repeating the caveats made earlier about the vexed term 'normality', all the projects either claim to be pursuing a policy of normalisation or are explicitly following a policy which can reasonably be claimed to be an implicit variant of normalisation. The Camden project, for instance, states its intention to make operational the Independent Development Council's ten principles to produce a service which:

1   values the client as a full citizen with rights and responsibilities, entitled to be consulted about his/her needs and to have a say about plans that are being made to meet those needs, no matter how severe his/her handicap may appear at first sight;
2   aims to promote the independence and to develop the skills and abilities of both clients and families;
3   aims to design, implement and evaluate a programme of help which is based on the unique needs of each individual;
4   aims to help the client to use ordinary services and resources of the local community, for instance primary care, education, health, social, employment, housing, welfare and recreational services;
5   aims to meet special needs arising from disabilities by means of local, fully co-ordinated, multidisciplinary, specialist services delivered by appropriately trained staff;
6   is easily accessible;
7   is delivered to the client's home, school, day centre or place of work;
8   is delivered regardless of age or severity of disability;
9   plans actively for people who are now living in residential institutions to return to the locality and use its services; and
10 is staffed by locally-based small teams who are available to visit families in their own homes and clients in their places of study and work.

The Derby project also espouses principles which are guided by normalisation although not spelt out in such degree of detail. Their two guiding principles of service delivery are that people with learning difficulties (i) have the same human value as anybody else and should be treated as individuals; and (ii) have a right to live like others in the community and need the opportunities this can create. Services are to be exactly as would be provided for ordinary people, and delivered to clients in their own homes, so far as possible. Clients are to make use of generic facilities in the community, including those for health care, education and leisure. Specialist services will be provided only when needs cannot be met elsewhere. (This is a very fine principle which indicates the paranoia often lurking behind 'normalisation': it is implied that elsewhere services are wilfully duplicated with the sole object of isolating people with learning difficulties.)

In the third place, by definition all projects are jointly planned and co-ordinated in order to qualify as pilot projects. In practice, they are no such thing. This partly arises from the fact that, since the aim is to produce social services-style care, the end result may not require a large input from the health service. But it also reflects a much more fundamental fact of project organisation, that in some places it really has been done by coalitions made up from different agencies, and in other places it has not. (We are talking about ownership of a project, rather than about whether it manages to call on other agencies as necessary.) Torbay, for instance, has been genuinely jointly organised and watched over since the very start. But Liverpool is very much a voluntary organisation project, accepting, somewhat reluctantly on both sides, a temporary piggy-back from the health authority.

The Somerset Mental Handicap Project

Somerset County Council has a strategic plan. Over a period of five years substantial numbers of people will move from the county's mental handicap hospitals to a multiple core-and-cluster pattern. Part of this widespread operation will be the discrete Care in the Community project, in which two core-and-cluster systems for people with learning difficulties will be established to transfer about 40 people from long-stay hospital care to a community setting. Clients will be selected by multidisciplinary teams. They will be encouraged to take an increasing part in domestic life and attend a range of day care provision.

The pilot project will come under the general auspices of the core house leaders based at Yeovil and Bridgwater. Plans have been formulated to set up local mental handicap teams (LMHTs), and also multidisciplinary teams for selecting long-stay patients for transfer to the core training unit and the community.

The relationship between health and social services. The future of services for people with learning difficulties in Somerset is therefore firmly within the social services department's ambit: the health service will have only a small continuing role. The central aim of national policy is to maintain commitment to the principles first espoused in *Better Services for the Mentally Handicapped* (Cmnd 4683, 1971): to develop co-ordinated health and social services in each locality, and to achieve a shift in responsibility and resources for the residential care of people with learning difficulties from health towards local authorities. The Somerset project is thus in line with national thinking; indeed, if anything it goes further down this particular road than the articulated policy prescribes.

The main impetus for the project has clearly come from the SSD, although key individuals in the health service have been important catalytic agents, and have firmly carried the health authority along with them. The putative pilot project was asked to confirm that local mental handicap teams would be established, and that the full range of NHS care would remain available to those clients who might need it. The project promoters naturally did confirm this. It remains to be seen to what extent an ambitious non-NHS venture will be able to involve NHS personnel at the operational rather than the planning level, or to what extent a clear attempt to effect a transfer of service responsibility to the local authority will succeed. Still, it is fair to say that at the higher strategic level joint working relationships are as good as the social services department consistently says it wants them to be.

Client population. National planning is a little confused about the extent of service needs which have to be met. The 1971 White Paper suggested a target of 55 hospital beds and 75 community residential places per 100,000 population aged over 16. The DHSS's 1980 review of services concluded that the White Paper probably overestimated the number of hospital places for adults which will eventually be required. Be that as it may, the new services in Somerset are designed to cope with transferred hospital patients, rather than to make any analysis of unmet or existing need in the county. Equally, the plans assume (and this is the main area in which there will be a continuing role for the NHS) that there are a number of people in the hospitals whose behaviour is so disordered that it would either bring them into conflict with the community or at least be quite unacceptable in a community setting. The danger is that resettling these people without adequate safe provision and/or training could discredit the initiative as a whole. The number of such people appears to be quite small, and for planning purposes it has been decided that Somerset Health Authority should aim to provide places for about 35 people with severe behaviour disorders. It is assumed that one or two small units would be required and that those people detained under the Mental Health Act 1983 would also be accepted. In so far as there is a confirmed national policy on the subject (it is still under study by the DHSS), this would seem to match it.

Community services. As mentioned above, local mental handicap teams will be established in each area before any of the clients move to the community. The full range of NHS care will continue to be available to those people who need it. The pilot project, like the whole scheme, is based on the core-and-cluster model. The two core training units, in Bridgwater and Yeovil, will provide flexible accommodation of domestic proportions for six residents, and communal facilities. It is assumed that the period of rehabilitation offered by each core house will depend on the abilities of the group, but would normally last no longer than a year, when the group will move to another living situation. In this way, over a five-year period, 30 people will move through each core house and on to newly-established cluster houses. At the end of five years the units will be used as a base of support for people with learning difficulties living in the community. The employing agency for all staff in these units is the SSD. There is a minimum expectation that day care of three days per week at the local adult training centre or day centre will be provided for each person.

This core-and-cluster approach is perhaps slightly behind the times. Many people now think that it compromises on the principle of normalisation. But there is no evidence that the Department is in the vanguard of such thinking. Community mental handicap teams are a feature to which the Department seems to be fully committed. But there is as yet no national census of them: nobody knows precisely how many there are, nor what their aims and resources are, still less what they really achieve. Some factions feel that they are a sop to the continuation of an outmoded (health service) model of care, and that if people with learning difficulties are really to integrate with the community on a 'normal' footing, the last thing they need is a specialist service. The Somerset project would thus seem to face a real danger that it will have a core-and-cluster network run by the SSD for ex-hospital patients, in parallel with an LMHT-dominated network of day services originally set up largely to cope with community demand. The LMHT will be an amalgam of health professionals and those parts of the 'old' SSD that existed before the prestigious new service came along and may well be understandably jealous of the resources being spent on hospital closures. It is not clear just how helpful the insistence that there should be such a team will actually prove to be.

Staffing and training. The project has budgeted for both training and research, and has established a full-time training post. But one clear example of local initiative has fallen foul of larger difficulties. Agreement was reached between the health authority and social services to develop a joint training establishment for mental handicap staff. Finance and premises were found. But the English National Board for Nursing, Midwifery and Health Visiting and the Central Council for Education and Training in Social Work have refused to co-operate, and have effectively squashed the proposal. This proposal closely follows practices that DHSS want to encourage. If local agencies are inhibited in the implementation of such policies by the intransigence of national bodies, then presumably the Department will eventually have to intervene. We have yet to see whether the necessary action will be taken.

Some remarks. There are two other key features of the Somerset project which should be noted. First, and beyond doubt, Somerset is a rural county, with no major conurbations, no inner-city problems (though rural deprivation ought not to be underestimated), and no huge outlying hospital colonies. Second, and harder precisely to substantiate, community and respite mental handicap services in Somerset are already of a high standard and intensity. In these circumstances, a scheme to close all hospitals and move to a county-wide network almost entirely based in the social services department, which promises a fine quality of care to all ex-patients whilst maintaining services to other people with learning difficulties who have never been in hospital, is plausible. Since, however, most of us do not live in the countryside, and too many people with learning difficulties do live in big hospitals, having come from big cities, the Somerset project will only promote change in national policy if it can produce interesting results at a micro-policy level. Such results are not yet available.

Policies and projects for people with a mental illness

The philosophy espoused in the White Paper, *Better Services for the Mentally Ill* (Cmnd 6233, 1975), lends strong support to prevention of mental illness, early recognition of problems, help for families, provision of suitable accommodation and housing, and social support. Involvement with and education of the local community are also given high priority. Subsequent papers, such as *Care in Action* (DHSS, 1981c), have also emphasised the objective of community care, with easy access to services and availability of a range of resources to match individual needs.

Because of the particular aims of the Care in the Community initiative and its programme of pilot projects, the eight projects for people with a mental illness are concerned with chronic sufferers who have been dependent on hospital services for some years, rather than with acutely ill people and concomitant issues of prevention and early recognition of problems. Many of the projects do, however, embrace a philosophy of non-institutional care and provision which is as close as possible in type and location to living at home. The Brent project, for example, plans to achieve this by providing a range of different supportive environments between which clients would be able to move as their needs change. Similarly, the Greenwich project aims to be flexible in making available both staffed and unstaffed accommodation between which clients will be able to move, with training and support provided for as long as necessary. The West Lancashire project, too, has planned for a flexible range of services including hostels, supported and independent flats, boarding houses and family placements to best

55

suit individual needs.

Strategic planning

Rationalisation of mental hospitals is advocated by *Care in Action* (DHSS, 1981c). Catchment areas would be reduced to the immediate district, inappropriately placed hospitals would be closed and staff re-employed elsewhere. Specialist provision for the elderly mentally ill would be available in every district.

This development is continued in a paper from the Mental Illness Policy Division of the DHSS which also accords a higher profile to regional health authorities (DHSS, 1983b). Each region should be able to offer a comprehensive range of accommodation and services, including secure and interim secure units. A clear exhortation is given to develop a regional strategy which includes hospital closure, but only where appropriate, and to plan carefully for perhaps five years ahead. The first step might be to align hospital catchment areas with district boundaries and to develop good services within the district. In a more recent statement from the Division (Cmnd 9674, 1985), psychiatric hospitals, where suitably placed, are expected to form a base for the local services. Inappropriately placed hospitals may be closed, but only after careful planning has taken place over a period of at least five years, in the context of a regional strategy. Money which is saved through the reduction of patient numbers should enable some progress to be made on this front, although it is recognised that substantial savings will not be made until hospitals are actually closed — and even then these savings are likely to be insufficient for a comprehensive community service (see Chapter 10).

The Buckinghamshire project is a good illustration of this strategic planning. The project is located within the framework of plans for mental illness services for the whole of the Oxford Regional Health Authority. The strategic plans intend to effect a significant change in the balance of care, away from hospital and towards the community. At least 65 patients must be discharged over the three years of the project for St John's Hospital in Aylesbury to keep to its schedule of closure by 1990, although it is hoped that perhaps 100 or so patients might actually be moved. One social services area and three district health authorities are involved, each of which plans to provide a range of accommodation, day care and recreational services. Any savings made at the hospital end will accrue to regional funds for financing further community developments.

Residential and day services

Although central government policy documents favour community care and flexibility of services, the practical advice about services they offer does not always match up to the intention. The model district service described in *Better Services for the Mentally Ill* is strongly based on the general hospital psychiatric unit which has a small number of beds and an important day hospital function. Medical facilities, such as ECT equipment and consulting rooms, are to be available in all the day hospitals. The social services' contribution to the district service is limited to a few rehabilitation hostels, a small number of staffed and unstaffed residences and day care 'to meet clients' immediate needs for shelter, occupation and social activity' (Cmnd 6233, 1975, para. 4.28). The more recent paper of 1985 accords greater priority to services provided by local authorities and other organisations in complementing NHS provision. 'Co-operation between all parties and co-ordination of provision are essential' (Cmnd 9674, 1985). Of course, it has always been the case that most people with mental illness live in their own homes in the community.

Although the greater part of the 1975 White Paper is concerned with acute services, there is a short section on long-term care of chronically ill people. Definitions and approximate numbers are given of 'old' and 'new' long-stay patients, but the only form of provision suggested is the hospital–hostel, demonstrations of which have been pioneered at the Maudsley Hospital and in Southampton. Some current models of good practice tend to favour ordinary housing for all, including those who suffer from severe and chronic conditions and who may have spent many years in hospital. The White Paper briefly mentions the possibility that ordinary housing might provide appropriate accommodation for people who need only a degree of companionship and support but does not extend the option to any with greater needs (Cmnd 6233, 1975). As far as employment is concerned, the DHSS recommendation is that special facilities should be used only where absolutely necessary and that general help for disabled people, through bodies such as the Manpower Services Commission, should provide help for most people.

The pilot projects are all geared towards chronically ill people who will need a degree of support for a long period of time, if not indefinitely. A wide variety of residential and other services are found within the programme. The Chichester project provides a hostel for up to 11 of the most dependent people and a few cluster houses, each for between four and six people who are a little more independent. These facilities are managed by a housing association. The project has been developed in close conjunction with the hospital which designated two wards for the preparation of residents for the hostel and group homes respectively. Once in the community, psychiatric out-patient facilities are available as they would be for any discharged patient. In addition, a day activity centre will be available for support and advice, and also as the base for the community rehabilitation team, which used the hospital in the first stages of the project.

The Warrington project contrasts somewhat. It is run by a voluntary organisation (Warrington Community Care) and consists mainly of a hostel with 24-hour supervision for 16 quite dependent people. Warrington Community Care, in common with some other organisations like the National Schizophrenia Fellowship, firmly believes that ordinary housing is *not* appropriate for the full range of people with psychiatric problems. The hostel building was formerly owned by the health authority but was handed over to a housing association which undertook conversion and continuing maintenance. Communal rooms in the hostel are provided for recreation and social activities. Each cluster of four bedrooms has its own lounge so that residents have a greater choice of communal areas during leisure time. In practice this has increased clients' privacy and independence. However, most residents are also encouraged to attend a nearby day centre which is run by an associated voluntary organisation. Sheltered employment is available on the hospital site and a workshop will be developed locally, funded by the European Community and promoted by the North West Fellowship. The residents make use of local medical facilities but have back-up from the hospital if emergencies arise.

In Waltham Forest, another project run by a voluntary organisation (MIND), all the housing is on a domestic scale and was explicitly planned around the principles of normalisation. These principles are a more prominent feature of Waltham Forest than of any of the other mental illness projects. Eighteen people will be accommodated in ordinary two-, three- or four-bedroom properties. They will not be expected to pass through a rehabilitation or half-way stage, but will be given permanent homes with training and support for as long as necessary. The project workers, who are employed by MIND, will undertake most of the assessment and selection of residents in accordance with the residents' wishes. A day facility is the co-ordinating link for the project, available to residents during day-times, evenings and weekends for training and leisure activities. Hospital and medical services, however, do not have a high profile.

Staffing

The 1975 White Paper (Cmnd 6233) discusses the contribution of medical staff at some length and that of nurses to a lesser extent, while social services staff, psychologists, occupational therapists and others are given only a brief mention.

In the 1983 and 1985 policy documents, the emphasis on staffing is rather different (DHSS, 1983b, 1985; Cmnd 9674, 1985). The community psychiatric nursing service is described as a very important component of community provision. The nurses work within a multi-disciplinary framework to provide after-care and to prevent unnecessary admissions to hospital. Nurse training should include preparation to work in a wide variety of settings, including residential care and the patient's own home. Social work is also given greater emphasis than in the 1975 paper: all districts should have access to specialist social workers who should contribute to the multidisciplinary forum in assessment, planning, caring and providing a link to the resources and services of the local community. The 1975 paper had limited its conception of social work involvement to a statement that 'most of them are concerned not only with the care of mentally ill people ... It is difficult to quantify the amount of time spent exclusively with the mentally ill as such' (Cmnd 6233, 1975, para. 9.17). It had simply recommended that in each social services department there should be *senior* staff with specialist training who were available to advise social work area teams. The importance of other key groups of staff, including occupational therapists, physiotherapists and psychologists, is mentioned in the 1985 paper.

The pattern of staffing within the pilot project programme shows considerable variety. The Chichester project has a larger proportion of health authority staff in the community than any other project. The hostel is staffed by health authority employees — and therefore predominantly nurses, although non-nurses are also considered — and supervised by a community psychiatric nurse. The cluster houses are unstaffed but are supervised by a worker employed by the housing association who is responsible to the local management committee. An occupational therapist assumes responsibility for the activity centre.

The projects in both Brent and Buckinghamshire encompass a range of facilities and employ a variety of staff. In both projects the health service staff tend to be based in developments within, or closely associated with, the hospitals while most of the community-based staff tend to be employed by social services. This pattern differs slightly from the guidelines contained within recent policy documents which have continued to emphasise the centrality of health service facilities within the community, backed up by a network of residential provision with social work and paramedical services widely available.

The staff in the Greenwich project — all employed by the local authority — include a project leader, an occupational therapist and residential workers. The project team undertake the selection, assessment and initial training of residents before they leave hospital and the same people continue to care for them in the community. Health care is provided by existing facilities in the area, to which all other members of the public have access.

The West Lancashire project is unusual in its use of project workers since a rehabilitation officer will operate both as an assessor of client needs and existing services and as a catalyst to new developments. The project will provide community care assistants to work alongside clients on a day-to-day basis but will draw on existing local services and rented accommodation in the area. All the project staff will be social services employees.

In the Waltham Forest project staff are employed by the voluntary organisation MIND, and are responsible both for initial selection and training in the hospital and for subsequent care after discharge. Each staff member was given the job title of 'resettlement worker' in order to avoid any suggestion of a particular leaning towards either health or social services. The choice of job title was intended to avoid some of the difficulties experienced by other projects in relation to recruitment of community staff. For example, the label of 'residential social worker' had caused some discontent among local nurses since it had seemed to imply that they were ineligible for the new post. Many projects, Waltham Forest included, hoped to attract a variety of people to the community posts in order to provide a mixture of backgrounds and experience.

Directions for the future

The practical guidelines in the policy documents concerning people with a mental illness are still dominated by the hospital and the medical profession, while attempting to embrace an objective of community care and the involvement of local people. Not that these features are irreconcilable; it is possible to provide hospital or medical care for those who need it and yet develop a more local and flexible service. Differences in philosophy, however, still prevail, particularly in the field of mental health, and these do not help in the provision of integrated services which are responsive to individual needs.

Another major problem for the development of alternatives to hospitals is the requirement for bridging money to cover the period of transition and for incentives to persuade the health service to transfer resources and responsibilities to other agencies. The 1985 paper glosses over the problem rather, asserting that 'most authorities have developed strategies for developing bridging funds and other financial mechanisms to assist the creation of new community services' (Cmnd 9674, 1985, para. 19). We return to these problems in Chapter 9. There are, of course, many more obstacles in the way of the development of a comprehensive and flexible pattern of community mental health services. One of the most prominent is the reaction of hospital staff to any proposed changes. Understandably, nursing and ancillary staff are worried about their jobs and their career paths in an increasingly uncertain future. Psychiatrists in particular have expressed disquiet over the inadequacy of some of the new community services, a view which may be strengthened by a more strategic worry over losing control of the mental health service. It would, of course, be dangerous to assume that this is the sole reason, for there are many instances outside the Care in the Community initiative where 'new' community services are obviously inadequate.

A further hindrance to the development of community services can be the response of people living in the neighbourhood. During the first years of the Care in the Community pilot project programme, local inhabitants banded together on a number of occasions to raise objections to the siting of a new hostel or day centre. One project which has begun to face difficulties in this area and which is making concerted efforts to overcome them is the West Berkshire Mental Illness project, on which we now focus. We return to the general question of public relations in Chapter 6.

The West Berkshire Mental Illness Project

The West Berkshire project will provide a staffed house as a permanent home for 12 long-stay patients, a day facility for at least 35 people and multidisciplinary teams of staff to work in the community. It also plans to make considerable use of existing local resources for accommodation, employment and day-time activity.

The general principles and goals which lie behind the project sit well with recent government policies. The project will develop in the context of a district plan to give community support to people with a mental illness and at the same time run down and eventually close an isolated mental hospital. The new pattern of services is based on the psychiatric unit of a general hospital in the centre of town. Closure of the mental hospital is not expected to be completed for at least ten years, and many of the highly dependent old long-stay patients will not move elsewhere. The latter expectation is in line with the policies of the DHSS (1983b), which express the view that only a proportion of long-stay patients could be appropriately placed in the community. However, the hospital does expect to close some wards within the next few years.

The catchment area of the hospital is already limited to that of the managing district, West Berkshire — in accord with one of the recommendations of *Care in Action* (DHSS, 1981c). This enables the project to simplify its selection procedures, since all residents of the hospital will be potential entrants, and no negotiations with other districts will be required.

The project is of necessity the result of joint planning between health and local authorities. This was a condition of receiving pilot project funding, but it has also led to a genuinely joint planning and management structure. The management team comprises four representatives from the health service (two consultants — one now the unit general manager — the director of nursing services and the unit administrator), four representatives from the social services department (which include a divisional director, an assistant divisional director and the project manager) and a member of MIND who represents all the various voluntary groups involved.

The general principle, endorsed by all recent government policy documents, of a wide range of services which are easily accessible to users and involve the people of the local community, is reflected in the aims of the West Berkshire project. In particular, a number of local voluntary organisations will provide services such as day centres and social clubs. In the first six months of the project some difficulties arose with the local community. A number of people in the area formed a group to protest against the proposed new day centre. Later, public meetings were held by the project team and a public education exercise was undertaken with the local press and local radio station. After much public relations work of this kind and more informal meetings with some of the nearest neighbours, permission was eventually given to go ahead with the development of the day facility. The project team have high hopes that the people of the neighbourhood will accept the day centre and its users, and that they will learn from the experience. Unfortunately, the hostel development has also suffered from objections by nearby residents. The project staff are tackling this situation in a similar manner, in the hope that fuller understanding of the clients and their problems will lead to acceptance or, at least, toleration.

Some of the practical aspects of the project also accord with the guidelines given in policy documents, particularly in *Better Services for the Mentally Ill* (Cmnd 6233, 1975). The new staffed house provides accommodation for 16 people and a programme to assist them with daily living skills. It will be managed by the SSD in conjunction with a housing association, and residents will be expected to attend one of a number of day facilities which are run by a variety of statutory and voluntary bodies. The new day facility provides accommodation for large and small group activities, staff offices and clinic rooms for consultant psychiatrists and other professionals such as psychologists and social workers. The combination of day centre activity with medical back-up and consultation was a specific recommendation of the White Paper, although there it was envisaged within a day hospital rather than within a social services-managed day centre.

The staffing balance of the project diverges somewhat from the guidelines of the White Paper. The project manager is a social services employee. A team based in the day facility will consist of social work and occupational therapy staff employed by the SSD and a charge nurse and a psychologist who will be employed by the DHA. A community team working from the centre will comprise eight social services staff (including social workers and occupational therapists) and ten health service staff (of which nine are community psychiatric nurses and one a psychologist). All staff will be employed and managed by their respective authority. The medical dominance of the model set out in the White Paper is diluted considerably and the contribution of other professions such as occupational therapy, psychology, social work and psychiatric nursing is given greater recognition.

The project encompasses additional practices and goals which have not been set out in any policy documents so far. Each client will be assessed by a multidisciplinary team before they leave hospital and an individual care plan will be drawn up. The report from the House of Commons Select Committee on the Social Services (1985) did make such a recommendation. Further, all clients will be given the opportunity to spend a period of several months in a rehabilitation unit before entry to the project. Regular reviews of progress will be carried out throughout the project and individual needs re-assessed on each occasion.

A clear aim of the West Berkshire project is to link together the various local agencies which already provide services for people with a mental illness. Representatives of all the relevant voluntary organisations were brought together to air their views and develop some common aims. Clients will have programmes developed which encompass a range of statutory and voluntary resources with the aim of providing an appropriate and flexible package for each individual. Key workers will ensure that the programmes are carried out and will take the responsibility for liaising between the different agencies.

Finally, the stated goals of the project include an improvement in both everyday skills and quality of life for the clients. Policy documents to date have affirmed a desire to encourage services which are comprehensive and flexible and which appropriately meet the needs of individuals, but they have not yet made any statements about improving the quality of life. The impetus to develop new services in the community and to reduce the capacity of the old institutions contains a number of assumptions. One such assumption must surely be that flexible locally-based services will help people to maintain their skills and to be happier in their daily lives.

Policies and projects for elderly people

Although some of the projects for elderly and elderly mentally infirm people funded under the Care in the Community initiative contribute to strategies of hospital closure, most do not. Their policy significance lies more in coping with the increase in the number of very elderly people in the coming years which will exert continued pressure on hospital facilities. The total number of elderly people is projected to increase by about 5 per cent between 1981 and 2001, in which period the number of people aged 75 and over is expected to grow by nearly 30 per cent (Office of Population Censuses and Surveys, 1983). Although only about 2 per cent of elderly people are in hospital at any one time, they occupy nearly half of the NHS beds, including 40 per cent of acute beds (Cmnd 8173, 1981, section 8.2).

Improved primary health care and acute hospital care, as well as the development of personal social services, are required to support elderly people in the community, and since elderly people may require several different services, close collaboration between services is essential. The broad objectives set by the DHSS in *Care in Action* for the provision of services to elderly people by health and local authorities are set out below (DHSS, 1981c, section 5.4).

1 To strengthen the primary and community care services, together with neighbourhood and voluntary support, to enable elderly people to live at home.
2 To encourage an active approach to treatment and rehabilitation to enable, wherever possible, elderly people to return to the community from hospital.
3 To maintain capacity in the general acute sector to deal with the increasing number of elderly patients.
4 To maintain an adequate provision for elderly people who require long-term hospital or residential care.

A growing interdependence between services for elderly people is emphasised by the DHSS. Community services have to respond to the results of a policy of brief hospital treatment and more active rehabilitation as well as the prevention of re-admission as far as possible. Health service planning must take account of existing local authority services and voluntary and private sector resources, perhaps using the joint planning machinery. The latter is seen as a suitable way to produce cost-effective and comprehensive service packages. The Care in the Community initiative, with its emphasis on the movement of identified people from hospital, contributes to the DHSS's overall objective of community care for elderly people, but less significantly than for other client groups.

Government policy for elderly people suffering from mental illness is one of a comprehensive, integrated service. The Health Advisory Service report *The Rising Tide* (1982) describes in detail the development of such a service. It proposes that a specialist psychogeriatric department (or department for the psychiatry of old age) would deliver hospital care for elderly patients with functional or organic psychiatric disorders. The same department would also cater for patients in the community suffering from dementia or functional disorders such as depression or anxiety. Elderly patients with chronic mental illnesses tend, at present, to be patients of the general psychiatry service although they could be absorbed into the psychogeriatric service as appropriate.

The main purpose of the type of psychogeriatric department proposed in *The Rising Tide* would be to provide treatment or hospital care for the most seriously ill people. Most elderly people suffering from mental illness live at home and receive care from their general practitioner and local authority services. A hospital psychogeriatric department could provide essential support and temporary relief to families, and advice to primary health and social services agencies. The need for sufficient residential and, particularly, in-patient care for elderly people with mental illness is recognised by the DHSS (1981c, sections 5.8 and 5.9), although the possibility of alternative approaches was raised in the 1981 consultative document (DHSS, 1981a, section 3.2).

The DHSS advise a multidisciplinary approach for both geriatric and psychogeriatric departments in which medical staff, nursing staff, occupational therapists, physiotherapists and social workers would work together. Clinical psychologists are also recommended for psychogeriatric departments.

Recent developments have broadened the scope for long-term care beyond the general aim of maintaining elderly people in their own homes. Three experimental NHS nursing home schemes have been set up as a possibly better alternative to hospital care for some patients. The DHSS is also encouraging health authorities to monitor the possibility of using independent nursing homes. Whereas these developments are taking place within the DHSS policy framework, the growth of private sector residential care would appear to conflict in part with the overall aim of integrated care, particularly since private residential homes often tend to be rather isolated from health and social services developments. Private sector sheltered housing schemes, however, which have grown since the publication of *Care in Action*, should provide the opportunity for elderly people to live in their own homes for longer (DHSS, 1981c, section 6.7).

Seven of the 28 pilot projects funded under the Care in the Community initiative cater for elderly people, three for those who are physically frail and four for those who are mentally infirm. One of the projects for physically frail elderly people — the Darlington project —

involves moving people from hospital back into independent accommodation, either their own homes or housing provided by the project. The other two projects for physically frail people — in Coventry and Winchester — provide sheltered housing with extra care. The four projects for mentally infirm people all use staffed residential homes. In Camberwell the home will be run by Age Concern, while in Hillingdon, St Helens and West Cumbria the statutory authorities are taking the responsibility.

The capital-intensive nature of the projects in Camberwell and St Helens is reflected in the extent of central funding for the capital elements of the two schemes (£706,000 for Camberwell and £559,620 for two-thirds of the St Helens scheme). Both of these projects have suffered from a number of delays and are not expected to move clients from hospital until the very end of the three-year period of pilot project funding. The *Care in the Community* consultative document refers to the possibility of (unspecified) alternative approaches to the care of elderly mentally infirm hospital patients (DHSS, 1981a), but the transfer of elderly mentally infirm people from hospital to residential care begs the question as to how far the four projects providing Part III accommodation are strictly offering care 'in the community'. Residential homes do not appear to qualify as community care provision according to *Growing Older* (Cmnd 8173, 1981, section 7.8) although the other policy documents may include them. However, such capital-intensive projects may be less vulnerable to the pressures on continued funding caused by pump-priming exercises (Webb and Wistow, 1985).

The Hillingdon project also provides resources to enhance an existing home care support service which aims to prevent, or at least delay, the admission of elderly people living in the community into residential homes. This should, in turn, free some residential places into which hospital patients will be able to move.

The four projects for elderly mentally infirm people are all designed to reduce demand for hospital places. Most will move patients from distant hospitals back to their former locality. One of the hospitals in the West Cumbria project is 50 miles from the residential home to which clients are moving. In St Helens the project forms part of a strategy for the eventual closure of Rainhill Hospital.

In the Darlington project it is hoped that savings can be made by the hospital from a more effective use of geriatric and acute beds. Such savings may then contribute to the continued funding of the project. The Winchester project, catering for ten clients, is unlikely to make an initial impact on the use of hospital beds, but ward closures may be possible in the future when more patients have been transferred.

Multidisciplinary assessment of clients features in all projects for the elderly, usually involving both health and social services staff. In the Camberwell project representatives of Age Concern Southwark will play a key role. Potential clients and their relatives are fully consulted in all projects.

The involvement of relatives in the care of clients is emphasised in all projects for elderly people. This is particularly important in those which specifically aim to move people back to the locality from where they were admitted. In the Darlington project most of the clients are moving back into their former homes. Some of the clients of the Hillingdon project are being moved from St Bernard's Hospital in Ealing back to their former locality. The project has enhanced its flexibility to achieve this end by providing places at five units within 'ordinary' old people's homes. As a consequence, taking account of former location places little constraint on the selection of clients for the project.

Individual care plans are a feature of all projects, although their planning and operation varies with the organisation of the scheme. Most have adopted a multidisciplinary approach. In the Coventry and Hillingdon projects each client will have a key worker to monitor their progress. The Darlington project has developed a sequential assessment procedure which involves the geriatric multidisciplinary assessment team, the project and the community nursing service, co-ordinated by a project service manager. When a referral has been accepted, a care plan is devised by the service manager in conjunction with the client, their family and various relevant professionals. The operation of care plans for clients includes the use of individual client budgets by service managers along the lines developed by the PSSRU in Gateshead and Kent (Davies and Challis, 1986; Challis, Chessum, Chesterman, Luckett and Woods, 1988).

A particular aim of the Darlington project is to concentrate services on clients through one key individual — the home care assistant — who is trained to undertake domestic and personal care tasks and provide support and advice to clients and their carers. This person may act as a helper to any of the professionals involved and also replaces the home help service. This is in accord with the suggestion in *Care in Action* that some district nurse functions may be undertaken by less highly qualified personnel (DHSS, 1981c, Appendix 2). The concentration of tasks also reduces the possible overlap in roles of different staff. Specialist therapists can be called in for individual clients, but the home care assistants will be able to undertake basic therapeutic procedures. This scheme will help to explore ways to extend the role of domiciliary services.

Each of the projects for elderly people intends to involve volunteers or voluntary organisations (DHSS, 1981c, Appendix 2). The Camberwell project is co-ordinated by a voluntary organisation — Age Concern Southwark — which hopes to use its close links with volunteers, paid local people and other voluntary organisations to provide services to clients and their relatives. Voluntary housing associations are involved in Darlington and in Winchester. In the Darlington project support for informal carers is an important part of the home care assistants' role. The Coventry scheme includes a day centre which encourages volunteer help.

Key issues in current policies for the priority groups

Policies for the three main client groups have tended to be articulated as general guidelines rather than as specific directives. Trends are observable over time, such as the growing emphasis on a local service network which provides a range of facilities close to people's homes. The practical steps that might be taken to achieve such a service are rarely spelt out in detail, however, and implementation of the changes, such as an alteration in the balance of staffing, occur only gradually. The *Care in the Community* circular has probably had a significant impact on such details, since it has made possible some changes in the way services are financed — inevitably a crucial factor (DHSS, 1983a). Other legislative changes which were not necessarily directed at these client groups but have affected the financing of care, such as the supplementary benefit regulations, are also likely to have influenced considerably the pattern of services provided on the ground.

The pilot projects developed under the Care in the Community initiative all provide, to some extent, illustrations of current government policy at the general level. All aim to contribute to a more locally-based network of services in which the various agencies and professions work more closely together. Great variation, however, may be seen within the programme. Models of care differ dramatically from project to project while maintaining a semblance of conformity to client group policies. Of course, a policy which advocates flexibility would be unlikely to foster only a narrow range of options. In addition the projects themselves vary greatly in scale and immediate aim. Some have planned to house perhaps a dozen people and to rely on nearby facilities to fulfil their other needs. Others intend to develop a complete service for 80 or so people within a locality, and yet others view themselves as a catalyst to extend the brief of existing services. Some plan to spend their money almost entirely on buildings, while others have opted for a revenue-based scheme for staffing. Yet all in some way wish to contribute to an overall pattern of local services for their particular client group.

Another feature of the projects — about which there is much variation — is the agency responsibility and the degree to which they intend to manage services jointly. Policy guidance from the centre on this point may not always have been interpreted with great accuracy. Some authorities have gone far down the road which leads away from health service ownership of schemes. In doing so they have begun to encounter opposition both locally and recently, to an extent, from the centre. It is only fair to say that policy guidance in this area has not always been crystal clear and that, of late, there has been an increasing exhortation to involve health service personnel and facilities at all levels. Joint planning and joint working within the projects — which will no doubt remain a contentious topic for some time to come — is the subject of the next chapter.

5. Promoting and managing joint ventures

All Care in the Community projects had to be, by definition, joint ventures in order to qualify for pilot project funding. Applications which might have originated in a local authority, a district health authority or a local voluntary organisation had to proceed through the joint planning channels. A number of schemes had been waiting on the shelf for some time, perhaps having been submitted more than once to different funding agencies. Others were devised directly in response to the invitation in the *Care in the Community* circular. But whatever their precise origins, projects arose out of local circumstances — although somewhat moulded by national policies and a central selection procedure — and must be viewed in their local contexts, of existing and changing relationships between local organisations.

Moreover, although organised under a national umbrella, projects are not managed nationally; they are managed locally, by a health or local authority, or a voluntary organisation, fitting in to the formal structure of local planning, quite distinct from the pilot programme. Also, by definition, they must in a formal sense be jointly planned and developed. That formal structure, however, is something which central government has been concerned to devise, implement, and then continuously change (some would say tinker with) for many years. Some of those changes have been described in Chapter 2.

Project development

What are the advantages of *joint* planning? What kind of incremental change in local organisations was expected by the promoters of the Care in the Community initiative, and why were particular kinds of bureaucratic constraint written into the circular?

In practice the 28 project packages have been put together by a variety of different agencies and combinations of agencies. They are roughly identifiable as those which are instigated by either health, social services or a voluntary agency, and those which have arisen out of joint working or some other kind of coalition. Since inter-agency co-operation is a condition of receipt of central funding — through the joint finance mechanism and through the selection procedure described in Chapter 3 — the extent to which projects can be single-agency affairs once they are off the mark is limited. Nevertheless, they have often been largely germinated in one agency, and some continue to have only minimal input from other agencies, or added impetus from only one other agency.

The Chichester mental illness project, for instance, was very much a health-led project, devised by professionals and administrators in Graylingwell Hospital and the district health authority. They planned the outline of rehabilitation in the hospital and took their ideas far enough to be able to give a coherent remit to a housing association for the facilities which would be needed in the community. This included accommodation both for patients and for the community rehabilitation team, which was effectively to move out of hospital with the patients.

On the other hand, in Torbay, a voluntary agency — the Parkview Society — directed by a coalition of representatives from all concerned local agencies and thus able to draw on resources from all of them and to plead its case easily through local joint bodies, had cut its teeth on setting up a hostel for people with a mental illness and now proposed to do so for people with learning difficulties. Although technically a voluntary enterprise, this is clearly a case of genuine joint working, with enough entrepreneurial flair to make use of the social security budget to meet local needs.

Three case studies

We shall now consider the development of some of the projects in a little more detail, using three of the pilot projects as case studies.

The *Brent* project was brought into being by a small number of people in the joint health care planning team. In particular, two recently appointed officers, in health and social services respectively, recognised the potential for collaboration and looked for a new project to work on. The *Care in the Community* circular came out at just this time and provided the ideal opportunity.

Mental illness was an area that had already aroused some concern, particularly on the health side, in relation to the local long-stay hospital and its management. Mental health provision consumed a substantial portion of the health service budget but took only a small share of the social services funds. Most of the money was bound up in hospital care and, although rehabilitation programmes were operating, they were hampered by a lack of community facilities into which to discharge people. An initiative was therefore needed, with pump-priming money, to facilitate a transfer of resources and to improve the effectiveness of the rehabilitation work.

In addition, some buildings were to be redeployed in the borough, having previously been children's homes and a mental health hostel. These opportunities were quickly seized on and channelled towards the project. This particular move was not uncontentious, however, and led to debate for some while over the availability of hostel places in Brent as a community resource. The health service trade union, COHSE, expressed some concern over the closure of health facilities and their replacement with social services facilities, which was described by some members as 'asset stripping'.

An outline plan of the project was developed by the two officers who saw the need to include at an early stage a number of other key actors in both authorities. In their own words, they 'carefully picked off people of a like mind whom they felt they could work with' and formed a small working group. Each group member took the responsibility for planning a part of the project. A psychologist who had wanted to set up something along these lines for some time planned the assessment, selection and rehabilitation operations in conjunction with the hospital rehabilitation committee and a recently appointed consultant. These people became an important link with the hospital side. Social services planners and officers took main responsibility for the community side. The planning group was characterised by great cohesion and enthusiasm. The individuals concerned all had a full-time commitment in addition to the project and consequently spent a great deal of their 'spare' time in meeting and developing ideas together.

Another important feature was probably the sheer determination of the group's chairman, who skilfully manoeuvred the plans through the necessary committees within the social services department. He was careful to involve certain significant individuals through informal lobbying and consultation, while keeping certain others at a distance. This is not to say that everything went smoothly, however, and difficulties and delays occurred throughout the early stages. Sources of these problems included staff recruitment, approval by committees and opposition from the trade union, COHSE.

The continuation of funding for the project after the three years of central funding will be ensured by a combination of social services, health district and regional health authority contributions and benefits to individual clients. Negotiations continue between these different authorities as to the proportion of funding each will contribute. Protracted debate over financial support will be a common feature of large projects where future sources of funding will be subject to change and uncertainty, such as the effects of rate-capping on social services budgets and constraints such as RAWP on the health side.

It is expected that the hospital will be able to close two wards by the end of the three-year period and that the savings generated will be transferred to the project.

Some of the buildings for the project will be provided by the housing department in Brent and some were made available by re-arrangements of social services facilities. More recently a number of voluntary housing associations have become involved and will provide the remainder of the residential accommodation. In addition, a number of clients have been placed with families in private homes in conjunction with the adult home-finding officer.

It is uncertain whether people will continue to be discharged from the hospital at the present rate. There are no definite plans for closure in the near future, although reduction in size is likely. In addition, estimates of the numbers of hospital residents who might be expected to be discharged vary widely within the project team. Many of the residents remaining in the hospital come from areas other than Brent, so future plans for them require planning and negotiation between the health district and a number of local authorities.

The Brent project is undoubtedly a joint venture between health and social services although it has clearly identifiable parts which are the responsibility of each separate authority. Within each setting, however, working as a joint project has influenced the existing practices. Joint assessment and multidisciplinary work, for instance, have become established methods of operation. The key feature in its development appears to have been the influence of individual personalities, all of whom stressed the importance of being able to work together. A further factor was probably the availability of buildings which were already owned by social services.

It should be noted here that putting a joint project into practice is far from easy. Managers have had to grapple with structural differences in the organisation and accountability of the two agencies as well as a cultural divide. The two parts of the project have developed at different rates, which led to a 'bottleneck' on the rehabilitation ward at one point before some of the community facilities became available. The joint operational group found it necessary to employ an external management consultant for their meetings, which helped them through some of the stickier patches of negotiation.

The *Derby* mental handicap project began jointly from a group of officers in the district health authority and social services department who decided that joint working was becoming a necessity for mental handicap services. The outline of a joint strategy had been considered two years before the *Care in the Community* circular came out, but no detailed planning occurred until then. The planning was undertaken largely by a development officer in social services and a psychologist on the health side. A partnership team of senior officers from both authorities was established, who were to take managerial responsibility for all developments.

It is probably fair to say that there had been some mistrust on both sides in previous years and that agreements about transfer of resources would have been unlikely to have been reached were it not for the impetus of the circular. The negotiations about resource transfer were based on an assumption of savings to be made in hospital by closing wards. In order to make sufficient savings, 100 patients must be discharged over a total period of six years, i.e. a further three years after central funding ceases. The number of patients discharged is reckoned on a different basis for purposes of central Care in the Community monitoring from the reckoning negotiated locally. One reason for this is that the district mental handicap unit consists not only of hospitals but also of several hostels and group houses in the community. The district is prepared to transfer money in respect of hostel residents who move to other accommodation, but the Care in the Community initiative is concerned solely with people who leave hospital, although the latter can include discharge to health service hostels and homes.

The complexity of counting patients stems largely from another key feature of the project: its very close links with other facilities which already existed in the area. Indeed, this feature could be held to be partly responsible for its existence, or at least for the scale of the enterprise. On the social services side the existence of an 'infrastructure' of facilities on which to build gave the project an extra degree of confidence. On the health side, since the hospitals already had a tradition of discharge to the community the project was not viewed as such a new innovation (or as great a threat) as it might have in a different locale.

The project itself provides teams of both health and social services staff in four sections of Derby, each led by a co-ordinator (who is a social services employee). Flats and group homes are acquired through the housing department and voluntary housing associations as the project develops. At first many people were discharged from hospital into hostels which had been established for some time. In the early stages of the project it was difficult for the research team to identify which of the people leaving hospital should be considered to be Care in the

Community clients as distinct from those who would have left anyway. Another feature which is problematic for research — although good as a model for practice — is the integration of project staff and their work with other facilities and clients in the community. It may be desirable from a service point of view to avoid the development of rigid boundaries between 'special project' and 'non-project' staff but, in this case, the nature of the funding necessitates that staff time and activities are accountable.

Some of the difficulties encountered by the project in its inception are common to many. Planning meant extra work for already busy senior people, so much had to be done in their spare time. The delay and uncertainty over knowing whether or not funding would be granted was irksome, as were the bureaucratic constraints — particularly in social services — which required many decisions to be passed through a number of committees.

Looking to the future, there is some concern on the health side over whether the community will be able to provide adequate specialist services such as physiotherapy, hydrotherapy and speech therapy. Another worry is the comparative costs, since calculations of the sum to be transferred per patient were made on the basis of 100 discharges in six years. If the projections are far out of line one authority or other will have to pick up an unexpectedly large bill.

The initial impetus for the *Liverpool* project came from a housing association which had previous experience of similar ventures elsewhere. The idea was developed in conjunction with a local Mencap group who acted in an advisory capacity. Together they had already planned a project — unconnected with the circular — which was having difficulty in obtaining funding. Later they joined with the local hospital which was able to identify some suitable clients and applied to the DHSS for financial backing under the Care in the Community initiative.

When the health authority became involved some procedural changes occurred which were particularly important in the light of the region's agreement to support the project after the three years of central funding. Eventually the various parties agreed that all of the staff would be employed and supervised by the health authority.

The Liverpool scheme moved clients from hospital more quickly than any other in the pilot project programme, probably because of its small scale and the availability of houses which had been purchased and partially adapted before the funding decision was made. This was achieved despite some delays encountered during the planning and decision-making by committees.

How projects manage themselves

The resulting projects are managed, once they have been set in motion, by a variety of agencies and combinations of agencies. All of these are controlled not merely by the amount of their funding but also by the procedures they may impose.

Management in this context does not mean the management of individual cases: that is discussed later in the chapters on care planning. Nor does it mean — largely speaking — the day-to-day management of capital assets or of personnel, nor attempts to manage the external environment in which projects have to work — their relations with the public, for instance. All these are dealt with in later chapters. Projects may be viewed as new ventures concerned to establish new networks of service provision, which must devise for themselves both systems for the integration of different parts of the network and means of ensuring the implementation of initial project aims.

The Maidstone project is attempting to apply a carefully-considered set of economic and other principles to service delivery itself. It arose in the first instance out of a desire in Kent Social Services Department to replicate for people with learning difficulties the successful approach developed in the Kent community care scheme for elderly people (Challis and Davies, 1986; Davies and Challis, 1986). The project is jointly managed by the health authority and Kent County Council. A joint service steering group co-ordinates and supports the project team, and contains relevant officers of the health and local authorities. But within this framework, responsibility for the overall implementation of the project rests with the area director of social services. On a day-to-day basis, the project is managed by the project co-ordinator, who has responsibility for liaison with other health and social services staff.

In the original Kent community care scheme a budget constraint was set for individual clients within which project officers were given responsibility to provide services as necessary. Needless to say, a procedure also had to be devised under which project officers could ask more senior staff to override budget constraints, where this seemed right for the particular client involved. On the other hand, many other clients were able to manage with fewer direct services.

Budgets of this kind have not previously been set for providers of services for people with learning difficulties. Review of financial limits, and the appropriateness of budgets more generally, has therefore to be a constant concern of the Maidstone steering group. At the same time, the previously evaluated community care scheme for elderly people found major benefits for clients and staff in the approach. One of the aims of the Maidstone project is to try to achieve those benefits for another client group. A budgetary system with valid price constraints and proper safeguards may take considerable time to fully develop.

Other large schemes have set themselves up in different fashions. In Somerset, ultimate responsibility for the project rests with the director of social services and the mental handicap action team which he chairs. On a day-to-day basis, the project team was responsible in its first stages to the senior assistant (mental handicap) who is a member of that team. Later a principal assistant was appointed, with two senior assistants. The scheme then in effect had a number of different overlapping management systems, much in the way that social services departments themselves usually do (and this reflects the fact that care of all people with learning difficulties in Somerset will be the responsibility of the SSD). It has that central command team, an established departmental structure of area offices, and a new set of local (i.e. community) mental handicap teams. A network of core-and-cluster systems in different parts of the county forms the main planning device, in conjunction with an existing network of 'enterprise centres' and other day services.

In Bolton, all staff involved in the project will be responsible in the normal way, within their own employing authorities, through their line managers. However it is also recognised that the departments involved have a shared responsibility for ensuring that the project money is used efficiently and effectively for the purposes intended. As a consequence, the following arrangements were made:

- Project co-ordinators were designated by both authorities, who would also act as liaison officers for DHSS and PSSRU.
- A network co-ordination and development group was established, reporting to chief officers and the JCC.
- Client needs for resources were determined by the individual programme planning (IPP) process and referred for action to the appropriate line manager in the normal way (notification of these needs is also being routinely referred to the network co-ordination and development group for monitoring purposes).
- The four project leaders, in association with the officers-in-charge, the rural training manager, the education support tutors and others, formulated *group* care plans, as group needs became apparent as individual needs were assessed (later, responsibility for co-ordination of individual care plans was handed over to a nominated key worker).
- Needs for project resources to meet group care plans were identified and referred for action as above.
- Project resources were controlled as much as was practicable by the staff providing the direct service to the clients.
- The joint treasurers were given six-monthly reports on expenditure.
- The health authority met the salaries and wages costs of those people employed by the health authority under the scheme (all other expenditure incurred by the project was covered through the

SSD-nominated budget holders who were the project co-ordinators from the health authority and social services department).

Formal arrangements in the Derby project (described earlier) were similarly devised. A partnership team, comprising a group of senior local authority and NHS officers, was responsible for the joint implementation and monitoring of a strategy of which the Care in the Community project is a key part. The partnership team reports to the joint care planning team of the joint consultative committee. Two sector development groups, again inter-agency, reported to the partnership team. IPP co-ordinators were responsible for individual and group care plans, and for monitoring their progress. The plans were drawn up by a multidisciplinary team of community staff, with assistance from hospital staff and relatives of clients.

In projects which are either smaller, and therefore able to achieve a certain independence from mainstream authority management oversight, or centred on voluntary organisations, different structures have been set up. As already mentioned, in the small-scale scheme in Torbay all the relevant statutory services are represented on the Parkview Society's management committee, and there is also cross-representation on the JCPT. Members have lines of communication into various agencies and under their guidance hostel staff are encouraged to form other links on a working level. Progress is monitored by the unit management group and senior management of social services within the joint care planning team for mental handicap. But in practice the professional leadership of the Parkview Society has considerable latitude to pursue agreed goals.

In the voluntary organisation-based model being set up simultaneously in several parts of Warwickshire under the oversight of joint planners led by a team in the social services department, local Mencap societies will have overall responsibility for the developments in their area. In practice, however, the management structure will include representatives both from the health authority and social services. A model management structure is in the process of recommendation to the Mencap societies. This is likely to be headed by a management committee with two members each from health and social services in each locality, together with six members of the local Mencap society. Where a management structure is already in operation for an existing hostel, some rationalisation of responsibilities may also take place, although separate financial accounts will be kept, at least in the early years of the initiative.

Problems of joint management

We have begun to build a picture of the arrangements made by local and district managers, the constraints from which they have arisen, and the service aims they have produced. We can now add to that an interim view of some of the difficulties that these plans are meeting, both at the local level and more globally, and some of the steps which practitioners might be best advised to take against the dangers.

Agency issues

The local climate of joint working and co-operation before a project is even mooted is a key factor in its future success. Political commitment of the relevant agencies to the new project is equally important. This is true both in the obvious sense, that the directly sponsoring agencies should be energetically committed, but also in the less direct sense, that other agencies whose willingness to participate can make or break the venture should be fully involved. For instance, a housing department should be aware of when and where it may be asked to contribute.

There are special difficulties when the project aims to move clients to a social services area which is outside the health authority area of the hospital from which the clients start. Some instances of mistrust between neighbouring health authorities have, at times, hindered negotiations. This is unlikely to make life any easier for other agencies, since although local joint working in the receiving area may be excellent, with the best will in the world misunderstandings are likely to occur between authorities which have not previously had diplomatic relations, never mind the degree of mutual co-operation at the client level needed to instigate proper services.

Project issues

There are a number of problems which arise simply from the fact that projects are developing within the somewhat artificial framework of a pilot programme. In the first place, although quite detailed outline plans had to be produced in order to win central funding, only those few first-round projects which were planning to go ahead anyway, by raising the money elsewhere, were in a position to forge ahead the minute they knew their proposal had been accepted. Others had to gear themselves up with the operational planning which could not sensibly be done on the off-chance of winning.

Second, both rounds of projects have inevitably had what, in the context of the usual planning horizons of health and local authorities, has been extremely short notice that they were to be funded at all. Long lead-in times are needed to set up the machinery to identify and assess clients, and to provide new services and facilities, or at least adapt existing provision. Some of the projects for elderly people, such as Camberwell and St Helens, which have planned to build new residential homes, provide extreme examples of this difficulty.

Third, the financial arrangements for the Care in the Community initiative are constraining. Having been provisionally allocated sums over three fiscal years, projects are required to use the money within just that period: they cannot allow their spending to spill over into fourth or later years. The combination of this with the practical absence of any project at all in the first weeks of funding, for the reasons already mentioned, has made life difficult for many senior project managers.

Cost-consciousness

Another major conflict, sharply illustrated by several of the pilot projects, arises for policy-makers — particularly at the local level — who need to think hard about the long-term consequences of planning services in response to client needs alone. The professional temptation — some would say obligation — to do this is very great. Nevertheless, as a simple matter of fact services will always be constrained by available resources. If planning to meet clients' needs is increasingly devolved to the key worker level, then perhaps knowledge of financial constraints should be as well, together with the responsibility to plan within them.

The practice of British social and health policy has not traditionally encouraged service planners and case managers to develop such cost-consciousness. Training is no doubt one part of the answer to this, as is managerial direction. But the value of changes in the incentive structure has to be emphasised. The incentives in question are by no means restricted to perks and pay rises. A clear lesson from the Care in the Community projects, as it has been from the Kent community care experiment (Challis and Davies, 1986; Davies and Challis, 1986), is that even very junior staff, and certainly middle rankers, will respond with enthusiasm to the increased responsibilities of devolved planning for services at the client level.

A note on models of care

The local structure of management could to some extent be regarded as one of the things that are on test in the PSSRU's research: within the 28 projects there are a number of different *models* of the management and delivery of care, at various levels. In principle these could be compared on the basis of cost and output data, thus enabling statements to be made about how different styles of management, or philosophies of care, make differences to the real lives of clients.

Clearly, there is a distinction between models of care delivery on the one hand and models of project organisation on the other. In other words, there are two related kinds of model: what the project does to its clients, and purely internal practices. (We assume throughout that 'project' is more than simply a linguistic device for financial or other purposes, and does signify some genuinely separate bureaucratic entity.) Both of these types of model are determined primarily by statements about practice at the client level. A project which sees itself as a core-and-cluster project manages itself as such, then expects both staff and clients to behave accordingly. So the set of models would be an identifiable list of options related to the available technology of care as viewed by practitioners, based on explicit classifications of practice.

We cannot attempt this here though, for a number of reasons. In the first place, there is no existing dictionary of all of the possible models from which projects could have drawn their philosophy and practices. Our study would therefore be incomplete. In the second place, projects were not simply selected or set up to exhibit and test characteristics of different models. Most projects are hybrids. Even if not a hybrid at the outset the implementation of any model seems to be subject to distortion by other parties or systems in the service context. The 28 projects do not provide a range of discrete examples of models of care and organisation and PSSRU's evaluation of the programme does not expect to deliver data in such a form.

At a lower level, however, PSSRU will be able to make quite pointed statements that have less to do with general principles and more to do with the bricks from which projects are built. We shall wish to comment on, for instance, the relationship that costs and outputs have with the kinds of facility used by clients (staffed homes versus unstaffed, and so on) and with professional and service inputs. (Does occupational therapy in the community seem to make a difference?) The characteristics of clients are of particular interest; any comments on effectiveness of facilities will have to take into account the widely differing needs of clients and groups of clients.

6.   Public relations

An important activity to which project managers need to give careful consideration is *public relations*. The Care in the Community projects are developing within an intricate context of service agencies, interest groups and individuals, each of which will affect, and be affected by, their progress. The relationship between projects and every agency and individual with which they come into contact is crucial. Public relations need to be interpreted as broadly as possible. The aims of public relations work will be to communicate, educate and inform where knowledge is lacking; to create an appropriate image and establish confidence in the project; and to develop and maintain good working relationships.

Hospitals and other service agencies

The very existence of new projects which aim to provide a different type of service incorporates an implicit criticism of those which they seek to replace. For this reason project personnel need to tread particularly carefully where relationships with hospitals are concerned.

The future of most hospitals has now been decided and spelt out in detail in regional and district strategic plans. Some hospitals are due to close within a few years, others will reduce in size and change their function, while others will remain and receive clients from hospitals running down elsewhere. Relationships with hospitals which are planned for run-down or closure are obviously particularly sensitive, since the future of existing staff is likely to be the most uncertain.

Where projects have been planned in conjunction with district strategies for the future of hospitals, there will probably be fewer problems of negotiation with authorities, at least at the management level. In other cases, where projects have developed independently from other mainstream local plans, considerable negotiation may be required to ensure long-term funding and access to essential resources which have not been built into the project. Schemes which emerged from joint working arrangements between authorities may be at an advantage in this area. In some cases the time-scale of planning has worked against the linking together of project and mainstream services. Some districts did not fully develop their plans until the project was already under way, which has meant that it has begun to progress along a different path from other services, although it may have fitted well with previous plans.

Good communication with authorities providing long-term funding will be particularly important. They will need to be informed of project details and progress, especially those changes of plan which have implications for staff numbers, and consequent costs. In the early days it is important to provide funding authorities with details of project intentions in order that a clear and understandable picture of the new services may be constructed. Continued representation from the authority on the project management committee may also benefit information flow in both directions.

Different regions and projects have found very different ways of reaching agreement over the long-term funding of the new services. In a few cases the health authority has agreed to support the full cost of replacement services. In other cases, a sum per resident will be transferred, usually the approximate average cost of a hospital place; this is the so-called 'dowry payment'. In yet other cases, only a proportion of hospital costs will be paid, on a sliding scale according (roughly) to the dependency level of the resident. Some projects will be supported according to their full revenue costs, provided that the agreed number of people are discharged over a three-year period. 'Dowry payments' are discussed again in Chapter 10.

Funding policies can encourage insensitive planning. For instance, in some cases continued support depends on a resident's borough of origin, even though they may no longer have any relative living there. Too strict an adherence to such policies may lead to inappropriate placements and will rapidly lower the project's credibility with other agencies.

The way in which a hospital run-down or closure is managed will influence a project's relationship with the hospital staff. Some hospitals have deliberately kept plans from their staff, assuming that such information will cause anxiety and disruption at all levels, preferring to wait until all decisions are finalised. In practice this does not seem to have been a very useful policy, since it soon becomes obvious that changes are afoot and rumours may be more distressing than fact. Uncertainty is naturally prevalent in such times of change. Some staff may feel that they have heard talk of closures so often in the past that it will never actually happen. Others have objected to the lack of consultation with staff in developing forward plans. Providing the maximum amount of clear and detailed information at all stages (through, say, fact sheets and meetings) is emerging as a good way forward. Better still would be consultation with representatives at all levels of the system throughout the period of planning and implementation. Even those who favour the development of community care and the run-down of hospitals may, at times, have doubts about the ability of new services to cope with all possible situations. Such doubts can be transmitted and magnified all too easily where future plans are not spelt out clearly.

Some hospitals have set out a no-redundancy policy for staff, which will help considerably in the acceptance of future services. Others have, in addition, determined that each member of staff will have the opportunity for individual discussion about their future and choice of where they will be employed.

Teams of workers in developing projects have not always found it easy to work alongside existing members of staff. There are particular difficulties where new services will be managed by an agency other than the NHS, such as a social services department. Differing conditions of service, salary scales, career structure and pension rights are obstacles to the transition of staff from one to the other. Nursing trade unions have raised formal objections and refused to co-operate with some projects in the belief that their members were not eligible for employment in the new schemes. Negotiation with trade unions is advisable at an early stage in order that some of these difficulties may be ironed out before the project gets under way. The titles attached to new posts have sometimes given quite misleading impressions to potential applicants. Even though a post may be managed by social services, projects have found it wise to describe it in a neutral fashion, rather than by a title such as 'residential social worker' which may imply that nursing staff cannot apply.

Consultants, too, may raise objections to new developments. They tend to have considerable power over decisions in hospitals and may even veto the discharge of individual patients after considerable rehabilitation work has been undertaken with them. It is therefore important to involve them in discussions as early as possible. Projects which are closely linked to more general plans for the hospital may be at an advantage here.

The objections and doubts which consultants and nursing staff may hold about a project stem from a mixture of motives. On one side they probably worry about their own future — their own 'territory' and professional identity — while on the other hand they may feel deep concern about whether the community services can cope. They may simply not know that the project intends to provide buildings, facilities and trained staff. Opportunities for hospital staff to mix with those of the project and to visit the developing community services may help to reassure them that their residents will not simply be 'dumped' in the community and expected to manage on their own.

Clients, too, are likely to find it even more difficult to visualise what community service might be like. It would be unreasonable to expect them to make major decisions about moving from hospital without extended contact with project staff and visits to the new facilities. Some community units, such as the hostel in the Warrington project, have guest rooms in which potential residents may stay overnight. Involvement of clients in decision-making about their future, with some of the challenges which it raises, is discussed more fully in Chapter 8.

On the other hand, some projects have helped the hospital in its development plans. In Brent, for example, the expansion and improvement of a rehabilitation ward and its work have provided a model for other parts of the hospital to follow. Training programmes on the ward have demonstrated gains in daily living skills in many residents, and periods of time spent in the community have enabled them to make use of local facilities. In addition a new system for assessment and early work with clients relies heavily on co-operative work with staff on long-stay wards. Considerable emphasis was placed on public relations work here: project staff approached each ward in turn, held extensive and informative meetings, instructed nurses in the use of assessment schedules, and encouraged visits to rehabilitation and, latterly, community facilities. Exercises of this kind are extremely time-consuming but the benefits gained are worthwhile.

Similarly, the demands of the Warrington project in preparing people for the hostel led to development of different rehabilitation practices in the hospital. Some of these practices may continue, even though all the project clients have now left. Other projects, such as Bolton, have acted as a catalyst to the development of services in some areas, and established a pattern which hospital plans may follow. In Somerset, the resettlement procedures and documentation established for the pilot project will be useful in other developments which are not centrally funded.

The structure of the project itself may influence its relationship with the hospital. It might be expected that large projects, which necessarily have a greater effect on the hospital, would encounter more problems. In fact, the reverse seems often to have been the case in many pilot projects. Small schemes have sometimes become submerged in the details of a hospital's future and progress has been held up for weeks or months before permission has been given to work with the residents. This may be partly due to the lesser involvement of small schemes in hospital strategic plans, and partly because of the lessened likelihood of negotiation with authorities at a senior level beforehand. Some hospitals are beginning to be more selective about the organisations with which they are prepared to communicate. Non-health agencies may find themselves kept out of discussions so it may become increasingly important for even small schemes to include NHS representatives on their management committee. This has to be counter-balanced by the risk of losing a degree of independence.

The appointment of a co-ordinator as soon as a project plan has been agreed has proved to be enormously helpful in many cases. A key person in this position is able to negotiate with all the necessary authorities, explore details of housing and other capital developments, and establish a public relations policy with all interested parties. Existing service managers, who may have been responsible for planning the project, rarely have the time to carry out all these necessary activities.

Recruitment of some project staff from the hospital of origin can also be most advantageous for projects. They may already know some of the clients, which can help, and will also know and be known to other hospital employees. Informal working relationships can be among a project's most valuable assets. In addition, the credibility of a project will be enhanced by the involvement of trusted and respected members of staff and by the overt demonstration of enthusiasm that employment within the project may suggest.

The performance of projects in achieving their aims is, of course, the best way of making a good impression. The ability to provide housing and day care services on time is initially important. Projects which began work with clients and were later unable to resettle anyone for long periods frequently found themselves the subject of criticism from hospital staff. Morale within the team and respect from others improved when the hold-ups were overcome and residents started to move out. Delays are inevitable at all stages, but some of these should perhaps be anticipated in the development of a realistic schedule, which can then be publicised widely throughout the project's service network.

The relationship between pilot projects and mainstream services is of interest here. It is likely to be advantageous to link in with other services so that people who move from hospital are not treated as an entirely separate group from people who are already living in the community. In the early days, though, projects may wish to develop along rather different lines and pursue models of practice which break away from the traditional mould. Allowing non-project clients to make use of certain facilities, such as day workshops and special education, may be a good way to begin to build up a useful relationship. Inevitably, though, this has to be balanced against the need to husband project resources to identified clients to ensure that specific goals are met.

Families and relatives

Opinions differ on the importance of involvement and consultation with clients' relatives. Some feel that their views should be considered at all stages and they should contribute to all major decisions. Indeed, the *Care in the Community* circular said: 'Projects should provide for prior assessment of the needs of the people concerned and take their wishes and those of their families into account.' Others, however, feel that relatives' views may not necessarily reflect the best interests of the client and the way should be made clear to override their views if necessary. There is a balance point to be found here, such that relatives' views have some influence over decisions but they do not have the ultimate right to determine the outcome.

Any assumptions made about the links that clients may have with a particular geographical area should be investigated before firm plans are made for resettlement. It may be the case that the family has since moved, so it will be important to discover where they are currently living.

If a policy decision is made to consult relatives of all clients, there are further differences of opinion over whether they should be contacted at an early stage or whether it is best left until later. Early contact has the advantage that proper consultation is possible, and relatives may have the opportunity to contribute to the care plan. On the other hand, the fears and anxieties held by parents about a move from hospital may be more difficult to deal with in the early days of a project when staff teams and project facilities are not yet fully established.

Families, particularly parents, may be anxious about plans to resettle their relatives from hospital for a number of reasons. They may fear that community services simply will not be able to provide adequate care for special needs, especially where children, young people and those with severe or multiple handicaps are concerned. Medical establishments have always been able to give a comforting and reassuring impression in which all those who come into contact may trust and feel secure. This is, in part, to be accounted for by professional expertise, but is also partly the result of professional mystique and image. Terms such as 'nursing care' (which in this context usually means intensive personal care) can be misleading, since the majority of tasks which it describes can be competently carried out by appropriately trained non-nurses. There can also be some confusion over what is meant by qualifications and training. In untraditional areas of service provision — and all of the Care in the Community projects come within this description — 'unqualified' does not necessarily mean 'untrained'. Indeed, many workers will have received a more appropriate training for their role than a formal qualification would have been able to provide.

Aside from articulated fears about the adequacy of new services there are probably some feelings which are more complex and more difficult to express. Parents of children with learning difficulties may have carried a burden of guilt for many years for having brought their children into the world and subsequently being unable to care for them. 'Needing to go into hospital' provides a practical solution which can be easier to accept emotionally than seeing their child in an ordinary house staffed by non-medical personnel.

Relatives of people with mental illness may have a different set of feelings about community services. In general, fewer families of people suffering from mental illness have kept in close touch with their relative than families of people with learning difficulties. In either case, families of people who have been in hospital for many years will have built up their own lives and established patterns in which the relative has no part. They may be extremely worried that they will now be expected to take back a major part of the responsibility, with all the commitment and upheaval that it would necessarily involve. Some families of people with mental illness would have had a very difficult time before the admission to hospital and now have no wish for them to live nearby, as this could mean a return to old times best forgotten.

A feeling which may not very often be expressed but can be evident in families who are not themselves materially well-off is an element of resentment. Most of the new houses and hostels to which residents move are comfortable and pleasant, and filled with good new furniture and fittings. This, as is often argued, is as it should be, but it may be considered rather unfair by those who have struggled hard all their lives to acquire a modest standard of living. Nor is it unheard of for staff, too, to express such feelings.

Once a decision has been made to contact relatives, there are a number of different strategies which are available. Some projects have simply sent letters to relatives of all the people concerned. In one case, the hospital insisted that the project sent letters to families of all potential dischargees — about 70 people — although they only planned to resettle 18. Others have held meetings for large numbers of parents and relatives. This can be a difficult forum to discuss individual problems, and generally may tend to exacerbate fears rather than allay them. Details of new services may not be easily understood by parents unless their own son or daughter is actually discussed. They will probably want to know how the changes will affect them personally rather than to learn about the general plans.

Most of the projects which have given the topic full consideration have come to the conclusion that individual contact with families is necessary. Working alongside hospital staff may be a good way to start since they may already know the family through visits to hospital. It may be necessary for project teams to be available at times (such as Sunday afternoons) when visits are made. Even if the first introduction does not come through ward staff, it is important to work together to ensure that the same message is given to parents from both hospital and project. Otherwise confusion over plans could lead to problems later on.

After an initial introduction to the family, project staff may need to visit as many as five or six times in order to establish a relationship, to go over the complex issues and feelings, and to determine the nature of their future involvement. Visits should not be placed too far apart, perhaps every two or three weeks, so that earlier work is not lost and information is not forgotten. It will be important to recognise the various motives and feelings which they may hold. Some families may decide to become actively involved in the project and to take part in planning meetings which concern their relative whereas others will be content for decisions to be made in their absence. They may appreciate the opportunity to visit new facilities — even if they are not complete — and to meet the staff team in order to gain reassurance that good services will be provided. Some projects have also begun their own newsletters for families and other interested parties. Undertaking intensive work of this nature with families has considerable implications for the workload of busy project workers. Planners will need to take this into account when estimates are made for staffing and resources.

In many hospitals relatives' groups have developed, often in conjunction with Leagues of Friends. Some of these have become affiliated to recently-established national organisations which have begun to take on a political and campaigning role. Some groups also have a professional membership, including members of the major trade unions, who tend to be opposed to hospital closures and, in turn, to community projects. Within such a setting, anxieties and doubts can multiply and lead to the development of a powerful force of opposition to community projects. After this word of warning we should note, however, that many of these groups share the aims of the Care in the Community programme; in particular, opposition to the indiscriminate discharge of people from long-stay hospitals into inadequate facilities, and support for the development of proper care plans before anyone leaves.

While many projects believe in the principle of involving relatives in as many decisions as possible, there can be problems. Individual programme planning and case review meetings are usually held at times convenient for staff rather than relatives. A parent may be expected to lose half or more of a day's work to attend such a meeting or they may need to make arrangements for child-minding and so on. Transport can be a problem, too, since not all relatives will have their own car and public transport to isolated hospitals can be slow, inconvenient and expensive.

On the positive side it should be noted that many parents and relatives have been a great asset to some of the projects. Even some who were initially opposed to any change have harnessed their interest in a constructive way and become useful and influential advocates. Some have subsequently been able to give support and encouragement to other families in similar positions to themselves. In other cases, projects have been able to help families to re-establish contact with their relative, and this has been a subsequent source of satisfaction to all concerned. The goodwill and help of families can greatly help a project to develop a positive image and a network of community support nearby.

Neighbourhood and community

Many people hold the view that it should not be necessary to ask permission to move into a neighbourhood simply because you happen to be elderly, or have learning difficulties or a mental illness. Small groups of people have managed to move to a new home in a domestic setting without anyone noticing or objecting. While this is based on a sound principle and certainly follows a rule which most of us would expect to apply to ourselves, there can be problems if attempts are made to copy it on too large a scale.

Larger residences are more likely to require planning permission for change of use and may need to register under the Registered Homes Act. The experiences of projects in this area are extremely varied — quite different responses have been received from local residents to different facilities even within the same project. In some cases an individual approach to neighbours has proved fruitful: project staff knocked on the doors of everyone living in the immediate vicinity, explained the project to them and received favourable and even helpful responses. In other cases exactly the same approach has led to powerful objections: neighbours organised petitions and insisted on a public meeting after which planning permission became very much more difficult to obtain. Feelings among neighbours can be very strong indeed. One group have taken their objections to their Health Service Commission and the local authority Ombudsman. The obstacle of planning permission varies enormously in different parts of the country. Some projects have managed to sidestep it entirely. Others have been held up for long periods by restrictions on the use of certain buildings and some house purchases have fallen through for this reason. Certainly the problem is reduced where ordinary housing is used. Local knowledge in advance may help to predict the likely response of a neighbourhood. In some cases public meetings have proved helpful, but more often they have raised more difficulties than they have solved.

The findings of a survey of community responses to 43 group homes for people with learning difficulties in the city of Boston, USA, confirm some of these anecdotal reports (Seltzer, 1984). Most of the group homes in Boston had been in operation for two or three years, and accommodated an average of six people, most of whom had previously lived in institutions. About half of the homes encountered opposition from the local community. The number of residents, their ages and levels of disability did not bear any relation to the community's response, but the strategies employed in establishing the home did seem to be important. Homes which had employed a 'high profile' strategy — activities such as public meetings, use of media and open houses — were significantly more likely to have encountered opposition. Protests from the neighbours were also received more often when information had been made available at an early stage, particularly during the six-month period before the home opened. In addition, more opposition was encountered in areas where property values were higher. Surprisingly, homes which received support from local people and homes which included local representation on their management and site-selection committees were no less likely to encounter opposition.

One frequently-reported reason for opposition is the fear of neighbours that their property will decrease in value. Analyses of the property market in a number of different areas in the USA have consistently shown this fear to be unfounded. A similar finding has been reported in five separate studies, published between 1978 and 1982 (Seltzer, 1984).

The type of organisation running the scheme may make a difference. Voluntary organisations can project a different image from statutory authorities and at the planning stage it is image and impression which count. Health and social services agencies may render a more reassuringly professional impression, although small voluntary organisations may be better able to move in unnoticed.

Some areas are not at all suitable to resettle people. Certain deprived and run-down areas of large cities, where unemployment is high and crime and vandalism are rife, cannot provide a good quality of life for anyone. It would be a misunderstanding of 'normalisation' to assume that such areas should be used simply because 'normal' people also live there and endure an impoverished lifestyle. Normalisation for people with disabilities should mean treating them as valued citizens and consequently enabling them to live in reasonably pleasant surroundings. Other areas, although not undesirable, may be unsuitable because of a lack of appropriate residential accommodation.

The number of residences and people to be resettled from hospital in any one area should be limited. Over-large buildings and the clustering of smaller houses in too small an area can easily lead to 'ghettos' or 'saturation' of an area which tends to make people with disabilities more conspicuous rather than less so, and consequently less easily accepted. Planners of projects will need to investigate the local area thoroughly and to find out whether other new services, such as residential homes for elderly people, are also being planned. Once a residence is established and people have moved in, it may be advantageous to get to know some of the immediate neighbours. This does not step outside the bounds of normal practice since most people would be expected to make contact with their neighbours before long. It can also be preferable to meet residents in person and to have the nature of the establishment explained openly, rather than picking up gossip and rumours which inevitably spread. Arranging for residents to make personal contact is a very different enterprise from asking permission beforehand on their behalf, and usually produces quite different reactions. Some projects have held parties or barbecues to which neighbours were invited, which then led to further contacts and the development of friendships.

Projects vary as to the priority they place on getting to know the neighbours. Some see it as a vital part of community integration and have made considerable efforts in that direction, whereas others have been content to allow residents and neighbours to ignore each other in peace. Both approaches are common in ordinary life: some people prefer to know everyone around them while others are happy to have little contact. Expectations of people with disabilities can differ, though; excessive noise or unusual behaviour may be less easily tolerated from former residents of hospitals than from a family of ordinary children. Again, personal contact can often help to clear up misunderstandings and provide reassurance.

Relationships with general community facilities are important. Local shopkeepers, publicans, police, clergy and others may appreciate a visit or a meeting when people have moved in. It may also help them to feel involved and to act on behalf of the project if necessary.

General practitioners (GPs) constitute a powerful group and can become a major obstacle to community developments if they so wish. Many GPs have refused to accept responsibility for people resettled from long-stay hospitals on the grounds that they are likely to place above-average demands on their time. (This is not necessarily the case, and often depends on the age of the people concerned.) At present there are no incentives to them to accept 'more demanding' people onto their lists and so decisions have tended to reflect the individual levels of interest and enthusiasm of particular GPs. Projects have tended to register their clients with GPs who are willing to take them but this tends to overload a few individuals. As more community services are established and hospitals run down, it may be necessary to develop guidelines on a wider scale for family practitioner committees to persuade GPs to co-operate. An insoluble problem which remains is that special arrangements to encourage health professionals require residents to be treated as special, working in direct opposition to principles of normalisation and integration.

General practitioners are one group who may gain from further education and information about Care in the Community and the needs of people with learning difficulties and mental illnesses. They can arrange to attend study days as part of their normal duties. Other interested groups might also benefit by being better informed about special need groups and community services. Pictures, films and videos shown to local audiences can be a powerful medium with which to convey messages so that they are not forgotten. Indeed, the level of knowledge among the general public still falls far short of ideal. The problems of ageing, learning difficulty and mental illness are often confused, and all are feared and misunderstood.

Studies of the knowledge and attitudes of the general public to the problems of disability, and particularly learning difficulty, have indicated cause for concern. A recent survey of over 1,300 teenagers discovered that only one-quarter had ever had any personal contact with a person with learning difficulties. Those who had had contact tended to be more knowledgeable about causes of learning difficulty and abilities of handicapped people, and were generally more willing to meet them and confident about how to react. The teenagers' social background also seemed to have an influence on their attitudes: those from lower-income families tended to be more accepting of the rights of people with learning difficulties to be treated as full members of the community and to mix socially with non-handicapped people (McConkey, McCormack and Naughton, 1983a).

Changing attitudes, however, seems to require more than simple proximity and non-interactive contact. Sinson (1985) has noted that residents of areas where people with learning difficulties (from an institution) 'wandered about freely' were no more likely to have had any real contact than people from areas without such an institution. Similarly, bringing the public into contact with people with learning difficulties through 'institutional tours' has found no evidence of improved attitudes, and may indeed serve to reinforce existing negative beliefs (Cleland and Chambers, 1959; LeUnes, Christiansen and Wilkerson, 1975).

The most successful programmes of education and attitude change have involved elements of education — including films and videos which 'modelled' appropriate ways of interacting with handicapped people — and structured interaction. It seems to be helpful if all participants in the programme are of equivalent age and social background, and if the activities are age-appropriate. It is also important to emphasise the skills and abilities of handicapped people, rather than their limitations (McConkey and McCormack, 1984). Educational packages, consisting of a series of such activities, have been tested out in a number of secondary schools and adult education colleges in Ireland (McConkey et al., 1983b).

While such programmes may be very useful in educating people for the future, the problem remains of how to reach the majority of the general public who do not attend school or college. Specialist television and radio programmes probably do not reach the people who have the greatest ignorance of disabilities and handicaps. Gradual, appropriate introduction of these topics into popular programmes, such as soap operas, could prove a powerful means of conveying messages to those who might not otherwise want to hear.

Further efforts to educate the community in general about these topics would be beneficial for all concerned.

7. Individual care planning: lessons from America and elsewhere

The Care in the Community initiative sets out to help long-term residents of hospitals to return to a new life in the community. The majority of the people concerned have come from mental handicap and psychiatric hospitals, although some elderly people are from geriatric and general hospitals. All are likely to continue to need care and support for a long period of time, if not indefinitely. Here we will focus on people with learning difficulties and mental illnesses, for whom the initiative is perhaps more pertinent, although many of the principles and practicalities discussed will be equally applicable to elderly people. For all client groups, we place very strong emphasis on the need for individual care planning or case management.

In this chapter we provide a comprehensive description of case management practices in America and elsewhere. The experiences in these other settings spotlight issues which have arisen in the Care in the Community programme. There is much to learn from the experience of case management programmes in America, if only because many of them have been in operation for ten years or more and relatively little is known about them in the UK. In Chapter 8 we look at experiences in the use of case management 'models' in some of the Care in the Community pilot projects.

Care in the Community: the need for planning and co-ordination

The kinds of support needed by people with learning difficulties or mental illnesses are many and varied. A recent survey of the service needs of a group of discharged psychiatric patients delineated a number of important areas. They included needs for medical care, counselling, leisure activities, financial support, help for relatives, activities of daily living, vocational rehabilitation, education and accommodation (Solomon, Gordon and Davis, 1984). A study by Lehman, Reed and Possidente (1983), in which clients were asked for their opinions about their needs for help, drew out a similar list of areas which spanned accommodation, employment, social life and mental health problems.

The kinds of community service which are beginning to develop to meet the needs of these people are also varied, and are likely to grow in an increasingly divergent manner. Recent government publications (DHSS, 1981c) have emphasised the objective of providing a wide range of services within each locality, with the flexibility necessary to meet the needs of different individuals. Already, community services are provided by a number of different agencies, from health service-managed hostels and day hospitals, social services-managed houses and day centres to housing association accommodation, further education, sheltered employment, voluntary sector social clubs and private homes. In principle, the availability of a range of such services has far greater potential for fulfilling the needs of individuals than an institution would have, with its standard routine and lack of flexibility over living environment and activities. On the other hand, the very divergence and flexibility of community provision, with its greater scope and choice, creates its own problems.

Where services are *not* all provided under one roof, or at least by one agency, the probability of someone missing out on something they need is very high. Even supposing that a particular locality contains a comprehensive set of services, a mentally disabled person is unlikely to be able to tap into the appropriate long-term support services without specialist help. Concern that people discharged from hospital may receive inadequate care led to one of the major recommendations of the House of Commons Select Committee on the Social Services (1985). They advised that no mentally disabled person should be discharged from hospital without a clearly-defined individual care plan and resources available to ensure its implementation. The care plan would have to span the full range of a person's needs, which implies that a careful assessment is required. Furthermore, someone must take responsibility for co-ordinating resources and must subsequently follow up to check whether needs have been met. It is important that a single worker take on this role over an extended period of time, so that people discharged from hospital may be followed up, and care continues as long as necessary.

96

What is case management?

Careful assessment of need, comprehensive care planning, co-ordination of services and follow-up — together these broadly define case management, a development which has become increasingly important in North America over the last few years. Its specific objectives and functions can vary considerably but the concept is a useful one, particularly in considering long-term care in the community.

The term *case management* appears in the health and welfare literature from the mid-1970s onwards. It has not yet emerged in British writings to any great extent, although it has much in common with the notion of *key worker* in settings such as social service teams (see for example Ferlie et al., 1985). Case management in America developed from the expansion of social services in the 1960s and a consequent complex of agencies providing care in a rather sketchy and unco-ordinated fashion. In the early 1970s the Department of Health Education and Welfare recognised the need for an improvement in their co-ordination and proposed certain legislative changes. They also funded a programme of demonstration projects to test various integration techniques (the Services Integration Targets of Opportunity projects). One feature common to most of these projects was a 'systems agent' or case manager to co-ordinate resources for individual clients.

A case management system is usually one in which the provision of services to meet the needs of individual clients is the responsibility of one agency or worker. The services themselves may be provided by different agencies but the case manager co-ordinates the services and ensures that needs are met. The American Joint Commission on Accreditation of Hospitals defines the case management task as assessment, planning, arranging and linking services, monitoring and advocacy. Many programmes assume that preceding activities of case funding and screening for eligibility also fall within its sphere.

The objectives of case management

A number of objectives tend to be ascribed to case management. It is interesting to note that advocates of the model have often shown enthusiasm for its potential usefulness from very different perspectives. For instance, one group which espouses the principles of *normalisation* recommends that services are planned and co-ordinated around the needs of individuals in a flexible manner, rather than people being slotted into existing services (Tyne, 1981). Achieving this goal means that a key worker, or case manager, must take responsibility for the co-ordination of services while at the same time acting as the individual's guide and helper. On the other hand, case management has also been

97

recommended by those who wish to improve efficiency, such that needs can be met without costs rising to an exorbitant level. There is no reason why different positions should not come to agree on the best way forward, but it is unusual for an alliance to develop between such divergent groups. Ramon (1982) has commented on the 'potency of untraditional alliances in bringing on reforms', although in a different context. (She was referring to the reform of psychiatric services in Italy.)

The most fundamental objectives of case management programmes share the general set of values which lie behind most social services and social work practice. Some of these are spelt out in practical guides for case managers (see Steinberg and Carter, 1983; National Association for Social Work, 1984). Workers are encouraged to be flexible, in order to respond to the varying needs of their clients and to develop appropriate and possibly imaginative combinations of services. They should appreciate that clients need to build on their own strengths and reach as great a degree of independence as possible, even if this means taking the occasional risk. Clients have rights to privacy and confidentiality which should be respected, and rights to express their own preferences which should be heard. Those who are most vulnerable will need the most help, and workers should aim to be helper, advocate and guide in a way that is sensitive and gives respect to the person's individual human dignity.

A look at the job descriptions of case managers in ten different settings revealed certain stated values in common. Those which appeared most frequently were the client's right to the least restrictive environment, and advocacy on the client's behalf. Values which could only be implicitly inferred from the job descriptions but also appeared frequently were: recognition of the client as an autonomous person; and accountability to the client and efficiency with regard to time, money and co-ordination (DeWeaver and Johnson, 1983).

Case management is also, in part, a method of planning and allocating care services. Consequently it must share some of the aims and objectives of service distribution in general, namely equity and efficiency. We will consider first the objective of efficiency which carries a number of implications.

· In order for a service to be efficient it must not only *effectively* provide for identified needs but it must also curtail services where they are not appropriate. Institutions frequently provide inefficient services, such as domestic help for people who can cope by themselves, and fail to provide other services, such as stimulating activities.

Several different aspects of efficiency which can be associated with particular case management tasks have been outlined by Davies and Challis (1986).

Input mix efficiency refers to an appropriate matching of resources to needs by the most suitable combination of resources. This is likely to imply an awareness of the cost of resources so that cost savings may be made, provided that outputs are maintained. One consequence of an input-efficient case management programme may be to alter the pattern of service consumption away from institutional and residential care in favour of community services (Beatrice, 1981). This has been the explicit aim of some case management programmes, particularly those concerned with frail elderly people. One project which achieved a more efficient use of resources was the Kent community care scheme (Davies and Challis, 1986), in which individual case managers had responsibility for client budgets with the flexibility to use them as they wished, and comprehensive information about the unit costs of services. (This enabled the substitution of some resources by others which were less expensive but were able to produce the same results.)

The tasks of comprehensive assessment, careful planning, co-ordination and monitoring all contribute to the degree of input mix efficiency achieved by a particular project.

Technical efficiency is achieved when a service maximises its effectiveness by using the most appropriate combination of inputs or resources. Regular monitoring of the degree of success in achieving welfare goals for clients and the use of resources is an important task for the achievement of technical efficiency. It may also be important to monitor and review the service itself at regular intervals to determine whether its overall aims are being realised.

Target efficiency is slightly different. It is a measure of the accuracy with which resources reach those for whom they were intended and implies equitable distribution according to need.

Horizontal target efficiency refers to the availability of a service to all those deemed to be in need of it. It depends on the awareness of agencies, potential clients and the general public about the existence of services and their aims. Good access to services is also important here. Success in this area depends on case finding and referral from other agencies, for which good communication and liaison within the locality are important.

Referral and case finding are not major activities in many of the Care in the Community projects since most have a pre-determined group of clients from particular long-stay hospitals. Only in a few projects do cases have to be found or referred through the hospital and even these activities are very different from the exercise of case finding in a non-institutional population.

Vertical target efficiency is a measure of the extent to which available services go to those who need them rather than to those who do not. (Like horizontal target efficiency, therefore, vertical target efficiency describes the efficiency with which service providers are able to distribute resources fairly and equitably.) The case management task on which it depends is screening, or selection for entry into the service programme. This is an important activity in some of the Care in the Community projects, particularly those which select on the basis of client characteristics, but it will be less important in projects whose selection decisions depend on geographical and local factors. Once again, the situation in these projects is quite different from that typically found in case management programmes for non-institutionalised people, since the major criterion for entry into the scheme is residence in a long-stay hospital which assumes, by definition, a need for the project and its services.

Output efficiency is the achievement of the ultimate service objectives. Assessment of a project's success in fulfilling its aims is discussed more fully in Chapter 11.

All the case management tasks of assessment, care planning, co-ordination and monitoring contribute to output efficiency. A thorough assessment is necessary to determine a client's needs in all areas of life, while careful planning should determine the most appropriate resources to meet those needs. Resources should then be provided in a co-ordinated and coherent fashion such that service gaps and overlaps are minimised. Follow-up and review are essential to ensure that needs are met as intended and, if not, that plans are altered accordingly.

Achievement of the objective of 'horizontal target efficiency' or fairness in service distribution requires that similar cases should be treated in similar ways, while 'vertical target efficiency' requires that different needs receive appropriately different service packages. This implies a thorough and competent assessment of need which is well standardised, so that the same criteria are applied to all cases at different points in time and in different locations. Some of the channelling projects in the USA have referred to a 'single point of entry' into the care system for all clients, as opposed to the commonly encountered situation in which many different agencies accept clients on the basis of their own particular criteria. In these projects one agency assessed all cases in a standard way and then determined which combination of services would best suit the needs of the individual, although the services themselves were provided by a variety of different agencies.

Some case management programmes have a further objective, namely that of service development. This may be a direct consequence

100

of case management work in areas where services are poorly developed. Through knowledge of client need, workers will be able to identify important shortfalls in provision and inform service planners about directions for new developments.

In summary, the main aim of case management is to meet the needs of clients in the most suitable and individualised way, rather than to fit people into the standard services which happen to be available. In addition, case management programmes frequently aspire to improve efficiency and to reduce the gaps and overlaps which often occur in a complex network of community services. Working from a central co-ordinating point increases the likelihood of equitable treatment, and good communications should make it easily accessible. Although case management may lead to an improvement in efficiency, costs may actually increase as more needs are identified and more services delivered (Intagliata, 1982). A final objective may be to develop new patterns of service and to advise planners about developments on a larger scale.

Variations in the case management model

Within the basic case management framework — referral, assessment, care planning, co-ordination of services, follow-up and continued monitoring — there are many possible variations. Programmes vary in the allocation and nature of tasks, the type of worker employed and the scope and influence of the case management function. In the USA the picture is further complicated by the assignment of the title 'case manager' to a variety of situations which would not conform to the description outlined above. It has been observed that 'the role of case manager is so widespread that it is unusual to find a health or social service agency that does not claim to provide case management services for its client' (Austin, 1983, p.17). For the sake of simplicity, the dimensions along which case management programmes might vary are discussed separately below, although in practice they influence each other and it will be necessary to cross-refer continually between dimensions.

A single worker or a combination of many

The question of whether a single worker should be responsible for all stages and activities pervades almost all of the other features of any case management system. It might appear that the obvious way to co-ordinate services is by the appointment of an individual case manager or key worker for each client, who could not only liaise with the various service agencies but also act as an advocate and helper. A single worker should be able to provide continuity, through the web of different service agencies and also over time, and would be a source of support to the client. This may be particularly important for people who need long-term care.

When other factors are taken into account, however, the picture becomes less clear. The practicality of whom to employ as a case manager, the balance of duties they should undertake, the scope of their responsibilities, their qualifications, status and management present difficulties for a single-worker model. A number of case management programmes in the USA have delegated some tasks to other workers and, occasionally, to other agencies. For instance, another agency may be contracted in to carry out the assessment of clients. This, too, presents problems as the original agency has less control over the contracted workers and their activities (Sterthous, 1983).

Degree of client contact

The basic framework of case finding, assessment, planning, co-ordination and monitoring assumes a degree of direct contact between the case manager and the client. There is, however, a considerable divergence of opinion over the extent to which case managers should be involved in direct work, or whether they should engage in direct work at all.

Lamb (1980) presents a case for workers to be therapists as well as brokers of services. He emphasises the role of helping the client through a complex system and stresses the advantage of keeping the situation as simple as possible by enabling the same worker to form the most important relationship with the client. He or she has no need to refer to another worker or agency. Other writers have pointed out that people with chronic mental illness need a stable and continuous relationship, which may help them to comply with the care programme which has been planned (Johnson and Rubin, 1983).

The case management model, introduced earlier, was developed by Davies and Challis (1986) to provide better community care for frail elderly people. Experienced workers with reduced caseloads carried out thorough assessments of the needs of clients, independently of the services which are normally available. The workers were given an unusually high degree of autonomy and flexibility in their work, and so were able to devise imaginative new solutions to some of the problems that were encountered. Case managers were encouraged to be precise in recording the services they provided and the reasons for them, and to monitor the effects at regular and frequent intervals. The workers' relationship with the client was an important feature both in a counselling context — if counselling was assessed to be a necessary service — and also in the provision of aids, adaptations and voluntary helpers in a sensitive and appropriate manner. Thus the case managers had to undertake a variety of direct and indirect tasks, some of which required in-depth professional knowledge and others which required basic interpersonal and administrative skills.

At this point — the involvement of the case manager in a variety of indirect tasks — opinions begin to diverge. Some writers have recommended that experienced caseworkers should carry out the more complex assessment and counselling tasks while arrangement and delivery of practical services and regular monitoring should be delegated to others. A problem that can arise when case managers provide most, or all, of the direct client contact themselves is the difficulty of ensuring that the balance of direct services is maintained in the most appropriate manner.

A further possibility is that the case manager almost never sees the client face to face. In this model, a pre-screening visit is carried out by an aide after which a thorough assessment is conducted by an outside agency, by contract. The case manager designs the care plan after some contact with the client, significant others and the care-providing agencies. Re-assessments and changes of plan may be negotiated by telephone or correspondence. The counselling aspects in this model are treated as a direct service that is obtained by contract.

It is possible that the extreme positions on whether or not case managers should also be highly involved in direct work with clients are taken by those with a medical perspective or a social/community work perspective. This division also becomes evident in discussion of other dimensions of case management variation.

From a more practical viewpoint, DeWeaver and Johnson (1983) point out that the location of the service in a rural or an urban setting makes a difference to the degree of client contact given by case managers. Specifically, rural case managers have to deliver a range of services themselves which would be otherwise available from other agencies and workers in an urban setting.

Case management specialisation and task sharing

Closely related to the issue of direct client contact is the extent to which the case management activities are the responsibility of a 'specialist' case manager rather than an existing worker who is already employed in another capacity. Specialisation will influence the types of task undertaken and the degree of sharing with other workers.

An example of a 'non-specialist' model of case management is the designation of key workers in a multidisciplinary team based in a psychiatric hospital. The key workers take on duties of liaison and co-ordination on behalf of their clients in addition to their normal duties of (say) nursing, social work and psychology with other clients. In this situation workers do not normally have the job title of 'case manager' but are labelled by their discipline of origin. Some of the case management tasks, particularly assessment, may be shared with other members of the team, or with the team as a whole. Austin (1983) has described case management in a non-specialist way as a function that can be incorporated into existing service systems without altering the relationships between providers.

Most of the case management programmes in the USA employ workers with the job title of case manager whose duties fit clearly within a 'specialist' framework. This has the advantage of clarity about liaison and co-ordination responsibilities, although some duties may be shared with other workers and agencies. One type of worker may focus on assessment and care planning, and another implements the care plans, possibly under the supervision of the original worker. The main problem with this model arises with long-term care groups, when the phases are not easy to separate and when formal assessment needs to be repeated at intervals in addition to continued checking up and monitoring.

In all of the variations in which tasks are shared the continuity of a single worker is lost, although other advantages develop. For instance, it becomes possible to make use of the special skills of particularly experienced workers during the phases for which they are most needed, without wasting their time carrying out more routine administrative tasks.

The size of the caseload will influence the range of tasks that an individual case manager is able to carry out and the amount of time he or she is able to devote to each. It is difficult to set down any firm guidelines as to caseload size, as the actual workload will vary with complexity and dependency of individual clients; it will be necessary to monitor the progress of highly dependent or unstable people at more frequent regular intervals. One important feature of the Kent community care scheme for the frail elderly was a reduced caseload, comparable in size to those of workers with vulnerable child care cases (Challis and Davies, 1984). In practice, case managers in the community care scheme were responsible for about 30 cases. Programmes which do not have a policy on caseloads may find themselves in an impossible position to perform a useful role. A Minnesota study found an average of 81 adult clients per case manager, with an average of 171 clients for every case aide when in stable community programmes. One of the highest case loads was 280.

Another feature built into the Kent community care scheme was peer group review, a formal means of promoting communication. Regular meetings of workers fulfilled a number of purposes. First they were to develop a form of 'quality assurance' (based on the ideas of business organisations which review their achievements on a regular basis), through discussion between representatives at all levels. Second, they were to disseminate ideas and innovations for practice, such as the recruitment of local helpers to befriend clients and carry out simple tasks for them to the benefit of both clients and helpers. Peer group meetings also encouraged the use of accurate recording and helped to foster an atmosphere of support and encouragement between the workers.

Professional status of the worker

An issue over which there is considerable debate is whether case managers should be professionally qualified or whether the critical liaison, co-ordination and monitoring tasks would be more appropriately carried out by unqualified workers.

The Kent community care scheme employed qualified and experienced workers who were able to carry out careful assessments and devise suitable plans to meet the needs of clients. It was seen to be important to employ workers of greater experience and status, in order to improve the quality of community services for elderly people who would normally have been allocated to unqualified workers. They were able to work more independently and to make decisions without recourse to a superior.

The other major reason for employing qualified professionals as case managers is their greater ability to command authority with the various service agencies among whom they need to work. The assessment and service planning decisions will at least need ratification by someone of professional status if they are to carry weight with other service providers, so the most efficient course may be for a professional to make the decisions in the first place.

Surveys of case managers in the USA have indicated a moderate degree of professional involvement. Kurtz, Bagarozzi and Pollane (1984) found that 58 per cent of those employed by mental health centres in the state of Georgia reported a professional identification, of which almost half were in social work, but only just over a third of these were formally qualified. The other major professional groups represented were nursing and psychology. Sterthous (1983) reported that ten out of 14 case management projects for elderly people in Pennsylvania employed professional staff, especially in assessment and care planning. Local factors such as availability and the needs of the particular client group largely determined whether or not professional staff were employed. Many projects used professional case managers only for assessment and planning while the more mundane tasks of service arranging, record keeping and follow-up were delegated to unqualified aides. Only three projects employed a single person to carry out the whole range of the case management tasks.

The employment of professionals is not without its problems. A study by Caragonne (1980) found that many professional case managers actually spent considerable time engaged in psychotherapy with their clients. These workers in particular tended to pay less attention to co-ordination and follow-up. Pelletier (1983) also reported that professionals were often unwilling to take on extra tasks which they felt did not accord with their training and status. These comments imply that the employment of a worker with the title 'case manager' does not, itself, solve any problems, and the importance of greater clarity of tasks and goals within any particular programme is paramount.

The obvious corollary is *which* profession is the most appropriate in case management? Many programmes employ social workers, although community nursing is also commonly encountered. Sterthous (1983) recommends the use of a small team consisting of a social worker and a nurse for the assessment and planning stages. The most appropriate style of assessment will probably depend on the type of client being provided for. In cases where there are medical problems, or liaison with health service agencies is particularly important, it may be most appropriate to employ nurses. Social workers may be most useful where families are involved and where other services, such as housing, welfare benefits and employment agencies, also feature. This categorisation does, to an extent, pre-judge and therefore preclude a comprehensive assessment.

A multidisciplinary team approach is frequently recommended for assessment, in order to combine the specialist skills and knowledge of a variety of professions. This could become very costly if team involvement continued beyond the planning stage. Many writers advise that the liaison and co-ordination functions are taken on by an unqualified (and less expensive) assistant who is less likely to spend much time in psychotherapy. This model has its disadvantages, since the continuity of a single worker is lost. Multidisciplinary teams can also have their own problems; for example, interprofessional rivalry can lead to conflict and the conclusions reached may reflect the interests of the most powerful members, rather than a synthesis of the team as a whole.

Form of recording

If the oft-cited management objectives — clear aims, continuity of provision, effectiveness, efficiency and equity — are to be achieved it is necessary to record decisions and plans in a systematic manner. One of the first attempts to produce a suitable recording format in the UK was Goldberg and Warburton's (1979) 'action research' study of a year's referrals to one social services office. A case review form was introduced on which workers recorded client needs, planned changes and social work activities at regular six-monthly intervals. It was found to be a useful record of work undertaken in the department, and it helped workers to specify their aims and tasks and to see individual needs within a broader context. The only drawback was in the categorisation of needs and actions which some workers found too restrictive.

The Kent community care scheme for the frail elderly employed a modified version of the case review form, to be completed by case managers at three-month intervals. It provided a structured and standardised record of the needs, plans and activities which could be referred to at a later date. At each review the client's needs were re-assessed and any changes of plan were noted. Both short- and long-term plans could be incorporated into the review procedure.

Individual programme planning has much in common with case review and case management. The IPP system, devised in the USA for work with people with learning difficulties and now in operation in many areas of Britain, has been described by Blunden (1980) and Kyle and Roche (1983). Its first principle is that services for people with learning difficulties should be planned individually, and by a team of professionals in consultation with the handicapped person and their family. The plan should be written down so that everyone's responsibilities are made clear, and it should be reviewed at regular intervals. The recording format differs from case review forms, being less structured and having fewer pre-coded categories, but the intention is very similar. The sequence of information-gathering, joint assessment, planning, implementation and follow-up are similar to those of case management. A 'key worker' is nominated who takes a role similar to that of a case manager, although direct work with the client and their family is emphasised more than liaison with other services. Co-ordination tends to be the responsibility of the team as whole.

The case review form that we designed for the Care in the Community pilot project programme is partly categorised, although the information recorded is qualitative and descriptive. Areas of need are specified, such as education, accommodation, personal care and leisure activities, and spaces for the recording of needs, requirements and action plans are set out. Each time a client's progress is reviewed the form completed at the last review may be consulted and care plans adjusted accordingly.

A possible disadvantage of structured, written review forms such as IPPs is that they may formalise and reduce the monitoring task to the extent that changes between reviews may be ignored. Some workers have observed that the process becomes 'too bureaucratic' and unable to adapt when a flexible response is required.

Control of resources

One objective of case management programmes is to improve efficiency while satisfactorily meeting the needs of clients. Input efficiency, in particular, implies keeping costs down, where possible, provided that an effective service is delivered. Case managers can have an influence on costs since, as Austin proposes:

> Fundamentally, developing a care plan is a resource allocation process involving a range of decisions about how many of what kinds of services a client will receive from which service providers. A case manager ... is operating as a resource allocator; and case management can be designed to enhance the manager's authority for this task (1983, p.24).

She goes on to say that the case manager's ability to allocate resources may be influenced by incentives. The sort of incentive that could be given to them is increased responsibility for planning services with control of a limited budget, to be drawn on at their own discretion. Some writers (Beatrice, 1981; Wray and Wieck, 1985) recommend the availability of such discretionary funds, on the assumption that funding decisions made closer to the point of service delivery are more effective and efficient.

The Kent community care scheme used this approach for people who were on the borderline of entering residential care. Social workers with specialist knowledge in the care of elderly people were employed as case managers and were given reduced caseloads. Their duties included the usual tasks of case management — case-finding and screening, assessment, care planning, monitoring and review — but also incorporated the additional feature of a budget constraint. Workers were given detailed costings (or 'shadow' prices) of all the services they co-ordinated, including both statutory services such as home help and other community resources which were to be charged against client-specific budgets, each limited to two-thirds of the cost of a residential place in the county. In addition, they were permitted to use the budget in a flexible way to devise new solutions to the problems of their clients. One solution, already referred to, was the recruitment of local helpers who visited the elderly people and carried out tasks which did not require any professional expertise. Some of these helpers were paid small amounts of money.

The scheme was able to improve the well-being of clients, as compared with a control group who received standard services, and at a lower cost. Rates of admission to residential care were reduced, as were mortality rates. Replications of the project (and developments of it) are now being carried out in other parts of the country with different geographical and demographic characteristics.

Influence over agencies

Financial incentives can be an important feature in the degree of co-operation between agencies. Case management involves the co-ordination of disparate and often unrelated agencies which may have no incentive to work together unless they are given a directive to do so or encouraged in some other way.

Case management programmes in the USA show considerable variation in the degree of control which the agency or worker has over service-providing agencies. Allocation of resources through a 'single point of entry' to the care system could considerably alter the balance of power within the system. But if the case management programme is managed by one organisation, such as social services, it may have limited authority over others, such as health services. An alternative model is one in which the case management agency does not have statutory authority over the allocation of resources but does have the capacity to purchase services. A third possibility is that the case management agency has neither statutory nor financial authority but has to rely on persuasion, negotiation and goodwill to obtain appropriate services for its clients.

It is important for case management agencies to have sufficient authority to obtain services, but without losing contact with service providers. The latter is necessary to maintain credibility at a local level.

Advocacy

Some case management models, such as that of the Joint Commission of Accreditation of Hospitals, include advocacy among the core tasks. Others (Etherington, 1984) view advocacy as a function more usefully undertaken by someone in a more independent position who is able to befriend the client and campaign on their behalf while, if necessary, criticising the service system for its shortcomings. The disadvantage of an independent advocate is that, without statutory responsibility, they will have less ability to obtain services for their client.

Overview of the variations of case management models

The variations of case management are complex. They are summarised briefly in Table 7.1, together with some of the advantages and

Table 7.1
Variable features of case management programmes

Feature	Advantages	Disadvantages
1 Single worker for all case management.	Continuity.	Lack of delegation of tasks to most appropriate workers.
2 Direct work with client.	Simplicity, continuity, support for client, better knowledge of client.	Conflicting tasks to be undertaken. Inappropriate balance of direct and indirect services.
3 'Specialist' case management workers.	Clarity about responsibilities of co-ordination employment.	More of a major reform for services and staff.
4 Tasks shared with other workers.	Make use of specialist skills. Experienced people not 'wasted' in mundane tasks.	Lack of continuity. More difficult to tie together continued assessment with service provision.
5 Restricted caseload.	More time to plan and carry out tasks effectively. More frequent monitoring.	
6 Peer group review.	Review achievements. Group support. Exchange of good ideas.	
7 Professionally qualified workers.	Appropriateness of social work skills. Ability to work and make decisions independently. Multi-professional teams for assessment.	Unwilling to do mundane tasks. Too great an emphasis on therapy. Which profession is appropriate? Loss of continuity where limited professional involvement. Difficult team dynamics.
8 Written recording format.	Improved clarity of aims and tasks. Consistency, continuity.	Over-bureaucratic. Over-formalises observation of progress. Pre-coded categories may be too restrictive.
9 Worker has control of resources.	More cost-effective resource allocation.	
10 Authority over service agencies.	Ability to obtain services.	Loss of credibility at local level.
11 Advocacy by independent person (e.g. voluntary worker).	No vested interests in service system, better able to represent client.	Lack of authority to obtain resources.

disadvantages of each variant. The choice of case management arrangement often appears to be determined by expedience — to make best use of the available resources and existing system while attempting to meet the clients' needs. The type of worker employed may depend on local availability and existing local relationships between agencies. Localities can also vary considerably in the availability of appropriate resources. In settings where services are highly inadequate or non-existent any attempt at co-ordination becomes somewhat futile. On the other hand, case managers may have considerable knowledge of client needs and local shortfalls in provision, and can therefore inform and advise planners about directions for future development. In these circumstances the role of case management has changed somewhat from the planning of services on the basis of individual needs, since the time-lag between assessment of need and provision of services will be considerable. This is particularly true for services such as residential accommodation, where the acquisition and alteration of new buildings can be a lengthy process.

Beatrice describes case management as a 'middle-ground' response which leads to some change in the service system but does not require an entire reconstruction of the financing and delivery of services. He describes it as a 'ground-up, muddling-through, practical approach ... rather than an elegant conceptual tool' (1981, p.159).

The style and shape of a case management programme will vary with the context within which it operates: a complex system will likely require a more complex case management model. In settings where resources are scarce, case managers may make use of their own time more as a service. Negotiation may require both statutory authority and good informal relationships. It will be important for planners to remember that the staff of most programmes are ordinary people and should not be expected to perform extraordinary feats all of the time.

Case management developments in Britain

While most of evidence about case management has come from the USA and Canada, a few more developments in the UK are beginning to emerge.

A major difficulty for the co-ordination of care services in Britain is the administrative division between the National Health Service and local authority social services and other departments. As we have already seen, even where areas are coterminous and where joint committees and planning teams operate, true joint working is rare, and care services tend to be managed by one or the other.

The consequences of the administrative division at the level of clients and case managers can be problematic. It will be easier to obtain services which are managed by the authority which employs the case manager. In cases where individual workers are permitted to make use of a flexible budget to procure services there may be particular difficulties over whose budget is being spent and who is ultimately responsible.

The successful use of case management in the Kent community care scheme, described earlier, took place in a context of largely social services care provision. The clients who entered the scheme all lived in their own homes or independent accommodation. The services that they would have otherwise been most likely to receive were assessment by a home help organiser or social work aide, and then home help, meals-on-wheels or Part III accommodation. They would have been somewhat less likely to receive nursing or health care, or to have been admitted to hospital. Since the services which the social workers/case managers had to co-ordinate were largely provided by social services, voluntary agencies and volunteers, the case managers were in a suitable position of authority in relation to the agencies. It was therefore relatively easy for them to co-ordinate an appropriate package of services for their clients.

Programmes for other long-term care groups, such as people with a mental illness, may be more difficult to co-ordinate for a variety of reasons. The people who enter the scheme are likely to be referred from a hospital or other health service agency. A social worker as case manager is likely to be in a less suitable position to obtain access to health services. Ideally, the case manager should be able to provide a package of health services, social services and voluntary provision which best suits the needs of the individual client. In practice, however, it may be the case that the contents of the package are largely determined by the wishes of the dominant professional interest. The interest may be all the stronger when clients were in health service care before they entered the scheme. On the other hand, the employment of nurses or other health service employees as case managers could lead to difficulties in obtaining services such as housing, day care, welfare benefits or employment.

One project in the south of England which planned to develop a case management system for discharged schizophrenic patients has experienced some initial difficulties (Gibbons, 1983). The programme was intended to reduce the drop-out rate from aftercare services and to enhance access to services by employment of case managers. During the first year the service agencies involved continued to experience rivalries and vested interests in relation to patient care. The case manager was seen to be a threat to the independence of the various organisations and to be pushing them in directions in which they did not wish to go.

112

Following this experience, the researchers recommended that such programmes should develop very slowly indeed and should work to win the co-operation of agencies by proving their worth, at first in very limited areas such as the monitoring of medication.

Individual programme planning has to date made greater in-roads in Britain than case management, particularly in services for people with learning difficulties, although clearly the objective of service planning on the basis of individual need and the concomitant activities of detailed assessment and continued monitoring accord with the aims and functions of case management. In IPP work a strong emphasis is placed on the involvement of the client and, where appropriate, the client's family. Although this is often also true in case management programmes, it has not often been highlighted as a major principle — particularly in the American studies — and often takes second place to co-ordination and liaison between agencies.

Another major focus of IPP work is on training and learning specific skills. This may be due to the influence of particular professions, notably psychology, in its development. Psychologists working with people with learning difficulties tend to be concerned mainly with assessment and training in living skills since this is where their particular expertise is able to make the greatest contribution. Case management, on the other hand, probably developed from an administrative or policy perspective rather than from one specific profession or discipline.

Most case management and IPP systems in Britain are at an early stage in their development. The Nimrod project in South Wales which uses an IPP system is being evaluated and will produce some evidence about its achievements over the next few years (Humphreys, Blunden, Wilson, Newman and Pagler, 1985). Many of the pilot projects in the Care in the Community programme have attempted to incorporate IPP or case management to co-ordinate services. A number of these developments and their various working practices, together with some of the problems which they face, are described in the following chapter.

8. Assessment and individual care planning in the Care in the Community projects

Almost all the varieties of individual care planning and co-ordination described in the previous chapter are represented in the Care in the Community programme. Models for client selection and assessment include single professional decisions, multidisciplinary teamwork, and the use of formal assessment schedules. Co-ordination of individual care plans is also achieved in a number of different ways.

Selection of clients for the projects and individual assessment of their needs are the critical first steps on which subsequent community care services depend. Case-finding is not as complicated here as it has been in some of the case management programmes described in the previous chapter since eligibility is limited to residents of one or a few hospitals. Community care in this context is understood to include residential care for most clients. Under other circumstances it has often been defined more narrowly. Multidisciplinary and multi-agency working feature in all projects to some extent, although the particular arrangements for doing so vary. In some cases they differ between areas within the same project. In many schemes the structure and style of assessment and care planning have evolved with the project and have undergone several revisions during its lifetime. The flexibility to manage such alterations and ability to review the degree of success in achieving their aims are key features of some of the most interesting projects. If the pilot programme is to provide useful lessons and demonstrations for others to follow, an honest review of successes and failures in this way is imperative.

Initial identification of clients

The fundamental principles and assumptions on which a project is based determine the group of people from which potential clients will be selected. Some schemes stipulated that everyone who originated from a particular district or borough would be resettled, regardless of their degree of disability or capacity for independent living. Such criteria tend to be more prominent where people with learning difficulties are concerned since normalisation — which would advocate equal opportunities for all — features more often in these projects.

Bolton, for instance, intends to eventually make community care available to all long-term mental handicap hospital residents who entered hospital from what is now the Metropolitan Borough of Bolton, whatever their degree of dependency. Only some of these people come within the remit of the Care in the Community initiative itself. Altogether 174 such people have been identified, 99 of them in Brockhall Hospital, Blackburn. Non-Bolton residents are also considered where there are strong friendship links with Bolton residents. Similarly, the target group for the Camden project is all those people in St Lawrence's Hospital, Croydon with a home address in the London Borough of Camden who are under the age of 45, regardless of the severity of their learning difficulty, physical condition or behavioural characteristics. There are 17 such people.

In the Derby scheme it was decided to resettle anyone from Aston Hall or Makeney Hospitals (outside Derby) who had, and retained, strong links with the city of Derby. The number of people that this could include is considerably larger than the scheme intends to take within the next few years, so initial selection will also rely on referral from ward staff. More recently the criteria for acceptance into the scheme have been revised such that ability and dependency levels will be taken into account.

Other projects have been planned from the outset on the basis that only people with a certain level of ability and with few physical or behavioural problems will be resettled. Most of these have made use of information from surveys, which have been carried out in many hospitals during the last two or three years. Mental handicap hospitals have tended to classify people according to Wessex or National Development Team categories (Kushlick, Blunden and Cox, 1973; National Development Team, 1982), while a range of assessments have been used in mental illness hospitals.

In Kidderminster, for example, a number of residents of Lea and Lea Castle Hospitals were identified who originated from the county of Hereford and Worcester and have been classified into Wessex categories I and II (National Development Team, 1982). People in these two categories have been defined as ambulant, continent and with reasonably good self-help skills. They should have either no behavioural problems or mild or only occasional problems which can be corrected with training. (Such assumptions, however, turned out to cause some problems for the project, as we shall see later.) In Somerset, where the project forms part of a county-wide development, a survey of all hospital residents has identified 146 people in Wessex categories I and II who should be most likely to leave within the next few years; only some of these people can be moved into the community as part of the demonstration programme.

The Darlington project for elderly people made use of information obtained in a census of Darlington Memorial Hospital patients in 1984 which identified 62 long-stay elderly patients who appeared to be suited to life in the community, given intensive domiciliary support. The Brent scheme also began from a survey of all residents of Shenley Hospital. Potential for discharge was estimated from a hospital assessment profile and a nurses' rating of living skills. A total of 88 patients from Brent were identified at this time as possibly suitable for discharge to the project. In addition to identification from the census, patients could be referred by ward staff who considered them suitable or they could refer themselves. These other channels made it possible for people who for some reason might have been missed by the census, or for whom the census information was no longer accurate.

By contrast, some of the other projects have planned to select people whose disabilities are more severe and who would not normally have been considered suitable for discharge to a placement in the community. In these projects the emphasis is on *demonstration*, and project managers — as well as government — clearly welcome the opportunity to explore new ways of providing care for groups of clients who are often neglected. In Waltham Forest, for example, it was decided to take people with chronic disabilities following an acute phase of mental illness, although not currently severely ill to the extent of requiring intensive nursing care. Each was resident in a continuing care ward in Claybury Hospital in north London. The project aims to identify and move people who would not otherwise have been selected for resettlement.

The West Berkshire project plans to resettle people with marked behaviour problems related to chronic mental illness who will be unable to fend for themselves in the community. The project intends to make use of survey information based on formal assessments, such as the REHAB schedule (Baker, 1983), but to identify people who score *below* rather than *above* a certain level of rehabilitation potential. In this way, it is hoped to make the best use of special Care in the Community facilities for people who might not otherwise have the opportunity to leave hospital, although others who are resident on particular wards may also be included.

Some of the smaller projects either do not have access to baseline survey information or are only able to take a very small number of the people suitable for resettlement. In these cases — for example in Liverpool and Torbay — much reliance is placed on referrals of patients from hospital staff, particularly consultants and nursing staff. The risk of missing people who might benefit from the project is high; in the terms described in the previous chapter, the 'horizontal target efficiency' is likely to be low. The procedure is likely to work best when a scheme has been planned in conjunction with the hospital, and when hospital staff are closely involved early in the planning phase.

None of these various means of initial identification of a group of people for selection has been without its problems. The principle of geographical links, as in Camden, can be misleading if relatives who once lived within the borough have moved away. It is important to ensure that such information is kept up to date and that connections with the home area are not simply *assumed* to be more meaningful than connections that have developed in the vicinity of the hospital. Policies which place funding responsibilities for community care with districts of origin may not, therefore, necessarily work in the best interests of clients. A further difficulty with reliance on geographical links has revealed itself in some of the smaller projects. A large number of people have been identified in a confusingly large number of different hospitals. In Islington, for example, project managers found themselves with a list of 360 potential clients but places for only eight. An additional set of criteria for suitability had to be established as a first step. It may be easier for small projects to target a single hospital from which to select their clients.

Survey information based on brief assessments, such as the Wessex or National Development Team schedules, have also proved misleading in some instances. The Kidderminster scheme began with a list of 57 people classified in Wessex categories I and II. Repeated surveys and discussion with hospital staff led — almost two years later — to the establishment of a working list of 33 people suitable for resettlement. Of these, only 22 were also part of the original group of 57, although the population of the hospitals had hardly changed (Bennett and Metcalf, 1987). Unreliability of such survey information for planning purposes is unlikely to be unique to Kidderminster. The Wessex schedule was intended as a descriptive tool for use in surveys of large populations, but it does not appear to be adequate for the classification of *individuals* for selection for resettlement programmes of the kind developed under the Care in the Community initiative. Other schedules which were designed for individual assessment may contribute usefully to decision-making about selection (see for example Challis and Shepherd, 1983).

Referral from hospital staff has its attendant problems, although some projects have developed a satisfactory system. Clients for the Buckinghamshire project are initially referred to the rehabilitation team by staff at St John's Hospital, Aylesbury. It may be significant that the project is closely tied to the strategic plan for the hospital and that communication between different staff groups seems to be particularly good. In Brent, project staff have succeeded in developing an assessment system on a ward-by-ward basis rather than by attempting to deal with the entire hospital at once. In addition, referrals may be accepted from ward staff or from clients themselves. Here considerable effort is put into 'public relations' exercises — early meetings with ward staff, visits to rehabilitation facilities, and joint work with individual clients.

The need for public relations work with hospitals has already been emphasised in Chapter 6, and is clearly important for the referral of *appropriate* clients to a scheme. One of the difficulties encountered in West Cumbria was the referral of patients with schizophrenia and other mental illnesses by consultants who were not fully aware of the project's focus on patients with senile dementia. This resulted in wholly inappropriate treatment for some individuals. In one project considerable time elapsed and tortuous negotiations were necessary before project staff were allowed access to the hospital at all. Uncertainty over the future of the hospital led to difficult working relationships, compounded by the involvement of a large number of districts each of which had their own resettlement proposals. In Greenwich, where communications between project and ward staff seem to work well, initial referrals from the hospital have generally been suitable. Even so, public relations work with clients was needed as few of the long-stay patients were willing to consider leaving before they knew more about the project.

In some hospitals inadequate consultation between project personnel and local district planners, and consequent misunderstandings, have given rise to the 'double booking' of some clients. Some people were resettled by their district of origin after Care in the Community project staff had been working with them for some months. In other cases, projects had developed lists of potential clients on which estimates of numbers were based, while the hospital had been preparing some of the same people for rehabilitation within their own schemes. Neither group apparently knew of the other's plans. In the case of one person, a sense of urgency over the need to resettle him quickly — before he became too institutionalised — produced parallel plans by the project and by the hospital. The opposite may occur in hospitals which are running down. Pressure may be put on the project to take people from particular wards which are due to close, even if the people are not suitable according to the criteria set by the project itself. An obvious point, but one worth repeating, is that communication is all important.

Selection and assessment

Virtually all projects make use of multidisciplinary and multi-agency working at some point during the selection or assessment process. It is possible to distinguish between those projects which focus on *selection* at this stage and those in which the focus is on *assessment* of individual needs.

Most of the smaller projects are able to offer only a limited range of facilities, such as group homes or a single hostel. For them it is important to select clients who will fit in well and for whom the project is an appropriate move. A number of the projects for people with a mental illness also tend to select for suitability at this stage, although a more detailed assessment of need will feature later, perhaps after a period of time in rehabilitation. In other projects the selection decision has already been made — either because of the emphasis on geographical links, and/or because hospital staff referrals have made decisions for them. In these cases the first decisions to be made by resettlement workers (or project leader or IPP co-ordinator), possibly in conjunction with hospital and community staff, are not *whether* to move a client but *where*.

Most projects, especially the large ones, have made use of formal assessment schedules. Some of the mental illness projects, such as Brent, Buckinghamshire and Chichester, have found it useful to develop a profile using schedules such as CAPE (Pattie and Gilleard, 1979) and REHAB (Baker, 1983). Decisions are never made on the basis of schedule scores alone but they may provide useful background information for (say) a multidisciplinary meeting. Some care must be taken in the use of formal assessments to predict the potential of individuals for independent living, particularly in the case of people with learning difficulties. In Bolton, for example, it was found that formal assessments completed in a hospital environment frequently underestimated the abilities which people could demonstrate in other settings. There was no substitute for getting to know people through personal contact and in a variety of different situations such as visits to community facilities.

The opinions of key professionals are always important. In most of the projects for elderly people a consultant makes the initial referral, after which suitability is discussed with hospital and project staff. In several of the projects for people with learning difficulties, before any

119

decision is made a key worker collects information from many different sources, such as hospital staff, professionals such as social workers and occupational therapists, and relatives, and from extensive personal contact with the individual. An individual programme planning meeting is usually called for this purpose, although in some cases, such as in Maidstone, the information is collated and it is not always considered necessary to hold a meeting.

Every project has laid stress on client involvement in selection and assessment decisions, while achieving it in many different ways. In Greenwich and Waltham Forest project workers spend some months getting to know clients in hospital and informing them about the project so that final decisions are made largely on the basis of self-selection. In other schemes, clients are asked by hospital nursing staff or consultants whether they would like to participate. In the Warrington project clients become licensees of a housing association on the basis of an agreement with Warrington Community Care, who receive and discuss written applications from clients themselves. An extensive preparation programme was offered to original applicants for the move to the community, and indeed to subsequent applicants. Applications to the project committee did not arrive out of the blue.

The IPP system was intended to enable clients, their relatives and professionals to come together and share knowledge and viewpoints in order that the best decisions could be made about goals and care plans. A recent report from the Nimrod project in South Wales, which pioneered the use of IPP systems, has indicated that the involvement of clients in IPP meetings can have its problems (Humphreys et al., 1985). Some clients find the meetings too large and are inhibited from speaking openly. Clients' opinions might be better elicited under more relaxed circumstances beforehand and information subsequently relayed to the meeting. Similar experiences have been reported in some Care in the Community projects. The Maidstone project team, for example, decided to sometimes forgo the formal IPP meetings and to obtain the information in other ways. Elsewhere — for example, in the Brent rehabilitation ward — clients are invited to attend part of the meeting if they wish, while much of the discussion takes place in their absence. If clients choose not to attend, a case manager ensures that they have the opportunity for discussion both before and after the meeting.

However much thought and care is devoted to attempts to elicit client views, it will be difficult to get at the 'truth' because so many institutional care processes are designed precisely to deny residents the rights to choose or make their views and preferences known. Some people with learning difficulties, if their communication skills are limited, may need to spend considerable time with a staff member in a variety of situations before their opinions can be obtained.

Those who are able to communicate may simply not have adequate knowledge or understanding of the alternatives to make decisions at an early stage. Greenwich staff have described the difficulty of getting people interested in the project when they have lived in hospital for many years. Similarly, in Buckinghamshire it was found that clients lacked the basic knowledge about community services to make informed choices. Few of them know about the future plans for the hospital. A trial period of a few weeks in a rehabilitation ward in the hospital grounds is offered in Brent, after which clients can return to their ward of origin if they wish. From the rehabilitation ward, frequent trips into the community can be arranged and extended visits made to the residential and day facilities of the project. Clients who miss out the rehabilitation stage also have extensive contact with project staff, including visits to the community. In other projects, such as in Bolton, it has been found useful to begin a community introduction programme many months before clients are discharged from hospital. They begin with day trips and later move to overnight stays in a special project house made available for this purpose. Before finally moving to the community, clients spend alternate weeks in hospital and in the house.

Trial periods and visits to the community are also useful for establishing compatibility between groups of people and determining whether any existing friendships are likely to be important. Many projects have stipulated the principle of resettling people *together* where friendship links are strong, and some have developed reciprocal, exchange agreements with nearby districts to take 'their' residents where friendships are significant. Putting this principle into practice can prove difficult; in Maidstone, friendships in hospital were not easy to determine and some that were assumed by staff to exist broke down very quickly after the move into the community.

It can also prove difficult to realise the principle of involving relatives in decision-making. This seems least problematic for elderly people, many of whom have families which are not only in frequent contact, but are pleased to take part in decisions about the future. People with a mental illness who have been in hospital for a long time are the least likely to have relatives who wish to be involved. Some relatives have stated quite clearly that they do not wish to maintain contact and are opposed to any move that will bring their family member back into close proximity. Of course, this is not the case for all, and others may welcome the opportunity to renew communications.

Some people with learning difficulties have lost touch with their families over the years of hospitalisation, and some have relatives who are extremely worried about the implications of a move into the community. Recent publicity about hospitals 'dumping' people has not helped, and families may fear that their relative will have no home to go to or will be left in the care of untrained and incompetent people. Considerable public relations work — explaining the project and introducing staff to relatives — may be necessary. This has been discussed more fully in Chapter 6.

It can be difficult to always abide by the principle of fitting services to individual needs, even where a range of facilities is planned. A compromise will usually have to be made to accommodate clients' needs in the services which happen to be available at the present time. The alternative — assessing needs and then waiting until the perfect placement is ready — may well be less desirable if the time-lag is long.

Rehabilitation

Rehabilitation practices vary widely. In some projects every client is expected to pass through the system in much the same way. In others, because the different clients may have different needs, so rehabilitation programmes must be tailored appropriately.

There is much debate about whether rehabilitation and training activities should take place in a specially designated unit, or whether clients should move directly to a permanent home in the community where training will be provided as necessary. The normalisation philosophy, which would not consider a half-way house to be an appropriate model of residence for anyone, is very influential in many of the projects for people with learning difficulties. With the other client groups, special rehabilitation units have often been set up or used, the assumed advantages outweighing the 'costs' of the disruption of multiple moves. Since many clients will have been selected for discharge long before they actually move, it would seem to be useful to spend the waiting time in constructive activities which will help to prepare them for the future.

Where such units are employed there may be advantages in siting them away from the hospital, since training in a realistic setting is seen to be more appropriate. On the other hand moving to a rehabilitation ward within a hospital may be less frightening to long-stay patients than the prospect of a move straight to community living. In Derby a useful compromise has been developed in which a small rehabilitation unit close to the hospital serves as a first step, and a second hostel a few miles away takes people at a more advanced stage. The obvious disadvantage is the disruption of lifestyle.

Some projects have managed to develop an assessment and rehabilitation system in the hospital which may continue to serve a useful function long after the demonstration project itself has come to an end. Good communication between hospital and project can have advantages for the hospital too. In a few projects more than one type of rehabilitation unit is available and clients can spend time in very different rehabilitation regimes. A structured training programme devised by the resettlement team may be most appropriate for some people. For others a self-contained unit on the hospital site is more suitable. where residents can be left very much on their own to learn to live as a group, but with support and back-up of normal hospital services. Assessment usually continues in all types of unit and reviews take place at regular intervals.

The length of time spent in rehabilitation can depend on project regime, individual need and, less appropriately, external pressures. A 'bottleneck' may occur if housing in the community is not available or, contrariwise, clients may be put under pressure to move on before they are ready if many community placements suddenly come on-stream. Hospital closure programmes will also hurry the rehabilitation process, pressurising staff to make room for the next wave of trainees from the long-stay wards.

Care planning and case management

Arrangements for care planning in the Care in the Community projects are varied, with case management arrangements being necessary only in the larger projects. Most of the small projects, which tend to offer a limited range of facilities, do not need to develop a complex system to co-ordinate client plans. Usually the smaller project employs a single care co-ordinator (variously known as a care assistant co-ordinator or project co-ordinator) who devises or oversees the plans, which are carried out by other workers. The co-ordinator may have some management responsibility.

Small projects may also employ a key worker system in which individual workers have most contact with particular clients, but without responsibility for care plans. Projects of this type have the advantage of simplicity and the workers tend to know all their colleagues and all the clients fairly well. On the other hand, they may not have sufficient access to resources such as day care and speech therapy, and so find themselves spending much of their time in negotiation with other agencies, in attempts to obtain these services. Such a role was probably not envisaged when the project first started.

A further problem encountered by one of the small projects which did not have a highly developed system for selection, assessment or care planning was insufficient information. Selection was the responsibility of hospital staff whose decisions would not necessarily have corres-ponded with those of the project. Clients entering the project were not well known to the workers, detailed care plans had not been developed and little information was sent with them. In one case, a client's blindness went undetected for some time as it had not been mentioned in the records.

Many of the larger projects use a care planning system, although local arrangements vary markedly and few would describe their activities as 'case management'. Some hinge on the use of a small number of workers who take overall responsibility for the care of their clients by seeing them through the processes of selection, assessment, care planning, service co-ordination and review. These were described in the previous chapter as 'specialist' case managers, in the sense that they are employed specifically to fulfil the co-ordination role. The Darlington project, for instance, employs 'service managers' who control plans and individual budgets. In Maidstone there are case managers who see clients through all the stages and have frequent personal contact with them. In Kidderminster the resettlement workers take on this role. They have main responsibility for assessment, placement and arrange-ment of services — and subsequent review — for all clients in a particular area and also take a major part in the liaison with, and development of, local services. The IPP co-ordinators in Derby are responsible for assessment, care planning and review for clients in their own area but they also each have a team of project workers based in that area. Although they are not formally line managers for the teams, they do have considerable responsibility for allocation of tasks and manage-ment of activities. One consequence of this is that the co-ordinators have less direct contact with clients once the initial selection process has been completed. Most projects have a central project manager or co-ordinator to guide the case managers, although this is not the case in Derby.

Case management in Brent could be described as non-specialist. Project workers of all kinds, such as staff nurses, community psychiatric nurses, social workers, psychologists and occupational therapists have case management responsibilities for a small number of clients. They do this in addition to the other duties which would normally be associated with their profession. The case managers do not always see clients through all of the project stages. Sometimes a member of the 'link team' case manages throughout the whole process, or a senior member of the community team takes the responsibility from an early stage (*after* selection and assessment by a multidisciplinary team and rehabilitation co-ordinator). In other cases a hospital worker begins the process while a community project worker takes over when the client moves out. The case manager is usually someone who knows the client well and has considerable direct contact, although that is not considered to be a central part of the case management role.

A mixed model is operated in Bolton. Before the client is discharged from hospital a project leader has the job of assessment, co-ordination and liaison with other, associated staff. The project leaders spend much time with the client but also have access to a staff team with whom they share the direct work. They also arrange and collect information for an IPP meeting before discharge. When outside hospital, a client's co-ordination and review is taken over by a client co-ordinator who is primarily employed as a community professional, such as a social worker or speech therapist. They will not necessarily have much personal contact with the client but take an administrative and monitoring role in addition to their professional duties. A principal worker is also nominated, who is probably a neighbourhood care worker, who knows the client well and has the most direct contact.

These different systems partly reflect local circumstances which require different solutions. Most of them have evolved as the project has grown, and some have been revised several times during the first two years. The Bolton project, for example, moved from a system of assessment teams (nurse and social worker) to one of project leaders and key workers, and later to the model described above. The Nimrod project in Wales has, after four years of operation, begun to change its methods. It appears to have moved slightly from a specialist model of key workers, who did all the co-ordination and also had most client contact work, to one in which some tasks were re-allocated along disciplinary lines. Administration and preparation of meetings appear to have been excessively time-consuming, as are effective liaison and communication (Humphreys et al., 1985).

Case management — involving assessment, co-ordination and review — is an unusual combination of activities and many Care in the Community workers may find themselves in unfamiliar situations. Many projects are also developing new and innovative patterns of service. Under these circumstances, support and supervision is crucial if staff are to feel secure in their work and to provide effective care. A system of regular staff meetings has been developed in Bolton for the various groups of staff involved. The system is itself reviewed from time to time and changes are made in response to any communication problems which might occur. Other than this, individual supervision takes place largely on an informal basis.

In Kidderminster the project team is quite small and workers are geographically isolated most of the time. Despite this, support and communication appear to be very effective, probably because the key people get along well and are able to make maximum use of regular individual supervisions and staff meetings. New ideas in service development are encouraged and workers are able to discuss views and experiences with each other. The Derby team is in a somewhat unusual position, having no project manager or co-ordinator to make strategic decisions. The IPP co-ordinators are individually supervised by their respective line managers in local social services offices, from whom support can be variable. Accountability in two directions can also be confusing. The co-ordinators' group, however, have developed a useful support structure for themselves. They meet weekly for discussion of cases, strategic decision-making and general mutual help and advice.

Staff support can be most difficult to achieve in the smallest projects. Where contact with mainstream services is strong, workers may have satisfactory back-up and supervision, but possibly insufficient independence. The project may become an extension of existing services rather than an opportunity to develop new practices. On the other hand, small projects may frequently find themselves very isolated. Staff whose previous experience may have been limited to a relatively junior position in a large hierarchy — such as in hospital — can suddenly find themselves in sole charge of a group of clients and workers with little outside help or expertise to call on.

The particular professional qualifications held by case managers or co-ordinators do not appear to be particularly important. Several projects employ a combination of social workers and nurses, which provides a useful mix of skills and experience. Those projects which employed nurses from the hospital have found their knowledge and existing relationships with staff and clients to be very helpful. Some case managers with no previous client group experience are also proving to be effective. This may indicate that attitudes, enthusiasm and common sense can be at least as important as qualifications.

Projects which employ specialist case managers (such as Derby, Kidderminster, Maidstone and parts of Bolton) have allocated them small caseloads in comparison with American case management programmes and the Kent community care scheme. In the Kent scheme, case managers each worked with 25 to 30 cases. This compares with a maximum of 20 in Derby (of whom ten may be living outside of hospital), up to ten (so far) in Maidstone, and up to a dozen in Kidderminster. In Bolton, project leaders have 20 cases in hospital and a team of workers to call on. Non-specialist case managers, such as in the Brent project, tend to have only three or four cases each, but these are in addition to their normal duties. Numbers alone may not prove to be a sensible way of making comparisons since the range of tasks undertaken varies so widely from project to project. In Kidderminster the workers are also involved in service development and negotiation with service agencies. Negotiation also features high on the list of activities in the Derby project. Care in the Community projects may well be far more complex exercises than any of the case management schemes which have been described in other places. It is undoubtedly true that case managers in Care in the Community projects are very busy and very active and generally work longer hours than stipulated in their contracts of employment.

Most projects have not yet reached a stage where reviews take place at regular intervals. Most assume that more frequent reviews are necessary during the early months of community living and that spacing them out will be possible when placements are firmly established and clients have settled down. Most projects make use of the PSSRU case review form on which they may record needs, requirements and plans in relation to particular areas of need, such as accommodation, domestic help and education. Some have planned to carry out formal reviews every three months, some every six months, while others plan to respond flexibly as needs arise. The Nimrod scheme found that it was not necessary to hold reviews every six months, as originally intended.

Only one project — Darlington — employs budget limits for its clients along the lines of the Kent community care scheme. Service managers will be able to provide statutory services, each with a shadow price attached, which will be deducted from an individual client's budget. Built-in flexibility will enable service managers to buy in non-statutory services, such as local volunteer help. This scheme is at an early stage as yet, so little evidence is available on how it is working. Case managers in the Maidstone project also work with individual budgets but so far they have not needed to keep a limit. The costs of placements and services for each client are worked out and recorded each week.

Access to non-project services is proving to be a problem in some cases. Small projects, in particular, may have to rely on goodwill and established relationships to obtain day care (as was the case in Winchester). Others are not so fortunate and care co-ordinators have sometimes spent many frustrating months in negotiation with other agencies in attempts to find day placements for their clients.

Some of the large projects have a wide variety of services available within their own project resources. The Bolton project, for example, is able to provide further education, rural training, daily living skills, teaching and also professional support such as speech therapy and physiotherapy. Other services are obtainable through the appropriate member of the team (for example, via a nurse for chiropody and psychiatric services) provided that links between project professional staff and mainstream services are well established. Some projects have not found it easy to obtain resources when needed and workers have felt that they had insufficient status and authority to negotiate effectively with other agencies. Recourse to a superior followed by decision-making at higher levels has proved to be a cumbersome and lengthy procedure.

Advocacy has not been emphasised as a particular feature of many of the projects, although ensuring that clients' views are represented at case reviews may be part of the case management role. A number of schemes attempt to recruit volunteer advocates for some of their clients. The Kidderminster team have helped to develop a citizen advocate scheme as a separate project. A paid co-ordinator (independently funded) will recruit and support volunteers who will advocate on the clients' behalf. It was seen to be important for them to be independent of the project and of statutory services in order to best represent the interests of the clients.

Assessment and care planning are undertaken in a variety of ways in the Care in the Community projects. In some cases the arrangements have been developed in response to particular local circumstances and in others projects were planned with a specific model of co-ordination in mind. Dispersed rural settings will require different arrangements from inner-city projects. Client characteristics will also make a difference. Many of the problems which have so far emerged in resettling people into the community have been resolved. In another two years we will be in a position to make some judgements about the comparative effectiveness of these different arrangements.

9. Community services in practice

Earlier chapters have chronicled in some detail recent policies for people who have a mental illness, learning difficulties or are elderly. Central to these policies has been the establishment of comprehensive community services, and care in an integrated rather than a segregated, institutional setting. To take mental health services, for example, *Care in Action* stated that one of the most urgent tasks was to

> make arrangements ... for the closure over the next ten years or so of those mental illness hospitals which are not well placed to provide a service reaching out into the community. Such closures should provide a source of staff, capital and revenue to support the development of the new pattern of health services (DHSS, 1981c, para. 5.9(c)).

But other official documents are categorical that it is *not* in itself government policy to close the mental illness hospitals, or for hospitals to encourage patients to leave unless there are satisfactory arrangements for their support (see for example Cmnd 9674, 1985, para. 18).

The *Care in the Community* circular (DHSS, 1983a) stresses that a move from hospital should be conditional, where possible, on the agreement of clients themselves and their families, and should be in their best interests. One aim of policy, then, would seem to be an improvement in the quality of clients' lives, and this in turn requires considerable resources to be diverted from institutions to provide the necessary follow-up, housing and local facilities.

Projects need to ensure that there is a comprehensive network of community services to replace all the relevant facilities provided in hospitals. The projects have approached this task in different ways. Most have tapped into existing services in the area, and many have also adapted them to suit the needs of people who have been in hospital. In some cases new services have been created to fill gaps in extant provision. Getting provision in the community right has also been far more time-consuming and problematic than most of the participants seem to have bargained for. Why this should be the case is not immediately obvious, although the fact that most projects break new ground and frequently involve liaison with a multitude of agencies must be significant.

We now turn to a closer look at the early experiences of some of the pilot projects, as clients have made the transition from hospital to the community. We discuss them under four heads: housing, income maintenance, staffing, and day care and leisure facilities.

Housing

The pilot projects have met housing needs in many different ways. The wide range of provision partly reflects the varied needs of different client groups and partly stems from divergent philosophies of care, varieties in local circumstances and the limits imposed by tight budgets. One end of the range is the purpose-built, highly staffed 30-place home which will be opened in St Helens for very dependent elderly mentally infirm people. The other end is the flexible programme for placing people with a mental illness in largely unstaffed ordinary housing in the West Lancashire project.

Housing plans have been determined by a number of factors. It would be naive to assume that a project could start from scratch and mould services to client needs in a vacuum. The local stock of available housing is proving to be a very important constraint. Less obviously, perhaps, the political environment influences whether a project makes use of local authority or private housing. In Maidstone, for example, the private sector is used because of a dearth of both public sector facilities and housing associations in the area. The West Lancashire project's plans to use Housing Corporation funding have been frustrated because the Corporation do not see their locality as a priority area.

The housing plans of the Bolton project also foundered for a while. After initially being assured of spare capacity within the local housing department, they discovered the stock to be mainly inappropriate family-type accommodation with insufficient ground-floor space to meet the needs of handicapped people. Other projects have experienced similar problems. Large capital investment in the partial or

130

complete creation of a housing infrastructure is sometimes inescapable. For example, in Chichester it was found that the capital costs of housing far exceeded the initial forecasts due to an underestimation of the price of large houses in the popular Bognor area. An early conclusion to emerge from the pilot programme is that the true cost of a new community service, which aims to respond to individual need, has not been recognised by policy-makers, particularly in local authorities and health districts. Funds should be made available both to convert existing housing stock and to put up new buildings where necessary.

Different philosophies of care will emphasise different forms of housing. There may be a tendency for planners to decide how other people should live on the basis of how they prefer to live themselves, but views dictated by own life experiences may not suit the quite different needs of (say) handicapped people. Domestic privacy is prized in our society. But it can spell isolation and despair for someone suffering from a mental illness. Other problems can arise when clients are grouped according to professional perceptions of friendship patterns. Staff who have known clients for years in a hospital may not be the best judges of compatibility in the community.

A major cause of unanticipated delay in many projects has been the need to comply with fire safety regulations. Projects did not foresee how regulations could actually work against the objective of client independence, where the philosophy of care involved an element of risk to the client. Fire extinguishers can be obtrusive and prevent the creation of a homely atmosphere, and some facilities would prefer to be without them. In West Cumbria, for example, an attempt at creating a homely atmosphere was thwarted when the fire officer insisted that reinforced glass be used in the windows. Strict fire regulations in hospital about the use of frying pans and the need for flame retardant clothing work against the process of rehabilitation. In larger community facilities, as a general rule, clients are not allowed to smoke in their own rooms because of fire risk. In providing a safe environment, the fire regulations — which will vary from locality to locality — limit personal freedom. The dilemma between the enforcement of rules to ensure safety and the need not to exclude elements of proper everyday risk from people's lives has therefore had to be resolved locally. A decision has to be made, in the best interests of clients, to place some bounds on the lengths to which 'normalisation' can be allowed.

But to look on the bright side of a gloomy picture, liaison with the local fire officer about a project's aims has been found to influence the way regulations are applied. Some projects have found it helpful to include extra specialists on their management committees — for example, the fire officer or planning officer or a representative of a housing association — to help foster a common understanding about the principles underlying a project and to ensure that regulations are applied sensitively and sensibly. Nevertheless, even trivial misunderstandings between professionals can frustrate the best intentions. The West Cumbria project planned for residents' doors to be painted different colours in order to help them to distinguish between different rooms. The instruction was carried out but the colours were such pale shades that the doors proved indistinguishable to staff, never mind to elderly confused residents.

The Registered Homes Act stimulated an important legislative change. It requires the monitoring and regulating of the standard of residential provision. But it does work against the aims of some projects and against the philosophy of normalisation. It imposes institutional standards on domestic properties. Official notices on walls, essential for safety according to the Act, diminish a homely atmosphere. These negative effects of the Act need to be recognised. There is, of course, a financial incentive to register since a higher rate of board-and-lodgings benefit is paid for clients in registered homes or those which are, in principle, registerable.

Several of the projects are developing adult homefinding services, or home placements. These enable some clients to live in an ordinary home with a family to care for them. A specialist member of the project team, such as a home placement officer, recruits the family carers and undertakes a careful selection and training procedure. Clients are then matched with the most suitable family who may spend some time getting to know them before the move takes place. The ethnic origin of clients and families is an important issue in the Brent project, so people are placed with carers of the same racial group wherever possible.

Income maintenance

Access to welfare benefits has been by no means straightforward. Many clients have not received consistent treatment from the local DHSS office and the task of finding out just what they are entitled to has been time-consuming and difficult. Time invested in seeking expert advice on welfare rights — from local welfare rights officers, from the Disability Alliance (London) or their *Disability Rights Handbook* (published annually) — may well prove its worth.

Social security benefits are proving crucial to the successful implementation of Care in the Community policies. Although projects differ in the type of service they aim to deliver, they all depend to some extent for their revenue on clients' statutory benefits. The hostel for people with learning difficulties at Torbay meets all its revenue costs from social security payments to residents. In Islington clients will hold the tenancies of their flats, and furnishing of all but the communal areas will be paid for by clients from supplementary benefit grants, with some assistance from ordinary social services funds. The major problem is that social security benefits do not constitute a stable source of income and yet many schemes are dependent on the receipt of adequate social security benefits for continuing revenue. Rates of benefit can fluctuate, not just because they are client-related, and benefit can be withdrawn. Concern is pervasive. The Select Committee reported:

> The Minister assured us that social security reviews would not be as it were pulling the rug from under those depending on social security entitlements to develop new community services ... We recommend that national, regional and local plans for community care include explicit reference to the role of social security entitlements and that such plans also indicate their effects on public expenditure (House of Commons Select Committee on Social Services, 1985, para. 22).

Such an uncertain source of income can cause major problems where budgets are tight. The revenue costs of the Warrington hostel for people with a mental illness are met from boarding-out allowances, but there were initial delays in building works. Clients were unable to leave hospital as planned, but staff had been appointed to schedule. As staff salaries had to be paid there was a temporary financial shortfall although fortunately, in this case, the health authority helped out with grant aid and the project was not endangered.

In Warrington, as in some other schemes, arrangements have been made with the local DHSS office for board-and-lodgings payments to be made directly to the scheme rather than to the individual. Others may see this as a restriction on the independence of clients although it is undoubtedly necessary for some people who cannot manage their own money.

Questions have been asked about the adequacy of benefits to replace the wide range of facilities offered free to residents of a hospital. Without sufficient income there is no possibility of clients buying equivalent services themselves. It is foolish to help clients move to the community to take advantage of a richer life if they do not have enough money to enjoy the wider range of opportunities. In practice many projects are struggling with a shortage of money for holidays and outings or large items of clothing and furniture, although some projects — Warrington is an example — have been able to make allowance for these from their own funds.

Employment can be a central aspect of income maintenance. The philosophy of many projects is that clients should have as full a life as possible, and this includes the opportunity to work. The problem is that the 'replacement ratio', the difference between payment for work and

133

benefits when not working, is very low for most clients of the Care in the Community projects. The ratio will be low (or even negative) for a number of reasons. Many clients are able to work only part-time or in only poorly paid employment and working may involve travelling expenses and other hidden costs which were not incurred before. Most significant is the fact that many of them need staff support, and projects may rely on social security benefits (at the higher rate) to pay for this. On the one hand, therefore, a project may depend on maximum benefit for its very existence, which could mean discouraging clients from seeking paid employment, while on the other hand attempting to provide as full a life as possible. In a society which values employment, the latter should override the former — clients should be helped to find work wherever possible — and care agencies will have to be prepared to make up any shortfall in revenue. Special solutions also need to be found to this employment disincentive problem for disabled people.

Some projects have helped smooth their own progress by striking up a good relationship with the local DHSS office. Negative responses and delays are probably inevitable when unexpected approaches are made for substantial benefit claims for large numbers of people. If the local office is informed of project intentions well in advance delays may be avoided.

Staffing

The success of any project will hinge on the quality of staff. At an early stage of the Care in the Community programme it became apparent that the move from hospital care would not only generate personnel problems in the new projects themselves, but would also be a catalyst for difficulties within existing services.

The first calculations of staffing requirements were made by those who wrote the speculative applications for pilot project funding. The resultant staffing structures were therefore estimated on the basis of hospital staff ratios and existing hostel and group home provision in the community. These were not necessarily appropriate and many projects realised later that they had underestimated their personnel requirements. In addition, projects have reported difficulty with recruitment. This may be due to the temporary nature of the project posts or perhaps their very novelty. It may partly result from the anomalies and differences in pay, pension rights, age of retirement, mileage allowances and fringe benefits such as car loans and relocation grants between health and social services agencies. The two organisations have quite different 'cultures', which encompass practices, regulations, philosophies of care and staff training.

The key to an effective service is responsiveness to client need which requires a flexibility not always easily achieved in practice, for staff can hardly be hired and fired on that basis. In Liverpool, for example, the project offers care and support on a 24-hour basis in the first instance, to be reduced as soon as circumstances allow. The philosophy of the Derby scheme is that it is staff and not clients who should adapt as needs change. In Chichester the core house will be staffed 24 hours a day but other houses will only be supervised where there is a continuing client need. In West Lancashire a round-the-clock service for people with a mental illness uses a team of rehabilitation officers and community care assistants to provide support as the situation demands. The Cambridge project for handicapped children employs professional foster parents who will live in the house with the children, and the Glossop scheme for physically handicapped people will be staffed by two paid community service volunteers who will occupy one flat in a block of four.

Delays recruiting staff have been widely reported, although this varies across the country and appears to depend partly on the responsiveness of the local labour market. The Maidstone project reported an initial delay in advertising posts due to a combination of late notification of DHSS funding and local bureaucracy. The temporary nature of the project posts has also complicated and delayed the appointments procedure. By the time the committee procedure was set in motion to approve the staffing requirements for the West Lancashire project, it was well into the first year of funding.

Many projects have thought long and hard about the type of staff they want to attract. A major difficulty has been the choice between health service and social service personnel. Some projects were concerned that health service personnel might be in danger of bringing institutionalised ideas to the new service while others emphasise the value of their previous experience and view them as an important resource to be cultivated. Suspicion can develop between the professions about job content, probably exacerbated by quite different philosophies of care. Although the differences between the two services will not easily be resolved, refusal to acknowledge the problems or to attempt to deal with them could seriously handicap the development of Care in the Community projects.

Responses to an advertisement are governed by a number of factors. Whether a project attracts applicants from health or social services, for example, can depend on where a job is advertised and what it is called. Geographical location is also important. For instance, the West Cumbria project found difficulty attracting suitable applicants for the post of officer-in-charge of home because local employment was unlikely to become available for an applicant's spouse at the same time. The price of housing can also be a disincentive to move to some areas.

The 'pilot' status of projects has affected the quality of the response in some areas. Some projects have reported a dearth of good quality candidates for middle management positions, which is not surprising in view of the risk to career prospects involved by employment on a temporary project (although some projects have arranged suitable secondments). On the other hand, special projects do often attract energetic, innovative and charismatic people. Professional staff, too, seem to be in short supply in many professions at the present time which is causing problems for new projects and for mainstream services.

For staff who move to the community stress may be a problem, caused by different methods of working and reduced support from seniors or peers once away from the hospital ward structure. Some projects did not allow enough staff time to cover for holidays and sickness, and consequently much overtime is being worked in many of the new community facilities. Individual staff have found the lack of back-up particularly stressful and one project has experienced an exceptionally high rate of staff turnover, perhaps as a direct result.

Reduced staff morale has also accompanied the run-down of large hospitals, with a knock-on effect on projects which depend on hospital staff for referrals and access to clients. Where closure is being mismanaged or insensitively handled, and where staff have little information about their future employment prospects, any attempt to move clients from hospital may be seen as a threat to livelihoods. Project personnel have often found themselves inadvertently in the direct line of fire for much displaced anger and it has been difficult initially to get support for the scheme.

Central to the forward planning of many projects are staff education and development. Some have included in their project design a course of training for new project personnel and information seminars to publicise the project. The Derby project, for example, has held individual programme planning workshops and 'working together' seminars for NHS and social services staff. There have also been workshops to look more generally at the integration of people with learning difficulties into the community. A 'Training for Change' module, devised by a training officer in the health authority, is being implemented in conjunction with social services personnel. In Bolton, three-week induction courses have been held for all centrally-funded staff in addition to further courses, some of which were locally developed and some bought in from elsewhere. In Winchester care attendants spend time working alongside nurses in the community and hospital as well as attending a course on lifting and a general induction course. The West Cumbria project ran a two-week induction course for staff which incorporated sessions on reality orientation and reminiscence therapy techniques (these are basic to the West Cumbrian project) as well as more routine activities.

If community-based services are to succeed in providing a new, and better, type of care they will require different combinations of staff and skills from those found in most hospital or social services settings. Multi-agency working in the community requires the breaking down of traditional professional barriers and greater understanding and trust on both sides. A change of attitude is a prerequisite for working in a different way, more often *with* the client than *for* the client. Training should be dynamic and responsive as staff needs alter, so that it becomes an integral part of the process of change.

Day care and leisure facilities

Most projects have included day care and leisure services in their forward plans even though, historically, the development of day services has been accorded low priority. The Select Committee Report on Community Care recognised that day care is at least as important as residential care. The Report also suggested that the definition of 'care' extends beyond 'nine to five' and weekdays, and that planning for community care should recognise this, together with its financial implications.

Some projects, Derby for example, define the provision of day care and leisure facilities as the whole range of facilities which are available in the community to anyone. This has proved difficult in some other areas where an assessment of extant facilities for day care has revealed woeful inadequacies. Adult training centres (ATCs), social education centres (SECs) and day centres encompass a range of different types of facility suited to clients with quite different types of need. The SECs are not suitable for people who are elderly or those who are really looking for employment. Many ATCs are themselves institutionalised and may be run by staff who feel threatened by the move towards community care. The relationship between new project services set up in parallel with those already in existence is a sensitive issue which can provoke obvious difficulties and tensions. Some projects have adopted a bias towards education, for example, or a strong emphasis on employment. Others have developed innovative forms of day care, such as the rural training scheme in Bolton which plans to encourage the physical well-being and social development of people with learning difficulties by training in agricultural and horticultural skills. Bolton also has an education service support scheme to develop individual learning programmes and make available to project clients educational facilities which are used by the population as a whole, thereby encouraging integration and promoting normalisation. The Kidderminster project employs training instructors who are attached to adult training centres throughout the county. They have succeeded in developing new day services in the form of work experience placements, leisure and recreational activities, independent living training and home teaching programmes. This diversity reflects to some extent the broad spectrum of needs for day care for people resettled in the community, an area which will require considerable thought and planning for some time to come.

Projects have chosen different types of location for their services. In Brent the core unit functions as a resource centre which provides a drop-in facility, structured activities and day care (including informal therapy sessions), covering between eight and 12 hours in each 24. The core unit also provides a focus for formal access to both health service and social services staff, to domiciliary support services and introduction to ordinary community education, leisure and general facilities. It is hoped that volunteer help will assist users of the centre by supplementing the skills of professional workers in specific areas. The West Lancashire project plans to provide a round-the-clock caring service by using a resource team to complement day-time staff, hence offering a support service at times and places conducive to a normal lifestyle. Within the team the role of the community care assistant is quite innovative, as it offers long-term help with budgeting, housing and consumer problems.

Projects do not always agree on the best way to deliver further education to their clients. Integrated classes may be closer to the principle of normalisation, but in some places people without handicaps have melted away from classes where integration has been attempted. Classes run for people with special needs avoid this eventuality and some projects prefer them, even though they run the danger of reinforcing negative attitudes towards a particular group. Even then, there is the problem that local colleges may not be prepared to accept clients with handicaps. If lengthy negotiation proves successful, there can still be problems where numbers are not large enough to make a viable class.

The pilot project programme is able to demonstrate a wide variety of types of residential accommodation, day care and professional support. Some are based strongly on the provision that already existed in the locality whereas others have started a new service from scratch, and have thus been able to develop quite new models of care and support. Integration of the new services with those already available, and with generic services, is an important question to be addressed within the next few years if community care is to be a reality. Another critical issue, particularly in larger and more comprehensive service networks, is the co-ordination of the various elements. Catering for diverse individual needs will necessarily require informed guidance through the service network and liaison with the various agencies on behalf of the individual, perhaps along the case management lines outlined in Chapters 7 and 8. The constraints imposed by tight budgets in all agencies will also have a powerful influence over the way services may be provided and linked together. Economic and financial questions are addressed in the following chapter.

10. Economic and financial questions

An important goal of the Care in the Community initiative is to investigate how *cost-effective* community services might be provided to meet the needs of the different groups of patients now in the process of being discharged from long-stay hospitals. In this chapter we look at the financial and economic aspects of the pilot projects and make some general observations about costs of care in hospital and community settings, although we are not yet able to reach any final evaluative conclusions about cost-effective community-based services.

Community care and the cost imperative

Chapter 2 has described how the notion of community care began to take hold in the late 1950s and 1960s. The impetus for community care stemmed from a number of perspectives, many of which encompassed a cost-effectiveness argument. Many of the existing hospital buildings were getting old and were in need of repair and replacement; their maintenance and running costs were swallowing large amounts of public money. New hospitals would be even more expensive to establish. An additional assumption appeared later, that community services should be able to provide better care than the old institutions. So both the cost argument and the effectiveness argument were influential.

On the cost side, it was argued for many years that community provision is cheap, certainly cheaper than hospital provision. *Better*

Services for the Mentally Ill (Cmnd 6233, 1975) is typical of many policy statements with its unequivocal but untested assumption that a community psychiatric service would be no more expensive, and probably cheaper, than the hospital provision it replaced. More recently a different view has emerged from the DHSS, though hedged with caveats: 'for some people community-based packages of care may not always be a less expensive or more effective alternative to residential or hospital provision' (DHSS, 1981b, p.20).

In the last couple of years we have seen the arrival of 'value for money audits' and the government's Financial Management Initiative. The aim is to encourage economy, effectiveness and efficiency. Economy is concerned with saving money or resources, and effectiveness concerns the achievement of service aims. Efficiency combines economy and effectiveness: it is concerned with achieving the most effective use of a given level of resources, or of minimising the cost of producing a given standard of service. Efficiency or 'cost-effectiveness', therefore, implies the consideration of *both* the costs and the results obtained (Knapp, 1984).

A further important criterion is the notion of equity — or fairness or justice. Without some consideration of this distributional objective — which in practical terms is often closely related to the goals of normalisation — the criteria of economy, effectiveness and efficiency can be argued to be insufficient for a full evaluation of services.

The emphasis on community care is based on three premises: ideologies, such as normalisation; relative cost; and effectiveness, incorporating the preferences and well-being of people with mental illnesses and learning difficulties and elderly persons and their relatives. Policy and planning questions must therefore ask how resources can be allocated to provide community care services which achieve cost-effectiveness whilst preserving certain standards of equity or justice. Precisely what kinds of service configuration are required in the community in order to achieve the best use of available resources?

The report of the House of Commons Social Services Committee (1985) made more than 100 recommendations. Four of these are important to the discussion of financing and cost-effectiveness, although none is original.

- The cost-neutral assumption that community services for the mentally disabled can be developed simply by transferring existing resources is naive and inhumane; adequate community care policies require a real increase in resources.
- Attempting to transfer resources with the least disabled or dependent people who are discharged from hospital will have serious repercussions for the more dependent people who are left behind.

141

- In the long term, local authorities should assume principal responsibility for all social care of mentally disabled people.
- An excessive reliance on social security payments to provide additional funding may threaten the long-term stability of the care system.

The Committee levelled some of its fiercest criticism at what it saw as the complacency of central government about financial issues. Joint finance has provided useful seed money in the past, but is now causing real difficulties in many areas. It should be retained, but it cannot make a major contribution to the hospital closure programme. Similarly, in their view the recent changes in joint finance rules and the legalising of 'dowry payments' are not sufficient in themselves to ensure major progress. What is required, according to the Select Committee report, is a large amount of bridging finance or 'double-funding' to allow community services to be developed until enough patients have been moved from hospital to permit significant savings to be made. Some money is already available for this purpose — in many areas through regional pools and the Care in the Community programme — which may go some way towards alleviating the problem. Some commentators feel that it may be more sensible to evaluate how cost-effectively — and, indeed, how equitably — this money is used before creating a new collection of yet more special funds.

Of course, resolving the question of bridging finance still leaves open the question as to whether community services can be financed adequately from hospital savings even if they materialise and are transferred to the local authority: two rather large assumptions in many instances. Many experienced professionals argue that appropriate services will be much more expensive than hospital care. There is some evidence to support this, but it is not necessarily conclusive because it has not been assembled on a consistent basis. In present economic circumstances it may be that conventional approaches to the problem are themselves inappropriate; it may be easier to win the argument for extra resources if it can be clearly demonstrated that more cost-effective alternatives have been tested.

Finance and structure of the Care in the Community projects

The initiative has arisen from a context of developments over many years, switching the balance from hospital to community care. It aims not only to move clients into the community, but to do so in a cost-effective manner which can be repeated by others. Each project must therefore be examined to discover how it works, what it costs, and whether it improves the well-being of clients. The costing exercise and cost-effectiveness analysis which are major parts of the PSSRU evaluation are outlined in the next chapter. Results from this evaluation will be available in due course. As the initiative proceeds we are able to observe and comment on the financial aspects of community projects and some of the problems they face. A key feature is the financial structure of projects, and how they mesh into local and national political economies. Funding packages have a number of different component parts.

Bridges

All the Care in the Community projects, by definition, are using some short-term funds (from DHSS) as what has elegantly been termed 'hump money'. Crudely speaking, £19 million of central hump money is spent on resettling about 800 people over three years. This figure does include some capital expenditures for facilities with a much longer life, and of course all the clients make use of existing facilities and other budgets. Several projects use other available district or regional sources, like the North West RHA's bridging fund for mentally handicapped people. It ought also to be said that virtually none of those budgets are 'bridging funds' in the ordinary sense, that is, money laid out to cover a temporary shortfall and *to be repaid later*. They are actually sinking funds.

Deals

A range of sources of funds are combined in about 28 different ways in the programme as a whole. First, to fund whatever is needed to rehabilitate pilot project clients and support them in the community in addition to the hump money. Second, to maintain those people in the community after the three-year pilot project. Third, to underwrite the costs of maintaining a continuing flow of people from the hospitals beyond the scope of, and after, the pilot project.

The sources of funds include direct pick-ups and indirect payments. In the first case the agency which ends up providing the service picks up the tab: the social services department pays for social workers, and so on. This is true for some part of every project. In addition, some parts of the project are financed indirectly by the agency of origin, or by a third party who feels responsible. These funds include regional funds, transfers between districts, transfers from local district to social services, transfers from a distant district to social services, either because a hospital of origin is in the outlying district or because patients 'belong' to the outlying district, and transfers from districts to voluntary organisations. Such transfers may be within or outside the joint finance mechanism.

What is interesting is not merely the range of sources, but also the manner of deal which is struck in each case. Transfers may be 'dowry payments' which recur annually, perhaps indefinitely, or one-off lump sums. They may be calculated on the basis of actual savings made in hospital, as in Derby or Brent, or on an estimate of current average hospital costs, as in the Maidstone project, or on the extra cost to the final agency of some specific extra service that will have to be provided. In Warwick, for instance, the SSD has produced a notional average costing for social education centre places. The district will transfer this amount with each client to the Mencap project, which will use it to buy SEC places from the social services department as necessary.

Other budgets

As remarked on earlier, supplementary, housing and other benefits are now a major source of finance for community care. Many clients in the programme receive supplementary benefit as an entitlement, in effect as the replacement for the 'hotel costs' previously picked up by the hospital. Outside the programme of pilot projects to a significant extent, and within the programme to a lesser extent, some authorities are seeking to reduce their own costs by placing clients in voluntary and private residential care and nursing homes. In these placements clients attract the board and lodgings allowance paid out of the national social security budget. The point is that social security budgets — like family practitioner committees' budgets — are not cash-limited. Several projects make 'creative' use of these budgets; that is, they use them in ways national policy-makers may not have intended, and may in some cases be distinctly uneasy about. But, as we have already observed, over-reliance on social security payments as the main source of project revenue can be problematic if not actually dangerous.

The national position here has changed already during the period of the initiative and may well change again. A particularly disturbing feature of the most recent change is the extent to which the new supplementary benefit rules may be thought to hinder 'normalisation'. The rates of benefit are now scaled in a way which financially penalises those who live on their own, away from paid carers.

The pursuit of cost-effectiveness

A major part of the DHSS rationale for the programme has been to fund projects which both look as if they will improve clients' lives and which, if successful, appear to be replicable by other authorities. Most commentators today would argue that community services can often be

144

more expensive than hospital provision, but probably more cost-effective. Thus, cost-effectiveness will undoubtedly enter considerations of replication.

It is argued that the community setting is preferred by most clients themselves and by most of their relatives and associates. (Of course, there will always remain people who need — or who prefer — the hospital setting.) The assumption of effectiveness depends, in part, on the argument that communities are not only capable, but also willing, to take responsibility for the care of people previously served in institutions. The number of people willing and able to *be* 'the community' in one sense or another has begun to change. We must always be careful to make the distinction between formally-organised provision and informal care by relatives and neighbours. The assumption of an untapped supply of informal care, which is costless to statutory agencies, may be highly misleading. Although most elderly, infirm or handicapped people are cared for by informal carers, usually family members, such care should not be considered as limitless. Many discharged hospital patients anyway have no relatives or neighbours to return to. And, of course, the changing economic situation of women may have affected the availability of volunteers and the ratio of possible carers to the number of people in need of care.

An element of the PSSRU's evaluation of the initiative must therefore be to move beyond anecdote to the careful interrogation of the cost-effectiveness assumption. Of considerable importance and interest to policy-makers are two related issues. First, the cost implications of the run-down of hospitals — and so the resources released, including the possibility in some places of selling off sites. Second, the relative cost-effectiveness of different community arrangements and service packages for clients. Although these two questions appear to be related, few of those involved in getting new or extended community services off the ground find it easy to believe that they can be wholly or largely financed by hospital savings, nor is that regarded as the central thrust of the programme.

Even if a cost-effectiveness advantage can be clearly established, local managers will often still have to find the actual cash difference. In the nature of the case, even average long-term savings from old, inadequate institutions are unlikely to be enough to finance new community provision — and in the short term they will most likely fall far short. This is where the social security budget may come in, but, of course, as an unreliable underpin for the care system. Outside the pilot programme the community arrangements which appear to be the most cost-effective are those which rely most heavily on family and other informal carers. This, too, is an unsatisfactory basis for the long-term planning of community care, or indeed the short-term organisation.

145

There are also what we might call the 'hidden' costs of community care which can often create disincentives to good practice. For example, keeping an elderly person in hospital involves no direct cost to relatives whereas payment must be made for accommodation in a home run by a social services department. Spouses or children may face a hefty, unaffordable burden, or the client's money may have to be spent on charges. However close a family, it is natural there will be mixed feelings over such a decision. Generally it is the fragmentation of funding of community packages of care which raises complex issues about efficiency incentives and case management responsibilities (see Chapter 6).

One of the smaller projects which has developed ordinary housing for a few people with mental handicaps provides an illustration of this diversity. The health district may have seen it as an opportunity to save some money since the houses were provided by a voluntary organisation, receiving charitable incomes and government grants, while most of the running costs were covered by residents' social security benefits. Staffing was provided and managed by the health service. Although the cost of the new houses to the health service was reduced, the total cost (including housing grants, social security and day care costs) was higher than it had been before. It is worth pointing out, however, that the advantages for the clients look to be considerable. They are able to take part in many more activities and have developed skills in areas where they had never before had the opportunity; tremendous changes in behaviour and abilities have been observed. Community provision in this case is not cheap, but it is almost certainly more cost-effective than hospital care.

Making savings

The comprehensive costing of hospital provision is only marginally less important than the costing of community provision in the short term — and is clearly crucial in the longer term if hospital resources released by run-down and closure are to be used to underwrite new developments in community provision. The Audit Commission has estimated that perhaps as much as 50 per cent of hospital costs are overheads and these will be little reduced as hospitals run down.

This raises a number of complex issues. First, 'savings' in a hospital are never simply objective facts. They are administrative agreements, subject to a range of institutional and political pressures. They cause changes in the level and style of services just as much as they result from them.

Second, the main element both in the definition of hospital savings and then in what is done with them is the simple conflict of interest over whether the 'gain' should accrue inside or outside the hospital. Health professionals are bound to prefer spending the same amount on fewer patients rather than deplete already inadequate budgets — to spread out the beds rather than close wards, as it were. One of the Care in the Community projects, Kidderminster, explicitly aims to develop and improve its hospital services alongside its community programme, using what is saved by closing Lea Hospital to help fund both arms of the strategy. In a number of other projects there is strong reason to suppose that, although solid agreements to transfer funds will be met, the running down of real resources on which hospital administrators have based their calculations may prove mysteriously difficult to realise. There will be a funding transfer, but not matched by a reduction in what hospitals actually plan to do.

Third is the issue of so-called 'dowry payments' — annual payments from the hospital budget of the region to DHAs or local authorities — which are generally calculated on the basis of assumptions about savings, although the arrangements vary from region to region. Many are worked out from the average hospital costs across a whole region or for individual institutions. Some dowries distinguish between NHS and non-NHS recipients — in Trent, for example, the non-NHS recipients receive only half the £12,000 dowry payable to NHS recipients — but only occasionally (as in West Midlands) is there a mechanism designed to reflect dependency differences among clients.

Dowry payments have been subject to a good deal of criticism of late, and do seem to lead to some problems. First, they can provide a disincentive for local authorities (and other non-health agencies) to participate in joint working schemes where these agencies receive lower payments. In many regions it is left to the discretion of the local health district to distribute an appropriate sum to other care-providing agencies, which clearly leaves the balance of power with the NHS. Such arrangements are unlikely to foster a change in the style of care away from traditional models.

Second, the exclusive focus on provision for people transferred from hospital — since it is only these people who attract the dowry payment — tends to divert attention (and resources) away from those who already live in the community. Many of the most deprived and needy cases are to be found in impoverished community settings with inadequate support. They, perhaps, should be of even greater concern than people who are at least being cared for (if inappropriately). Although the Care in the Community initiative was aimed specifically at people in hospital, and has nothing to say about people outside, they should not be forgotten in any discussion of community care as a whole.

A third point concerns the uniformity of the dowry sum, regardless of the characteristics of the individuals, which provides disincentive for districts to move higher dependency patients into their own community services. 'Dowry payments are not related to dependency levels in the case of transfers within the health service' (Wistow and Hardy, 1986, p.108).

Averages and individuals

Any resettlement scheme is likely to begin by taking rather less dependent people first (in some instances it is *only* the more able people who are moved), whose hospital care will cost rather less than the hospital average. For example, a published report of the movement of long-stay psychiatric patients from Hellingly Hospital in East Sussex to a staffed hostel in the local community — outside the Care in the Community programme — quoted cost savings of £10,833 per patient year (Raafat, 1986). These costs are probably the *average* costs across all wards and all levels of resident dependency. The patients moved from Hellingly 'required little support from the hospital', needed no supervision at night and carried out most of the domestic work themselves. These factors all suggest that they were costing the hospital considerably less than £10,833 each per year. Indeed, Wright and Haycox (1984) have found that ward costs can vary by as much as a factor of four. (Although this study was of a mental handicap hospital, the principle remains the same.) Rehabilitation wards can be more costly on staff time and other resources than are some other wards, but are still likely to be less expensive than the average.

Clients moving to the community in the early years of discharge programmes will be less dependent in terms of skills, behavioural problems, physical characteristics and capabilities than those remaining in the hospital. This is a feature of most similar transitions and closure programmes. It is not altogether surprising since the development of good community services is still a new venture and changes will be made more smoothly and quickly for those people whose needs are more easily met. This will reduce the initial bridging costs of new community services. The problems arise later because most projects ultimately wish to move clients with a range of abilities and such selective resettlement can greatly complicate the negotiation of financial responsibility particularly for those who are left behind.

It is also the case that the average cost of a package of services varies with the 'dependency' of clients, even though the majority of extant dowry arrangements do not build in a dependency-varying element. If, then, it is the more dependent people who tend to be found in hospital settings (on average and in the early years) and, other things being equal, higher dependency generates higher costs, then the resource implications of a move to community-based services will be rather

148

different from those suggested by a simple comparison of present average cost figures.

These two assumptions can be summarised with the help of Figure 10.1 which demonstrates some of the cost implications of a shift to community provision. The two lines drawn in the figure represent the average costs of hospital provision (ACH) and community care (ACK) as an increasing function of dependency. For simplicity it has been assumed that the cost of hospital care is greater than the cost of community care at all levels of dependency. The 'average degrees of dependency' of clients *currently* accommodated in hospital and in the community are denoted as DH and DK respectively. Associated with them will be the average costs. It is these two mean average cost figures (denoted CH and CK) that will emerge from the hospital and community costings described above. If a client with dependency DH (the average among the hospital population) is successfully moved, the subsequent cost will not be the present average community cost CK, but will be the larger amount CM. The total savings released by moving people from hospital to community care, therefore, will be exaggerated by the simple (mean) average cost figures prepared for clients *currently* in care (even if these costs include the omitted services discussed earlier).

Furthermore, when a client of dependency between DK and DH (*less* than average dependency in hospital but *more* than average in the community) is moved from a hospital to a community setting — as so often happens — there will be an increase in the (mean) average cost of both services. The mean hospital cost will rise because one of the less dependent people has left and the mean community cost will rise because someone more dependent than the average there has joined. Despite this apparent inflation in both settings, however, the *total* expenditure will fall in this simple example, because the individual moved is actually costing less in the community than they did in hospital.

The assumption that hospital care is always more expensive than community care can be relaxed without altering the thrust of the argument. Indeed, this would strengthen it. This is illustrated in Figure 10.2. Assume that above a certain level of dependency (DA) the average cost of community provision exceeds that of hospital provision. This might be because in order to achieve a certain degree of 'success' (in terms of client welfare), placements need a great deal of peripatetic and other health care support, social services provision and so on. In this case, moving 'very dependent' clients from hospital to community settings will actually *raise* average cost from CH to CB for these clients and also raise the total cost of service provision.

Figure 10.1

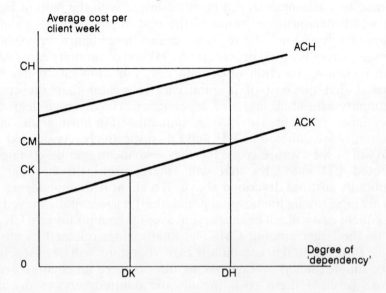

Average cost per client week

CH

CM

CK

ACH

ACK

Degree of 'dependency'

0   DK   DH

Figure 10.2

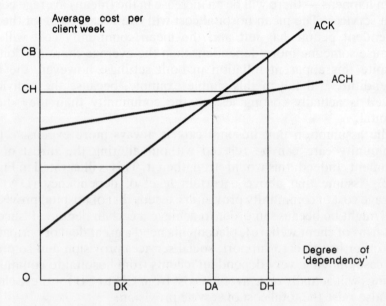

Average cost per client week

CB

CH

ACK

ACH

Degree of 'dependency'

O   DK   DA   DH

These two figures can explain in large measure the real cost inflation experienced by both hospital and community services in the last few years. As an increasingly large proportion of the hospital population moves into community provision the differences in average dependency and other characteristics will narrow, but individual client costs in the two settings will rise.

The observed cost inflation within the hospital setting will be picked up as part of the transition cost although it may not really be a transitional cost element itself, but simply the result of what has elsewhere been referred to as a 'creaming' process. Many hospitals and health authorities have begun to express disquiet over the selective resettlement of the 'best' patients. This disquiet arises for both financial reasons outlined above and in relation to the continuing role of the hospital. The hospital would necessarily become a more specialised service, perhaps for those with particular medical or behavioural problems. Hospitals are concerned that most of their resources would have moved with the resettled people, together with the more enthusiastic and the best qualified staff, leaving behind a 'second-rate' service for 'second-rate' people.

Irrespective of this 'creaming' process, hospital cost inflation is inevitable during a process of run-down towards eventual closure as the (quasi-fixed) overhead cost element has to be spread across a smaller and smaller number of in-patients.

This discussion gives a flavour of the problem: there is a clear need to relate cost to client characteristics and, of course, to other factors, particularly effectiveness. This can only be undertaken reliably within a comprehensive evaluative design and armed with appropriate multi-variate statistical techniques.

Conclusion

In this chapter we have briefly looked at some of the economic issues that arise — or should arise — in the debate on community care, particularly in view of the increasing pressure to take cost considerations into account. Such considerations can only be meaningful in the light of a proper cost-effectiveness study in which both sides of the equation are carefully examined. The variety of funding packages which arise in the Care in the Community projects provides illustrations of many general issues which are pertinent to the provision of long-term care in general. We have been able to highlight some of the issues such as the 'hidden' costs of community care, the problems of transfers and 'dowry' negotiations, and the pitfalls of too close a reliance on average cost measures. The assumption that community services for long-stay patients can be developed simply by transferring existing resources is unrealistic. *Genuine* community care policies require a *genuine* increase in resources.

11. Monitoring and evaluation

Chapter 3 pointed out that the monitoring of the initiative has not been a piece of hands-off research. The *Care in the Community* circular stipulated that the pilot programme would be monitored by the PSSRU, and one condition of receiving central funding was that projects should co-operate with the research team, by helping them to achieve reasonable access to clients, facilities and staff.

The PSSRU was commissioned by the DHSS to publicise the initiative, to monitor the projects and to provide a more detailed evaluation of the costs of community services and their effects on individuals. In terms of publicity or promotion, it was important to ensure that experience built up from the pilot projects would be disseminated widely. The publicity role consists of a newsletter published approximately twice yearly, seminars, conferences and the provision of general information in response to numerous requests.

Monitoring activities comprise regular visits, special conferences for project personnel and the reporting back of basic information on progress. Descriptive and narrative information about progress and problems are reported in the newsletter and at various conferences, in order that others may learn about the obstacles encountered in operations of this kind, together with some of the solutions which have been found.

For monitoring purposes we have collected descriptive information about what projects, at their inception, thought that they might be setting out to do. In practice it soon became clear that asking local

153

managers such questions, and asking them at meetings where several agencies sat at the same table, actually made them focus clearly, often apparently for the first time, on what management of the project would mean. In other words, the asking of such questions to some extent shaped the project itself. This was not entirely unintended. Conferences for project personnel have been held periodically throughout the years of the initiative, largely to enable them to exchange practice information, and for us to gather it. To some extent consensus views emerged from these (although this was not essential), and the first conference in particular (April 1984) influenced the research instrumentation developed by PSSRU.

We make a general distinction between monitoring and evaluation activities in the context of the Care in the Community programme. The information collected in monitoring is more likely to be routinely available from projects by the virtue of it being necessary for their own use. The time-scale of collection, analysis/synthesis and dissemination of information is much shorter and is, therefore, better able to be assimilated by schemes and used to influence practice. This brings monitoring close to an evaluation model often described as 'action research'. Evaluation activity is more likely to be based on a clear theoretical framework from which questions will be designed to test hypotheses. Monitoring information tends to be designed in order to meet practical and immediate needs.

Techniques and instruments employed in monitoring tend not to have been developed and tested in a rigorous scientific manner. Ease of use and manageability take higher priority than reliability and pre-coded formats. Information is often qualitative in form — for example, narrative reports of meetings, focused interviews and descriptions of care plans — as compared with the detailed quantitative information that is more prevalent in our evaluative work. Of course, the division between the use of qualitative and quantitative data is not totally clear-cut — many of the monitoring and research instruments and eventual evaluative conclusions contain both kinds of information. Many of our activities feed into both monitoring and evaluation and necessarily complement each other.

The evaluation framework

The evaluation is concerned with a number of questions which arise from the *Care in the Community* circular: 'Ministers wish to encourage a programme of pilot projects, to explore and evaluate different approaches to moving people and resources into community care. It will be important to demonstrate methods which are both beneficial to the

Box 11.1
Evaluation questions

1   What are the objectives of the initiative? Have they been achieved?

2   What are the objectives of individual pilot projects? Have they been achieved?

3   For what types of clients did projects intend to provide? How did experiences compare with intentions? Why did intention and actuality differ? How well did referral systems perform?

4   What are the implications of different staffing arrangements for the administration and running of the projects? What are the characteristics of staff recruited to projects (including previous employment)?

5   What is the relationship between the usage and style of case management arrangements and: organisational and agency context, project management structure and style, and other relevant factors? What factors in the case review process are identified as important by project staff? How effective is the case review process for setting and modifying individual clients' care plans?

6   What are the major obstacles in planning a pilot project? In implementation? In running? What means have been found to get around these various problems? What factors affect the speed with which projects get underway?

7   What means did projects use to prepare and persuade hospital patients to move into the community? What works best for what 'sort' of client?

8   What are the costs of community care? What is the distribution of the cost burden between agencies and individuals? What, for example, is the extent of the reliance on social security budgets?

9   What are the costs of hospital provision?

10 What are the set-up costs of community facilities? What 'front-loading' problems arise in establishing such services?

11 What are the sources of cost variation within and between community settings?

12 How do the costs of hospital and community care compare? To what extent are differences in cost (if there are any) attributable to differences in clientele? What are the implications of any cost differences (standardised or not for clientele differences) for the funding of community services?

13 How do the characteristics of clients change over time?

14 What factors account for changes in client characteristics between hospital and community settings?

15 What factors account for variations in output? Can the multiple dimensions of output be reduced to one or a small number of summary indicators?

16 In projects providing a range of community facilities, what factors affect the placement of clients in specific locations?

17 What factors and characteristics of clients are associated with the 'early loss' (return to hospital) of clients from community facilities?

18 Under what circumstances do clients engage in a greater variety of activities and spend more time being occupied?

19 What do the process, cost and outcome results tell us about the cost-effectiveness of alternative community care arrangements for the various client groups?

people concerned and cost-effective' (DHSS, 1983a, para. 11). From this we wish to ask of each project:

- Does it improve the well-being of clients?
- What does it cost?
- How does it work?

Our aim is to provide policy guidance about the circumstances in which cost-effective community services are provided to meet the needs of particular groups of long-stay hospital patients. In practice, of course, projects do not tackle the challenge at such a high level of generality, and useful policy guidance will be similarly much more specific, not least because different lessons may need to be drawn for different client groups. The evaluation agenda which spans these client group differences has been further elaborated by listing the most important groups of questions (see Box 11.1).

The research strategy comprises a modular framework in the sense that not all parts of it will be relevant to all of the projects. It is deliberately constructed at a level of generality which makes it suitable for the programme as a whole rather than for a particular scheme, and it can be modified for individual projects. To collect some of the more detailed information about the topics listed in Box 11.1 we depend heavily on the interest and participation of the projects themselves. To this end, we have gone to considerable lengths to consult projects and others in the field. We also aimed to develop some instruments which are useful to projects themselves. An example is the case review form, described below.

We also felt it was important to draw attention to the considerable enthusiasm for evaluation locally which could be supported by quite small amounts of new research money, targeted to individual schemes. In the event, both the Department and the Rowntree Trust accepted this advice and have funded additional studies which are more focused than the PSSRU approach could afford to be given its programme-wide responsibilities.

The broad framework of the investigation can be subdivided into four topics: *outcomes*, *services in practice*, *costs* and *process*. Although it may appear to be complicated and to require a large effort and commitment from project staff, its component parts are reasonably simple. Any single group of staff or clients will only be concerned with a few instruments. In some cases we ask project managers to complete forms or to participate in an interview, in others we question care staff. For some information we ask clients their views and make direct observations of service settings and the activities which take place there.

The general topics are suggested by the production of welfare model (Davies and Knapp, 1981; Knapp, 1984; Davies, 1985). This is an

156

analogy to the economic theory of production which has been developed in the PSSRU to take into account all aspects of the process of providing social care and related services and their consequences. It describes as 'inputs' both *resources* such as buildings and staff, and *non-resource* factors such as regime and management procedures, and characteristics of clients. Both 'intermediate' and 'final' outputs result from the production process. Final outputs are the ultimate goals of welfare provision, such as improvements in the quality of life of clients. Intermediate outputs are those which may be of interest in themselves but are essentially important only in the likelihood of their being associated with final outputs. Examples of these are the services received by clients and the quality of provision. The evaluation of the Care in the Community initiative aims to draw some conclusions about the relationships between the kinds of input and output in the projects.

In the following sections we will outline the principal features of the research instruments employed for each of the four topics, and describe how we are making use of them in practice (see Figure 11.1).

Outcomes

Outcomes, or results, of the projects form the major part of the 'effectiveness' side of the cost-effectiveness reckoning. The actual results will need to be compared with the desired results, or service objectives. The exact nature of those objectives may depend on whose point of view we take. Interested groups include the government, funding bodies including the DHSS, service managers, practitioners and (importantly) the clients themselves and their friends and relatives. We should always aim to be clear about whose perspective guides our approach.

The assessment of effectiveness is complex from any point of view. Most people would agree that services should aim to meet a range of different needs of their clients, such as material needs for shelter, warmth and nourishment, occupation or engagement in activity, satisfying social contact with other people, training for skills in daily living and the opportunity to exercise some choice and control in their lives.

Normalisation may also be an explicit objective of some projects, although it will not necessarily be so, and its meaning has frequently been misunderstood. Essentially, it concerns the value that society places on stigmatised groups of people, such as those with learning difficulties, such that they are not treated as *less worthy* than ordinary citizens. More recent interpretations of the normalisation principle tend to emphasise *positive discrimination* in favour of people with learning difficulties and

Figure 11.1
The research framework

Topic	Information collected	Method
Outcomes	Morale and life satisfaction	Client interview
	Skills and behaviour	Researchers interview care staff
	Social contacts	Care staff record
	Time budget	Care staff record
	Personal presentation	Researcher observation
	Significant events	Project record
Services in practice	Environment questionnaire	Staff complete
	Environment checklist	Researcher completes
	Background information and case review	Project record
	Staff record 1	Project manager completes
	Staff record 2	Individual staff complete
	Staff time budget	Individual staff complete
Costs	Service receipt questionnaire	Researchers interview care staff
	Service pricing	Researchers interview/ask from management
	Wards costing	
	Funding issues and transitional costs	Narrative information from visits and interviews
Process	Project plans and progress	Original application, project description documents, annual reports
	Project development and management	Researchers interview project managers and initiators
	Case management	Researchers interview case managers
	Case review	Project record
	Progress, problems and issues	Narrative from visits, interviews and conferences

consequently the provision of better-than-average services, in order to compensate for their position of disadvantage. Normalisation places particular emphasis on the need for opportunities to develop and maintain a broad range of skills in one's personal life. It also strongly favours the development of *individual* service packages, suited to the needs of a particular person. These features appear to be more important than the question of whether environments and settings are 'normal' or 'ordinary'.

Another way to describe the major objective of a service for people who leave hospital is the maintenance or improvement of their 'quality of life'. This is a difficult objective to define, but it is probably most usefully considered in terms of meeting the various needs of individuals, from material needs to more personal needs such as choice and privacy.

We aim to form a judgement about clients' quality of life, as far as possible in comparison with their previous life in hospital. Many different approaches to measuring this have been developed, each with its own advantages and disadvantages. But there is widespread consensus that a number of different domains of outcome should be included. We have adopted the following sets of outcome measures with the aim of covering all the client groups included in the pilot programme:

- Morale and life satisfaction
- Skills and behaviour
- Social contacts
- Daily activities
- Personal presentation
- Significant events

These measures are employed before the client leaves hospital and again when they have been living in the community for between nine months and a year. It is the *change* in clients' characteristics or circumstances over this period which gives us our indication of outcome.

Morale and life satisfaction. We place a high priority on finding out clients' views. We thus conduct an interview with the client in which we aim to ask about feelings, likes and dislikes, worries and so on. It is difficult to discover the opinions of some people, however, especially when their ability to communicate is limited. For some we tend to rely on non-verbal cues and attempt to back up our observations with other measures.

Few previous studies have attempted to measure the morale or satisfaction of people with mental illness or learning difficulties. Some have measured self-esteem via techniques such as the Kelly grid

(Fransella and Bannister, 1977); others have asked specific questions about circumstances, such as staff, other patients, free time and privacy. The degree of sophistication of instruments seems to be higher in work with elderly people, and a number of global measures of happiness have been developed. We have approached the problem eclectically. Our interview schedule is a combination of some standardised scales developed by other workers with questions of our own added to them.

The first section, of eight simple questions, serves a variety of purposes. It is intended to put the person at ease, as the questions are easily answered and lead in to the more difficult ones that follow. This approach is recommended by Sigelman and colleagues (1981) and Wyngaarden (1981) who have interviewed large numbers of people with learning difficulties. At the same time, we discover whether the person is likely to be able to answer many of the later questions, since they become increasingly more complex as the interview proceeds.

The next section is based partly on Seltzer and Seltzer's (1983) satisfaction questionnaire for people with learning difficulties and partly on Wykes' (1982) assessment of satisfaction with services. The questions are presented in an open-ended format, following the recommendation of Sigelman et al. (1981). Open-ended questions tend to elicit a lower overall response, but with greater validity than either a yes/no or a multiple choice format.

The third section, social contacts, is taken directly from the Interview Schedule for Social Interaction (Henderson, 1981), which is one of the few social network schedules to ask about *quality* of contacts as well as the overall number.

In section four, Cantrill's Ladder (1965) is added as a brief global measure of morale. The entire morale subscale of the Psychosocial Functioning Inventory (Feragne, Longabaugh and Stevenson, 1983), which is well validated and reasonably practical, is also employed. It was developed for use with elderly people but we have found it useful for a wider range of client groups.

The 12 'health' questions in section five comprise the depression inventory of Snaith, Ahmed, Melita and Hamilton (1971). This inventory was intended for use with the general population, to detect fairly short periods of depressive illness or prolonged periods of sadness, and is a useful addition to the assessment of morale. It is similar to the General Health Questionnaire, but is probably more appropriate for a population of varied age. The final question about health is taken from the General Household Survey of 1980 (OPCS, 1982).

Skills and behaviour. Here we interview a member of staff who knows the client well. The interview covers a broad range of self-care activities, domestic skills, physical health and mobility (such as use of public

160

transport and shopping), mental functioning, and behaviour problems. We have chosen to interview an informant rather than the clients themselves since — to give one example — symptoms tend to be under-reported and impairments in social functioning misrepresented by people suffering from schizophrenia.

It is important to monitor a person's behaviour and role performance. Indicators of their ability to survive in the world outside hospital include ability to look after themselves, perform everyday tasks such as shopping, and get along with others. Such abilities may improve following a rehabilitation or training programme, or with widening experience of community living. In addition, the progress of mental illness itself has to be monitored. It is dangerous to *assume* that a move from hospital will necessarily lead to an improvement in condition; indeed there may be some deterioration immediately following a move. (Some of these outcome domains will overlap. For instance, feeling sad and frequent crying are normally included in measures of symptoms, or mental functioning, although they would also be reported in a measure of morale and general satisfaction with life.)

For people with learning difficulties we need to have some repeated measure of skills and behaviour — to ensure that at least their skills do not deteriorate — although we do not have to assume that improved quality of life is necessarily paralleled by an improvement in skills. This very question, and in particular the extent to which handicapped people can be expected to improve their skills, is still a matter of some debate. It seems likely that in a new situation different opportunities may present themselves for demonstrating potential abilities, and even for learning some new ones. However, some people may develop too slowly, if at all, for our measures to record any change over the period of between nine and 12 months from discharge.

Existing schedules to measure skills and behaviour tend either to be too detailed and specific for our needs or to lack the sensitivity necessary to monitor changes. Most have been developed with a particular client group in mind, whereas we need to use one which will be suitable for a variety of people with mental illness or learning difficulties and elderly people. We have therefore taken a well-formed existing instrument — the Social Performance Scale — as a central core, to which extra items have been added from other schedules. This scale was developed in the Medical Research Council Unit at the Institute of Psychiatry, has been used in many research studies and is constantly being revised and updated. Using the September 1983 revision we will be able to compare scores on the Scale with other research studies. An earlier version is presented in the study reported by Wykes (1982).

Some aspects of mental and physical functioning, which fit concep-tually most neatly into this domain, are better assessed in an interview with the client, and so they are included in the morale and satisfaction interview. Examples of these are depression, subjective assessment of general health, and cognitive functioning.

Social contacts. We aim to obtain a record of social contacts over a limited period, particularly the frequency and nature of contacts with friends, relatives, members of the local community and care professionals such as doctors and occupational therapists. Such information gives an indication of the degree of social isolation, a factor often described as a classic feature of an impoverished institutional life.

To obtain information about a client's social contacts, a record form is completed by someone with good knowledge of their movements. The form spans a period of up to a month. Some clients who live in fairly independent circumstances are asked to complete their own record forms. Generally, however, most forms are completed by care staff. But because it is also important to know a client's view of the importance of their social contacts we have included some questions on contacts and friendships — and whether or not they are satisfactory — in the client interview.

Daily activities. We aim here for an objective record of activity — a measure of what a client is doing from moment to moment, whether occupied with a task, a leisure activity, interacting with another person or just doing nothing. It is commonly assumed that many people in institutions spend long periods of time doing nothing. This may or may not be correct. Our concern is to explore how the pattern of daily activities changes after the move from hospital to the community and how it varies between community settings.

The fullest description of activity would of course be obtained by detailed observation, on the basis of time-sampling at periods of, say, one or two minutes for a period of several days. This technique has been employed in several research projects, such as that of Dalgleish and Matthews (1981; see also Mansell, Jenkins, Felce and de Kock, 1984). Observations at this level of detail have not been possible in the Care in the Community programme but where possible we have employed a 'time budget' approach. A member of the care staff records the various activities of an individual client over a two-day period. In some projects the time periods were left open-ended, so that they would be determined by the client and the activity. In other projects observations are made at half-hourly intervals. In both cases behaviour is classified into six types of activity:

- essential functions, such as meals, washing, bathing, toilet, dentist, chiropody,
- work and occupational therapy,

162

- television and radio,
- other leisure activities,
- nothing or sleeping,
- social interaction.

The two techniques will be compared at the end of the study in terms of ease of use and quality of information. In a few projects the time budgets are supplemented with detailed observations carried out by a researcher. This will enable some estimation of the validity of recording made by care staff.

The most independent clients pose the greatest problems in the recording of activity. They tend to spend their time in a variety of settings, many of which will not be staffed. Some of these people have been asked to keep their own activity diaries, others are able to describe their day during the morale interview.

Personal presentation. We assess personal presentation ourselves, by observation. We are interested in whether clients look after themselves and take care over their appearance, at least to a standard which would pass as 'normal'. In some large hospitals, and sometimes in the community, people stand out as different by virtue of their ill-fitting clothing and unkempt appearance. This may influence the reactions of local people once someone moves into the community. For example, neighbours may be more willing to accept a group of clients if they look neat and cared for than if they look dirty, untidy and obviously unusual. This local reaction could have consequences for the eventual 'success' or 'failure' of a project. Whether or not this is the case, a change in the way people present themselves over time may be regarded as an outcome in itself. Different facilities place different degrees of emphasis on self-care and may vary in the availability of, for instance, person-alised clothing and mirrors.

We have therefore produced a checklist covering important aspects of personal presentation which would be obvious to anyone meeting a client for the first time. This covers the appropriateness and condition of clothing, cleanliness and general impression. Value assumptions are problematic here — perhaps more so than in most outcome dimensions. In addition, a research difficulty arises in that the context within which individuals present themselves is very relevant; the 'normal' style of dress may vary with different localities. Alternatively, people may, at least for a period of time, wish to assert their individuality by refusing to conform to conventional standards of appearance.

Significant events. We ask project staff to keep a record of the major events encountered by each client. Significant events or changes of plan during the project period are recorded by someone in close contact with them, such as a member of care staff or a case manager. Such events may include an illness, accident or return to hospital. The death of a close relative, for instance, would be likely to affect the client in some way. There may be nothing to record for many people.

Services in practice

The dimensions discussed above — morale, skills and behaviour, social contacts, daily activities, personal presentation and significant events — are all elements of final output. Changes along these dimensions are changes in the well-being of individual clients, and each of them is an explicit objective of either national or local policy. Intermediate outputs are slightly different. Rather than ends in themselves, these are means to ends. They include, therefore, the services provided by projects, gauged in terms of both quality and quantity. Thus the picture of each project needs to be built up from details of the main elements of the new services. This requires three things: a description of any accommodation provided, particularly the physical and social environments; second, the services received by individual clients; and third, information about the staff, their training and experience, and their responsibilities and job satisfaction.

Physical and social environment

Services are assessed in terms of the physical environment they provide and also the social environment, ambience or care regime. For this purpose we have developed an environment questionnaire for hospital wards, residential establishments in the community and centres for day-time and leisure activity. Items were developed from previous work in the field. A small number of key sources are particularly relevant. Raynes, Pratt and Roses (1979) developed a number of scales in their study of children's homes, including a Revised Resident Management Practices schedule based on earlier research and on Goffman's ideas about institutions. PASS is an elaborate schedule, developed in America, which requires extensive training to administer and which is based firmly on principles of normalisation. The Hospital and Hostel Practices Profile was originally designed by Apte (1968) and has since been used in revised form (see Wykes, 1982) to measure restrictiveness of regime. The questionnaire we employ is completed by a member of staff of the facility, often the person in charge. It is supplemented by a checklist, completed by a member of the research team, on which subjective impressions of physical facilities and certain aspects of regime are recorded.

Individual services received — case review

All of the 28 projects have been asked to complete a case review form for individual clients at intervals of approximately six months. It is intended that this will become a useful instrument for practice as well as being a research tool. The form was designed on the basis of Individual Programme Plans (Blunden, 1980) but with a greater emphasis on services and resources. It was developed by the PSSRU in conjunction with a small number of first-round projects. The form is not pre-coded but is structured in terms of areas of need, such as accommodation, personal care and education. The respondent (usually a case manager) is asked to record needs and problems, resources required and plans for action — both for staff and clients.

Projects keep copies of this form for their own use, and refer back to previous records at each review. It informs us about the services which are provided for individuals, other services which are planned and about any needs which cannot be met. Monitoring systems of this kind may prove to be very useful for service planning since they are able to generate information about group needs and point to directions for new developments. We have left the form open-ended but a coding framework for classification of types of service is being developed, to feed into the other parts of the analysis. Case review material will also be scrutinised in a longitudinal context, in order that evidence about processes of care planning in projects may be examined.

Staffing

A crucial part of the research agenda concerns project staff. We need to know about staff numbers (and ratios), the training and experience they have received, whether they have received special training for this project, and their duties. This information is collected on a staff record form, completed by project managers. It concerns all staff funded by the project and all others with a significant input, even though funded from elsewhere. Volunteers are also included. In this way we can develop an accurate picture of the total staffing needs of a project.

We are also interested in the opinions of those who care for project clients. Attitudes of staff have been shown to be associated with certain types of interaction with clients. A second record form is completed by individual members of staff, which covers some aspects of staff responsibility and patterns of communication. It also includes a short job satisfaction scale, based on previous research which isolated the most important factors (Dyer and Hoffenberg, 1975). This form is sent to us in confidence, in order to enable staff to relate their opinions and feelings without fear of the information reaching other members of the project.

165

In some projects the staff views of their responsibilities are supplemented by a time-budget survey of individual activities over a sample period of one week.

Costs

General issues about costs and their assessment were discussed in Chapter 10. In order to compare the costs of services, whether the community as an alternative to hospital, or between a variety of community settings, it is imperative to avoid some of the common pitfalls in cost assessment.

Comprehensive costings. All costs need to be taken into account whether or not they fall to the agency or project primarily responsible for a service. This means that costs incurred by local authorities (social services, education and housing departments), health authorities, social security agencies, voluntary organisations and, of course, clients and their relatives need to be included. The 'hidden' costs can often be as large if not larger than the directly observed costs of a particular facility, such as a hostel or residential establishment. The costing of hospital and community services therefore involves combining estimates of the resources used at each stage of each project for each client with valuations of the costs of those resources. When the data are analysed, a number of different calculations will be made of how the cost of projects falls on different agencies. For example, they will show the cost to *local authorities* of implementing Care in the Community, initially and in the longer term, so that authorities can decide whether they can afford to follow the pilot projects' example. They will also show the cost to the *public purse* of the facilities provided, compared with estimated hospital costs. This will show the extra public cost, if any, of community care, for comparison with benefits to patients transferred. The main bulk of analysis will be aimed at the assessment of the cost-effectiveness at the individual level of the many different processes of service intervention.

Moving beyond averages. Even if costing is comprehensive there is a danger that it will be based on average costs per patient rather than marginal costs. This frequently occurs when hospital costs are being considered. The need to move beyond average cost measures is crucial in relation to both hospital and community facilities. The first groups of clients moved from hospital settings into the community are likely to be rather less dependent than those that remain behind — in terms of skills, behavioural problems, physical characteristics and capabilities, etc. (In some instances it is *only* the more able people who are moved.)

166

Their hospital care will be costing — in both accounting and opportunity cost terms — rather less than the hospital average. The general point is that the characteristics of clients (such as level of ability, frequency and nature of the problem behaviour and age) have implications for the cost of services, so it is important to take them into account in any cost comparison.

Comparing like with like. For sensible cost comparisons to be made between hospital and community settings — and within the range of community programmes — a number of conditions need to be satisfied. Two are particularly relevant at the design stage of the evaluation: the breadth of the cost definition must be consistent in the two settings, and exogenous influences on the cost of a service or a complete package of services must be held constant or 'partialled-out' in so far as this is possible. The latter requires collection of detailed information on client characteristics and a number of other cost determinants. Some of the cost determinants have their primary influence at the facility level (hostel scale and occupancy, for example); others at the individual level (client skills and behaviour, for example).

Methodology

We are costing community services for individual clients. This involves, first, the collection of information about all services used by each client, including those provided by the project and those obtained from elsewhere. Later, prices are attached to the individual services, derived from the appropriate agency accounts.

Service receipt information is collected when the individual has been living in the community for between nine months and a year, that is, at the same time as we collect the follow-up outcome measures. A questionnaire — developed in conjunction with a costing study of psychiatric services in North East Thames Regional Health Authority — covers accommodation, staff cover, services attended, domiciliary visits, personal finance and informal care. Normally a member of staff who has case management responsibility for the client holds all of the important information but sometimes it is necessary to ask two or three different people. The prices of those services need to be collected locally, as national figures vary widely between parts of the country and between agencies. Most agencies already hold unit cost data of the type required, based on the financial year 1986–87.

Hospital costs will be disaggregated, as far as this is possible, to ward level. Research by Wright and Haycox (1984) has shown that ward costing is possible for approximately 75 per cent of total costs. Staffing accounts for most of this but services such as catering, laundry and maintenance must also be included. Costs for transport, drugs and medical equipment can be assessed by actual ward usage over a specified period. It is important to include any inputs from other agencies such as social services or education departments or the voluntary sector. Many hospitals are undergoing significant changes at this time — in factors such as capacity, occupancy and resident characteristics, staffing and level of maintenance — which will affect their costs. All reports of cost assessment should therefore reflect this shifting state and remind readers of the instability of current cost estimates.

Process

Any demonstration project worthy of its name is dynamic; it continues to evolve over time. We need to be able to capture this important facet of the initiative. If there are to be transferable lessons from the demonstration projects we need to know how they work. We are interested therefore in all levels, from the strategic organisation and development of the project to the most specific individual care plan, in the style and technique of working which are involved, and the goals and assumptions of organisers and carers which lie behind them. We must discover what processes of intervention at the level of actual service delivery are associated with the most cost-effective outcomes for clients.

Project management

In our evaluation of the initiative, we aim to provide a full account of how projects began, and of how they relate to the wider service context. This is a description of the implementation relationship between policy and action, an examination of the translation of ideas into practice.

Project documentation is the first material to feed into the process analysis. The questionnaires which formed the basis of applications to the DHSS for project funding, together with any available background papers, have been carefully examined. From these documents we have drawn up a detailed description of each project: its clients and their selection; buildings and services to be provided; staffing, management and financial arrangements. A meeting was held with each project at an early stage to agree on the details of the project description as a joint statement. This enabled us to clarify important aspects of the scheme and to set down its goals. A *protocol*, setting out the terms for co-operation between the project and the PSSRU, was also agreed early in the life of each project. We are also fortunate that the format for annual reports to the DHSS enables information to be presented in a structured manner. Syntheses of these reports provide a continuous assessment of progress during the pilot period and a final summary will be drawn together at the end. We shall return to the initial description at the end of the project in order to compare achievement with intention.

A further and important aspect of the process work is the questioning of key actors about the project, its plans and its progress. We interview project managers and others who played a significant part in its development, focusing on the context and history of the project; its philosophy and goals; management and administrative practices; problems, conflicts and lessons learned; and relations with the local community. We repeat some of these loosely-structured interviews throughout the three-year life of the project. Additional information about processes is obtained from a variety of less formal sources. Each visit to a project offers valuable insights, as do the twice-yearly conferences for projects. In this way we are able to trace the story of project development and the views of its main participants.

Case management

The case review system described earlier also forms part of our process analysis at the client level. Our analysis of completed forms looks not only at which services are received by each client but also at the method of assessment and review. Background information about the client tells us basic details such as age, length of stay in hospital and reason for admission (if known), while the case review form gives some detail about the case manager and the other people involved in making decisions.

Scrutiny of case review forms is supplemented by interviews with case managers. A focused interview — as for project managers — has been devised, in which we ask about important aspects of the case management role. It covers, for instance, employment, training and qualifications, caseload; areas of responsibility and how tasks are carried out; relationships with agencies and professions and general views about the work. We are particularly interested in the systems devised for assessment of individual need and the co-ordination of services, the ways in which projects ascertain the views of clients and their relatives, and how these can be used in conjunction with the views of professionals to produce optimal plans. We examine how case managers obtain and co-ordinate services for clients for whom they are responsible and the problems they encounter.

Providing new systems of community services for this type of client has scarcely been attempted on this scale before. From our studies we hope to derive useful lessons for others who may attempt similar

169

ventures. Even where mishaps occur or ideas cannot be implemented as planned, our descriptions should prove helpful, if only to warn others before similar mistakes are made elsewhere. They may also help other project initiators to place their own similar mistakes in perspective.

Implementation of the research design

The research framework outlined above is being used, then, as the basis for a longitudinal study. By starting in the hospitals and subsequently following the careers of clients in community services we will in effect be able to undertake a series of 'before–after' comparisons of individuals, the services they receive and the associated costs. But our research project can only go some way towards a full evaluation of effectiveness and cost-effectiveness. Ideally we would want to determine the extent to which observed changes in client well-being were attributable to the receipt of the service under consideration. We are not able to examine these changes in comparison with the alternative of 'doing nothing' — in this case, leaving the clients in their hospital settings — but we are able to compare effectiveness *across* the 28 pilot projects. Our evaluation is not, therefore, an effectiveness or cost-effectiveness comparison of hospital and community care, but a study of alternative ways of providing community living for discharged hospital patients. Clients in the projects were clearly not randomly selected, as the classic experimental design would require, but our research design is able to take advantage of a series of *natural* experiments in which similar clients are moved to *different* community settings in different areas of the country.

We do not dispute the need for research which compares hospital and community services, but our interests and our brief are rather different. The future of most mental handicap and psychiatric hospitals has by now largely been decided and set down in regional strategic plans. Many have been scheduled for closure or run-down. It follows that the most important policy question which we should aim to address is not *whether* certain long-stay hospital patients should be discharged, but into *what type* of community provision. We are able to compare different styles of working and services provided for clients with similar characteristics and thereby infer cost-effectiveness lessons. The main comparisons will be between change measures in different situations and settings. By the end of the pilot programme we will have collected information about a very large range of residential and other facilities, staff teams and so on which will be examined in relation to outcomes.

Beyond the measures of changes and their variation from project to project some control or comparison groups will be available in a few cases. In some projects, such as Darlington and Derby, which have research resources available locally, it has been possible to implement controlled studies in which comparisons may be made between clients within and outside the project.

It is clear from the foregoing that our choice of instrumentation was constrained to a degree by the multiplicity of requirements placed on it. It had to be applicable to a wide variety of people, from frail elderly persons to those with residual mental illnesses, to those with severe learning difficulties. It had to be transportable between 28 different project settings, brief and easy to use over large numbers of clients and yet sensitive enough to record detailed changes in particular characteristics. For a different type of task, say an in-depth study of one or two projects, we would probably have chosen differently. Despite these research blemishes and other lacunae, the evaluation of the Care in the Community initiative will be rich in information about how effective and cost-effective community services can be organised and delivered to meet the needs of both independent and dependent persons leaving long-stay hospitals. As the list of research questions in Box 11.1 graphically illustrates, the evaluation takes a very broad sweep in approaching the issues of effectiveness and cost-effectiveness and, although bolstered by quantitative measures of various kinds, the eventual answers will be greatly influenced by the close links maintained between researchers and projects over a period of years. This is certainly not 'hands off' research, nor does it conform to the demanding requirements of the controlled experiment so prevalent in outcome studies of psychiatric and related services. Nevertheless, at the end of the day, the evaluative research will offer unparalleled insights into the planning, implementation and consequences of 28 different community care projects.

12. Emerging issues

We have described the genesis of the Care in the Community initiative and its programme of 28 pilot projects, together with some of the obstacles and difficulties encountered during their planning and co-ordination, and the monitoring and evaluative frameworks that have been adopted. What issues have emerged now that projects are up and running?

The tremendous variety of types of care and models of organisation involved in the 28 pilot projects makes certain kinds of generalisation difficult. However, they enable general suggestions to be made over a wide range of important issues. Projects vary in their scale from those which deal with nearly 100 people, to others which deal with only three; from those which concentrate on only one facility (a hostel for people with learning difficulties for instance), to those, like Bolton's Neighbourhood Network, which cover all aspects of the lives of a large number of clients; and from those which regard themselves as testing new ideas in care to those which have consciously adopted well-tried procedures and styles of service delivery. Projects also vary in their managerial superstructure. Lead agencies have sometimes been the health authority, sometimes a local authority or voluntary body, and there have been cases not merely of joint initiation of schemes but also of continued genuine collaboration, and of collaboration forced by circumstances at the coal-face.

172

Progress and problems

Many of the emerging issues raised in this final chapter have already appeared in earlier chapters but have not been elaborated on. The focus, inevitably, is on problems which projects face since it is these which make the news; smooth running never makes the headlines. But it will be important at the end of the initiative — and it is important now — to emphasise the successes and achievements of the Care in the Community programme. The 28 projects have made real advances in their local areas. New community services which are jointly planned and implemented, which often include innovative practices, which always involve models of case management and review, and which are constructively monitored are — by their very existence — indicators of major achievement. As Tables 3.1 and 3.2 showed, by March 1987, 456 people had moved out to the community, out of a planned total of 896. This underestimates the true progress of the programme because the numbers of people involved accelerates in the later stages of the projects, and of course they continue after their central funding ceases. In very many other ways — particularly in influencing the quality of the lives of clients — the pilot projects are already giving every indication of success. However, we must really await the results of the outcome evaluation, and of other research questions, before hard and fast conclusions can be drawn. What follows, then, is biased toward some of the problems which seem to be both widespread and soluble with forethought.

Finance

Financial problems have been examined in Chapters 5 and 10. We have seen how initial delays in launching the pilot programme meant that some projects were unable to spend money straight away. It has not been possible for slippage to be carried over beyond the three years of central funding. A clear lesson from this is that demonstration projects need adequate planning time after the funding decision has been made in order to finalise details and to undertake preliminary administrative work.

Negotiation over the longer-term funding of schemes has been tortuous. The need for real growth in spending for services for the priority groups has begun to be recognised. As the Short Committee has said (House of Commons Social Services Committee, 1985), and as we will be able to test in our evaluative work, genuine community care appears to require a genuine increase in resources. The transfer of funds from health to local authorities has also required careful negotiation. Some agreements have been based on average hospital costs or some other — and no less arbitrary — proportion of hospital costings. Some transfers have been based on the cost of new services. Who is to fill the gap if transferred funds are not sufficient? The prospect of this gap can be a major disincentive.

Moving the least dependent people first may allow Care in the Community to start on the cheap. This, however, is the beginning of a vicious spiral of difficulties:

1   Small hospitals would be closed before large ones, because certain kinds of funds can only be recouped by closing entire institutions, so it makes economic sense to start with the smallest and therefore quickest.
2   The less dependent people would be moved out, leaving the more dependent who need the most intensive input from skilled professional staff.
3   The brighter staff would read the writing on the wall and the more marketable will have their talents bought up soonest. They would go to the new exciting services, not necessarily where the need is greatest.

The net effect could be disastrous: for many years a large residue of the most needy people would be looked after by the least talented staff in the worst institutions. But how do policies avoid the vicious spiral, and at whose expense? Planners for hospital and community services must consider these problems and devise strategies which look ahead beyond the immediate future.

Many community schemes have found their original estimates to be unrealistic. Many have needed more money, revenue for staffing in particular, since dependency needs have often been higher than expected. Capital costs have also escalated, due to rising house prices and additional building works for adaptations and refurbishing. Other areas of activity in developing services have proved unexpectedly high. Transport costs are a good example, particularly where the hospital is distant from the area of resettlement and project workers need to make frequent visits over the period of transition. Visits and outings are costly in mileage and in staff time.

Transitional costs of new schemes entail not only the 'double funding' required to put a new service in place before the old one can be removed, but additional activities and costs on top. These include administration and planning, developing staff teams and management systems, recruitment, training, acquisition of buildings, client assessment and rehabilitation training.

Obtaining the full social security benefit entitlements for clients has not been straightforward in all cases. Schemes which rely heavily on social security monies for their income will run into problems if occupancy falls for any reason. In addition, there are inconsistencies and grey areas within the benefits system, such as attendance allowance for which eligibility varies according to the discretion of the local office. Even within the same project some clients have been awarded this allowance while others with similar needs have been refused. Personal money is crucial for a good quality of life in the community and benefit levels can be hard for anyone to live on. Projects have often needed to subsidise their clients for large items or extras such as holidays.

The lack of incentives for clients to work, resulting from a benefit system which penalises part-time and low-wage earners, can be discouraging to good practice. The 'therapeutic earnings allowance' enables certain people to earn up to £26 (at 1987 levels) without losing their benefits, but many are not eligible. Some schemes have found ways of providing 'gifts' instead of money, but this is unsatisfactory as a long-term solution.

Excessive reliance on social security benefits to provide additional funding may, then, threaten the long-term stability of the care system. It may, on the other hand, have been the only (accidental) mechanism by which very substantial extra funding could have been concentrated on this relatively small area of the system. To put it differently, few governments have been forward in the provision of new money for new forms of community care. But where local entrepreneurship has legitimately used the social security system (although perhaps in ways which policy-makers did not intend) it is highly unlikely that the rug will be pulled from under their feet. When the system is altered, as it will be, ways will be found by central planners of continuing to support these ventures.

Time-scales

Nearly all projects have found that every step has taken far longer than was anticipated. This was partly because of the lottery aspect of applying for special project money, since many projects had to spend considerable time simply working out the details of their plans. Additionally, as we have seen, buildings have been a major source of delay. Many project managers have been continually surprised by the length of time it takes to design and erect buildings or have adaptations done. Builders have a tendency to be 'economical with the truth' and local authorities in particular often find the sustained concentration needed to make new premises happen simply beyond them. Over-optimism about how long the search for suitable sites and premises would take has probably contributed to the failure to provide housing on schedule. Committee cycles, planning permission and fire regulations (and the builder's men unaccountably being at another site) can make a three-year project a tiny step down the long road to travel before clients have anywhere to go. Eighteen months is probably a reasonable estimate of the time taken to buy, convert, furnish and equip existing buildings for project use, and new buildings take even longer.

But matters are not necessarily any easier if projects aim to move people into ordinary housing accommodation. Housing departments, after all, have their own priorities. Some housing officers are not particularly keen that people leaving hospital should take up scarce special needs housing. After all, a hospital place generally includes a roof over your head. If social services plan to move you to the community, should not social services provide a new roof as part of the planned package? In other words, at the very least, social services officials should consult their housing colleagues in the very early stages of planning a community care project.

The launching of the Care in the Community projects coincided with major changes in the regulations governing residential care and nursing homes. Last-minute changes were forced in the design of community facilities; for instance, in the sizes of bedrooms. Planning permission can be a minefield for anybody, of course. The ease with which it is granted seems to vary from district council to district council. Friends on the planning committee appear to make life a lot easier.

Fire officers too can be variable in their recommendations. Fire regulations themselves seem in some districts to be merely the starting point for protracted haggling. The ways in which obtrusive fire precautions can militate against a policy of normalisation are obvious: ordinary houses do not have red notices on the walls and double-thick spring-loaded doors. One also cannot help remembering that elderly people in homes are now many times as safe from fire as the average citizen; and that whilst no child has died in a fire in a school in recent years, several thousand have been badly injured by fire doors. Nevertheless, it has to be acknowledged that some former hospital patients are not amongst the most careful citizens. And project planners should know in advance that housing association and NHS properties have to meet very stringent building standards of all kinds. There is little excuse for the planner who is surprised by these requirements.

All things considered, many projects have ended up by making a compromise between the ideal buildings to meet the needs of their clients and those which happen to be available locally at an affordable price. This is obviously easier in areas where housing is plentiful and where the authorities involved already have resources which need to be used.

Staff recruitment has also been a problem in most areas. Some authorities have been unable to appoint, or even advertise, until a series of committees have met and approved the new posts — even though the money has been available. Later, attracting qualified staff has been vexatious. New community nurses, social workers and psychologists have all been slow to materialise, and in some places appointments have simply not been made at all. It may be that the services of good people are so much in demand that they have no need to incur the risks of short-term funded enterprises, although many 'mainstream' services face similar problems.

Whatever the reason for delays in projects, the effects on clients who have been prepared for a new life have ranged from disappointment to disaster. There have been several instances of patients deciding that they wish to remain in hospital after promised new homes have not materialised. In one case, a whole rehabilitation ward mutinied and refused to have anything more to do with community preparation. Tragically, there have also been a very few deaths in the programme, mostly of elderly people for whom the stress of a prolonged wait may have been too much. A few months of preparation before the move may be helpful for some, younger people with learning difficulties for instance, but for elderly people it is probably wise to shorten the preparation period and minimise the level of anxiety.

Projects ideally need to produce a management timetable from day one (to be revised as schedules alter, but to remain as a guideline), setting out what services they expect to deliver, to which clients, in what facilities, when, and (most of all) what has to be done in the intermediate stages to achieve these goals.

What does Care in the Community mean for hospitals?

National policy for the future of mental handicap and mental illness hospitals is, as we saw in Chapter 4, far from clear-cut. There is, let us say, a broad understanding that the large mental handicap hospitals will virtually all be closed by the end of the century. But it is explicitly not an objective of central government policy at the moment to close the mental illness hospitals. Closure is regarded as a secondary consequence of the development of community care (which certainly is an objective). The role of the hospital in the face of the growing problem of who will care for elderly people over the next 50 years is even more vexed.

Actual plans to close hospitals, furthermore, are made in difficult political contexts, by planners with one eye on the unions and the other on new developments in the health service — general management or whatever. Too often there has been a failure to recognise the paramount need to plan for the future of each individual patient, which in practice implies development of strategic systems which include safeguarding futures. The unfortunate result has been evidenced by stories in the press of destitute ex-patients sleeping rough or ending up in prisons. The opposite situation has occurred in some areas, that is the 'double booking' of certain individuals into parallel schemes run by the managing health district and the project.

The attitude of existing staff to the new service plans has been a cause for concern in some areas. Nursing and ancillary staff in particular can feel resentment and fear towards a community project which they may regard as a threat to their future livelihood, as indeed in many cases it really is. This may be exacerbated by the difference between hospital and field agency cultures, and their different models of care. Nurses' reactions stem from a combination of genuine concern — they may assume that project staff are untrained and ignorant — and the perceived threat to their own professional identity. Nurse training schools will also have to move to the community. Disbelief in the reality of the strategic plans can exacerbate feelings of insecurity (see Chapter 6).

Psychiatrists can be a difficult group to work alongside although some have made constructive suggestions and others have at times been leaders in the movement away from institutions. The objections some have made have been a mixture of the genuine and the defensive, no doubt shaped by different models of care which are employed by the different professions. Psychiatrists do wield considerable power, though, and can hold sway over major decisions and can veto discharges. Project staff have been refused access to wards in some cases.

Ancillary staff should not be forgotten although they are rarely included in decision-making, and are unrepresented on almost all planning bodies. There are some honourable exceptions where the unions have been consulted about closures. Another group which has often been ignored comprises the relatives of clients. There has been a backlash in favour of hospital care stimulated by relatives' groups such as Rescare. The importance of this should not be underestimated.

Progress in dealing with hospitals seems to be best achieved where all the relevant parties are consulted and made to feel involved at an early stage.

Project staff

Project staff, of course, can be moving into what to them is a completely different type of work. Their responsibilities may be breaking new ground entirely, or at least untried in that particular locality. It is therefore sometimes difficult for recruiters to know what they are looking for either in managers, co-ordinators, professionals or direct care staff. Personality and attitudes will often prove to be more important than qualifications and experience.

Many projects started out with the aim of recruiting a mixture of staff, from a variety of health service, social services and other backgrounds. The different conditions of employment and career structures in these agencies have become major obstacles to the employment of certain groups. For example, health service staff are eligible for retirement pensions some years earlier than social services staff. In addition, a move out of the health service for a few years would not confer any career gains if an individual ever wished to return. Considerations such as these have made it difficult for projects to recruit existing hospital staff — who frequently have the advantage of knowing the clients and the local context — and have sometimes led to organised refusal to co-operate with the project. Some relaxation of the rules from the centre could make life easier for community care development as a whole.

Project co-ordination and management are pivotal factors. The designation of a full- or nearly full-time co-ordinator at an early stage seems to have been enormously helpful in those projects which took this step. The co-ordinator could be involved in finalising project plans and liaising with other agencies such as housing. If the appointment of the full-time co-ordinator is left too late, or if those responsible for initiation of the scheme move away, the shape of the project is liable to change markedly from its original conception, and not necessarily for the better. As ideas turn into reality and new people make their mark so changes and developments are inevitable, but maintaining some continuity looks to be crucial.

Lines of accountability are not always clear in jointly-owned schemes. Some projects have designated co-ordinators in both health and social services, although line management responsibilities may still run in (at least) two different directions, to the project and to the mainsteam authority. Individual members of staff may find themselves torn between the project on the one hand and the mainstream (their official employer) on the other. Both are important: a project must operate in an internally consistent fashion, but it would be unwise for the project to stray too far from its parent body either. A few projects have needed to revise their management arrangements on a number of occasions during the course of central funding, and certainly thereafter, in the light of conflicting pressures from local line managers.

Staff training — and in particular joint training — is something of a vexed question at the present time. It is one of those questions that generates rather more heat than light. For example, the Somerset scheme had agreement at all levels in both the health service and social services to a joint training scheme. Although it is now in operation the English National Board for Nursing, Midwifery and Health Visitors and the Central Council for the Education and Training of Social Workers have been unable to reach agreement in order to approve it. This is clearly not a local problem. It is a national issue with which central government has failed to come to grips.

Just what sort of training is most appropriate, especially for front-line care staff, is not entirely clear. The lack of a formal qualification need not imply a lack of appropriate training. Indeed, many schemes have developed their own training package which they believe to be more useful than anything which can be bought in from elsewhere. It is worth repeating that most long-term care of dependent people has always been carried out by 'informal carers' who receive no training at all. Some training bodies now advocate a model in which all basic care is provided by unqualified people, with close support and back-up from established professionals.

High levels of stress are almost universal. Work in these projects seems to be demanding in a special way which is difficult to explain, but is probably to do with the many different kinds of stress which are encountered in the same day. Managers still face the demands (and, of course, rewards) of regular client contact, but must also exercise line-management responsibility for staff coming from a variety of back-grounds and with whom they are in constant close contact (a new skill for many). They additionally have to undertake budgetary planning (also new to many) and take responsibility for the success or otherwise of the whole venture. Multiple lines of accountability are the norm. All of this takes place within tight financial and time constraints, so managers need to have enough double vision to see all steps in a project both in tactical and strategic lights.

Front-line care staff who work in or manage the activities of, say, group homes are also subject to new stresses and anxieties. Relatively junior staff, who might previously have worked within the protective umbrella of a large institution, are suddenly in sole charge of a group of residents. Shift patterns can mean long and inconvenient hours, often in very intensive contact with the people in their care. Some projects have experienced an excessively high turnover of front-line staff, probably as a direct consequence of the stressful work pattern, especially where back-up and support are not well organised. Care staff are crucial resources on which hangs the success of a community project. They need effective supervision and support from the start. The opportunity for 'peer' supervision and support through staff meetings may also provide valuable guidance and reassurance.

Staff management structures and practices in new ventures such as these are also critical. Lines of communication and accountability have to be clear: something which is easily stated, but not so easily achieved. The structures of many projects have been established only gradually, subject to revision from time to time on the basis of experience.

Management staff turnover is a general feature of the health and social services and the set of pilot projects are no exception. In the final stages of several first-round projects, very able staff in key posts have moved on to other jobs. Nobody would criticise those individuals for sensibly planning their own careers. But the damage, however limited, which must ensue when projects fail to keep such people should perhaps be cause for concern. Some projects have found it hard to maintain their initial momentum and others have changed direction. Arguably though, the local loss may be to the general good. It must help the diffusion and development of community care ideas enormously that, for instance, a joint planner who became project co-ordinator of the Buckinghamshire mental illness scheme should use that experience to set up projects for people with learning difficulties in the West Country; that the leader of the community mental handicap team in Islington should take up the Directorship of the National Downs Syndrome Society; or closest to home, that the manager who played a formative role in the Chichester mental illness scheme should move to the project manager post in the Berkshire second-round project and then on to management of community mental health services in Cornwall.

Multidisciplinary working brings many advantages. Multidisciplinary teams have the advantage of putting different skills and perspectives to work on a problem, thus enabling a fuller picture of the individual to emerge, including their needs and the possible solutions. A perhaps surprising finding is that members of the multidisciplinary team, who necessarily have to spend more of their working hours in meetings, do not reduce their direct client contact. In fact, the reverse appears to be the case (Huxley, 1985). On the other side of the coin, establishment of an effective multidisciplinary team is never easy, and mistrust between professions does not disappear overnight. Most disciplines, at some level or other, continue to harbour insecurities about the exclusiveness of their particular skills and the existence of the niche which they occupy. Teams may find it necessary to delineate some duties very clearly so that each profession retains an area which is unique to them, while allowing other activities to be shared between members more or less equally.

There is scope for the introduction of new kinds of incentive, particularly for middle managers or team leaders, in the development of new patterns of care. Staff have been shown to respond with interest and enthusiasm to flexible arrangements in which responsibility (including budgetary responsibility) is devolved to those closer to the client (Challis and Davies, 1986; Davies and Challis, 1986).

The local context

Geographical factors have sometimes been paramount. Other things being equal, coterminosity of agency boundaries should simplify working arrangements. Warwickshire Social Services Department surely has a harder pitch to bat on, bowled at by four health authorities, than does Somerset, whose health service colleagues have virtually identical territory and whose headquarters are in the same building. But it would be a mistake to assume that the geographical factor dominates even in joint working at senior levels. At least as important seem to be the general climate of co-operation, the history of similar ventures in the area in the past, and the extent to which the political environment favours initiatives for particular client groups. Individual professionals, officers or politicians can be crucial catalysts.

Working within a network of existing agencies can be a complicated business, and becoming part of the 'community' as well makes the task positively Herculean. The position of staff who have to answer to two different lines of command has been mentioned already. The opposite pitfall to avoid is one of isolating the new project from established agencies, which has its own disadvantages.

Access to resources can be difficult where projects are isolated, and fundamental requirements such as day care and medical attention have not always been forthcoming. Even large projects which provide many services themselves will need to call on outside professional help occasionally or make use of, say, local education facilities. Nor will too much segregation help when clients want to mix with local people. A specialist service run entirely for people from hospital will continue to be seen as separate unless efforts are made to share some activities or facilities with people who already live in the area.

Case management and key worker systems are central to most of the pilot projects, with their concomitant case review and monitoring implications. These are particularly important in a multi-agency context, as we saw in Chapters 7 and 8.

Tapping into the primary health care services has not always been straightforward. Many GPs appear reluctant to take people they view as 'high risk' onto their panels. As the community care movement grows it may be necessary for some encouragement — financial or otherwise — to be given to GPs to accept responsibility for people with special needs, perhaps through family practitioner committees.

Public relations, with the local community in particular, were discussed in Chapter 6. There is no simple formula to guide a project in its approach to the neighbours but personal contact or silence seems to be preferred to, and more successful than, a 'high profile' announcement. This is consistent with maintaining the greatest possible degree of respect for the individual clients concerned. There is, however, still a need for further education of the general public about people who have a mental illness, learning difficulties or problems associated with ageing. A multiplicity of approaches is required if attitudes and levels of understanding are to improve, as they must, before it is too late.

Matters of practice

There are many issues around the possible models and techniques for providing community services for people with long-term needs. We can only raise a few of them here — those which have become prominent in the early days of the programme — but no doubt many more will emerge over the years to follow.

The much-debated notion of *normalisation* is in the forefront of almost all community care developments. Normalisation as a philosophy colours and influences all aspects of service delivery, outlined below and elsewhere. Debate over the degree of risk or safety that should be allowed is one example; how far to encourage someone to dress acceptably or fashionably is another. But this philosophy is probably misunderstood by many. The messengers of the normalisation creed, themselves, advise that it should not be written as a set of rules 'on tablets of stone', but rather used as a value base from which certain general principles emerge naturally. The fundamental notion is the full appreciation and valuation of all people as essentially human, instead of labelling some as a race apart, by virtue of handicap or other special characteristics. From this follow the rights of all to human dignity, choice, privacy (where desired) and services designed to fit one's individual configuration of needs. The normalisation philosophy has undoubtedly had a tremendous impact in the last few years on our perception of the services we provide for people and the ideals towards which they should aim.

But there are dangers, too. These arise particularly in the partial understanding of the principles which often encourages inflexible solutions — such as removal of childish possessions for all or the provision of uniformly ordinary housing — or, worse, the acceptance of poor standards of living because 'normal' people have to endure them — such as resettlement in deprived inner-city housing estates where no one is valued. Of course, it is impossible to disentangle one's own values from such judgements and this subjectivity has been a cause of much dispute.

The inclusion of a rehabilitation stage in the resettlement programme is another point on which opinions differ. Should all training (in daily living skills, dealing with people outside, and so on) take place in one's own home, once resettled — and thus minimise the number of disruptive moves — or does it make moving easier to take it in small steps at a time? Probably, as ever, different solutions suit different people.

A hospital, of course, has its own sense of 'community': the very sense of 'belongingness', of having a position and a role, greeting familiar faces on a walk around the grounds, dropping in to the social club or another ward for a chat and, perhaps, helping to deliver the post or the laundry. It will not be easy for community services to be fashioned to immediately replace all of this, though most of us manage to develop networks which are meaningful to us in different ways, and do not necessarily depend on immediate proximity to home. Developing a sense of 'community' *in* the community will take time. Perhaps the notion of 'asylum' should be raised at this point. Does it really describe a place or is it more a state of mind? And is a crowded hospital actually the best place to provide it?

Day care is an enormously important element of community care. It may be, for many people, a more powerful key to 'normal' life than their place of residence. One of the first questions we tend to ask, on meeting someone for the first time, is 'what do you do?', not 'where do you live?' Day care is also a most important route for getting to know people and making friends.

Day centres often combine (and confuse) the functions of training (for what?), work, education, occupation, entertainment, social interaction and leisure. People need most of these at different times and they should probably not necessarily be provided in the same setting. Some schemes have begun to develop innovative new forms of day care, such as work placements and home teaching. These may also enable people with learning difficulties, for instance, to become closely involved with ordinary members of the community. Colleges of further education can be another way to stimulate contact with 'normal' people. Some provide special needs classes while in other areas clients may, with a helper, attend ordinary classes.

Individual assessment and programme planning, which have been discussed at length in Chapter 8, are also critical features of any resettlement programme. It may be difficult to find the best way of asking clients what they want; staff are not always ready to *ask* rather than *tell* them what is best. The ideal procedure may take many weeks or months of intensive work. Review meetings can be inhibiting, and the requirement for the client to enact the dual roles of both participant and subject of the meeting can be a hard part for anyone to play. Some projects are worried that establishment of a review system is in itself insufficient for keeping alive the critical assessment of procedures. There is a danger that the system of meetings and filling forms could become just another routine procedure, to be carried out perfunctorily with the spirit behind it lost. A standard means for assessment and review is probably a necessary but not sufficient condition for effective appraisal of methods and achievements.

Relatives are also important for the success of community services and should be encouraged to participate in assessment, review and planning wherever possible. There can sometimes be conflicts of interest over which relatives should probably not have the casting vote. Where they want to be involved, it may be helpful to arrange meetings at times which suit them, and in places which are accessible.

This leads to the broader issue of client or citizen advocacy. It is almost inevitable, given the 1986 Disabled Persons Act and the plethora of local initiatives, that citizen advocacy will grow in importance as a means to safeguard the rights of vulnerable individuals and as a vital link with the community in its true sense. Whilst they may appear threatening, community projects should be looking to encourage local advocacy arrangements.

A partially objective commentator (such as a locally-based researcher) has proved to be valuable in some schemes by observing features, including problems, which are invisible to those staff who are deeply immersed in day-to-day work with clients and services. Feedback and discussion along the lines of 'action research' may help to dissolve some seemingly insoluble problems, indicate new directions for development or simply act as a sounding board to improve the understanding of what is happening in the project.

Pilot projects and their status

Demonstration projects and their functions were discussed in Chapter 3. We pointed out that demonstration or pilot programmes of this kind can, and perhaps should, be used to prepare the way for policy changes, to permit experimentation with methods and to carefully consider their relative usefulness. Ideally this would happen prior to any major redirection of policy. Yet during the pilot period of the Care in the Community initiative, policy events elsewhere have already joined and to an extent taken over the trail they were to blaze. Most localities already have strategic plans, at varying stages of development, for community services for the priority groups.

Many of the projects, nevertheless, have gone further down the community care road than the 'mainstream' services which surround them. Useful lessons are emerging, particularly at the level of specific methods of operation and techniques of implementation, even though the results of a full evaluation may appear too late for some authorities. The large projects, in particular, are exploring new strategies for the management and delivery of community services on a scale which has never before been attempted.

One central lesson to be learnt from the pilot projects already is that it is clearly possible for creative innovators to put together new packages of services, facilities and agencies — new at least to the local context in which they take place — which can be tailored to the individual needs of clients and which give every indication of enhancing the quality of life. Often these projects make use of funds from a variety of sources, sometimes intended by policy-makers for quite different ends. Housing and voluntary associations, for instance, can be prompted by entrepreneurial personnel from health or local authority to make interesting use of supplementary benefit entitlements to provide good new services for small numbers of clients.

It is also clear that, however much the non-statutory sector may grow in the foreseeable future, the main responsibility for those mentally disabled and elderly persons who need professional intervention will continue to lie with the statutory agencies. A sea-change in the nature of services to be delivered, as envisaged by all political parties and embodied in the Care in the Community programme, must therefore imply that the huge agencies involved should adapt to the new situation. Inevitable though this is, it will also be gradual. A conflict therefore already exists, and may well grow, between *creative marginal intervention* and *incremental adaptation of large organisations*. Reconciling, or at least diverting, this conflict is a major task for both local and national policy-makers. The projects themselves might most usefully merge into the mainstream, thus contributing to an incremental change. On the other hand, some will probably remain on the fringes as something of an oddity, continually reminding the main authorities of the alternatives which are possible.

Special projects, and changes of direction, need both impetus from the grassroots and commitment and authority from above if they are to succeed. Maintaining that impetus will be a challenge in the years to come; special projects and new ideas can stimulate enthusiasm at all levels, but the real questions about success must be asked once the novelty has worn off.

Whatever the future holds for the 28 projects with which we have had the privilege to work, we are certain of one thing. Our association with them prompts us to endorse the view expressed by the Audit Commission that there is no shortage of people in all walks of life who are committed to the development of community care. The stickiest problem for the future is perhaps that bright examples of innovation and enterprise remain outnumbered by others which exhibit a singular blend of confusion and inertia. The continuing challenge for public policy, therefore, is to find effective means of harnessing the talent and goodwill of those resourceful individuals and agencies who — given the opportunity — have proved they can make care in the community a reality.

186

References

R.Z. Apte (1968), *Halfway Houses: A New Dilemma in Community Care*, Bell, London.

Audit Commission (1986), *Making a Reality of Community Care*, HMSO, London.

C. Austin (1983), 'Case management in long-term care: options and opportunities', *Health and Social Work*, 8, 16–30.

R. Baker (1983), *A Rating Scale for Long Stay Patients*, Vine Publishing Co., Aberdeen.

M. Bayley (1973), *Mental Handicap and Community Care*, Routledge and Kegan Paul, London.

D.F. Beatrice (1981), 'Case management: a policy option for long-term care', in J. Callahan and S. Wallack (eds), *Reforming the Long-term Care System*, Lexington Books, Lexington, Mass.

C.E. Bennett and M.W. Metcalf (1987), 'Identifying people suitable for resettlement into community facilities', *Mental Handicap*, 15:4, 140–143.

R. Blunden (1980), 'Individual plans for mentally handicapped people: A draft procedural guide', Ely Hospital Applied Research Unit, Cardiff.

H. Cantrill (1965), *The Pattern of Human Concerns*, Rutgers University Press, New Brunswick, NJ.

P. Caragonne (1980), 'An analysis of the function of the case manager in four mental health social services settings', Report of the Case Management Research Project, Austin, Texas.

D.J. Challis and B.P. Davies (1984), 'Community care schemes: a development in the home care of the frail elderly', in J.G. Evans and F.I. Caird (eds), *Advanced Geriatric Medicine 4*, Pitman, London.

D.J. Challis and B.P. Davies (1986), *Case Management in Community Care*, Gower, Aldershot.

D.J. Challis and R. Shepherd (1983), 'An assessment of the potential for community living of mentally handicapped patients in hospital', *British Journal of Social Work*, 13, 501–520.

D.J. Challis, R. Chessum, J. Chesterman, R. Luckett and B. Woods (1988), 'Community care for the frail elderly: an urban experiment', *British Journal of Social Work*, 18 Supplement, 13–42.

C. Cleland and W. Chambers (1959), 'Experimental modification of attitudes as a function of an institutional tour', *American Journal of Mental Deficiency*, 64, 124.

Cmnd 3703 (1968), *Report of the Committee on Local Authority and Allied Personal Services (The Seebohm Report)*, HMSO, London.

Cmnd 4683 (1971), *Better Services for the Mentally Handicapped*, HMSO, London.

Cmnd 6233 (1975), *Better Services for the Mentally Ill*, HMSO, London.

Cmnd 7468 (1979), *Report of the Committee of Enquiry into Mental Handicap Nursing and Care (Jay Report)*, HMSO, London.

Cmnd 8173 (1981), *Growing Older*, HMSO, London.

Cmnd 9674 (1985), *Community Care*, Government Response to the Second Report from the Social Services Committee, 1984–85 Session, HMSO, London.

Comptroller and Auditor General (1981/2), *Report on Appropriation Accounts, 1981–82, Volume 8*, HMSO, London.

M. Dalgleish and R. Matthews (1981), 'Some effects of staffing levels and group size in the quality of day care for severely mentally handicapped adults', *British Journal of Mental Subnormality*, 17, 30–35.

B.P. Davies (1980), *The Cost-effectiveness Imperative, the Social Services, and Volunteers*, Occasional Paper No. 1, The Volunteer Centre, Berkhamsted.

B.P. Davies (1985), 'Production of welfare approach', PSSRU Discussion Paper 400, University of Kent at Canterbury.

B.P. Davies and D.J. Challis (1986), *Matching Resources to Needs in Community Care*, Gower, Aldershot.

B.P. Davies and M.R.J. Knapp (1981), *Old People's Homes and the Production of Welfare*, Routledge and Kegan Paul, London.

Department of Health and Social Security (1976), *Priorities for Health and Personal Social Services in England*, HMSO, London.

Department of Health and Social Security (1978), *A Happier Old Age*, HMSO, London.

Department of Health and Social Security (1980), *Mental Handicap: Progress, Problems and Priorities*, HMSO, London.

Department of Health and Social Security (1981a), *Care in the Community: A Consultative Document*, HMSO, London.

Department of Health and Social Security (1981b), *Community Care*, HMSO, London.

Department of Health and Social Security (1981c), *Care in Action*, HMSO, London.

Department of Health and Social Security (1983a), *Care in the Community*, HC(83)6, LAC(83)5, HMSO, London.

Department of Health and Social Security (1983b), 'Mental illness: policies for prevention, treatment, rehabilitation and care', Unpublished paper prepared by the Mental Illness Policy Division, March 1983, DHSS, London.

Department of Health and Social Security (1983c), *NHS Management Inquiry (Griffiths Report)*, DHSS, London.

Department of Health and Social Security (1985), *Progress in Partnership*, Report of the Working Group in Joint Planning, HMSO, London.

Department of Health and Social Security (1986a), 'Collaboration between the NHS, local government and voluntary organisations: joint planning and collaboration', draft circular, DHSS, London.

Department of Health and Social Security (1986b), *Public Expenditure on the Social Services: Response by the Government to the Fourth Report from the Social Services Committee Session 1985–86*, Cm. 27, HMSO, London.

Department of Health and Social Security (1987), *Public Support for Residential Care: Report of a Joint Central and Local Government Working Party (Firth Report)*, DHSS Leaflets, Stanmore, Middlesex.

K. DeWeaver and P.J. Johnson (1983), 'Case management in rural areas for the developmentally disabled', *Human Services in the Rural Environment*, 8:4, 23–31.

Disability Alliance (1987), *Disability Rights Handbook*, Disability Alliance, London.

J. Dyer and M. Hoffenberg (1975), 'Evaluating the quality of working life', in L. Davies and A. Cherns, *The Quality of Working Life, Vol. 1*, Free Press, Macmillan, New York.

A. Enthoven (1985), *Reflections on the Management of the National Health Service*, Occasional Paper 5, Nuffield Provincial Hospitals Trust, London.

S. Etherington (1984), 'Community mental health workers', *Open Mind*, 11, October–November.

M.A. Feragne, R. Longabaugh and J.F. Stevenson (1983), 'The Psychosocial Functioning Inventory', *Evaluation and the Health Professions*, 6:3, 25–48.

E. Ferlie (1982), 'Sourcebook of innovations in community care of the elderly', Discussion Paper 261, Personal Social Services Research Unit, University of Kent, Canterbury.

E.B. Ferlie, D.J. Challis and B.P. Davies (1985), 'Innovation in the care of the elderly: the role of joint finance', in A. Butler (ed.), *Ageing: Recent Advances and Creative Responses*, Croom Helm, London.

E.B. Ferlie, D.J. Challis and B.P. Davies (1988), *Efficiency-Improving Innovation in the Community Care of the Elderly*, Gower, Aldershot.

F. Fransella and D. Bannister (1977), *A Manual for the Repertory Grid Technique*, Academic Press, London.

J. Gibbons (1983), *Care of Schizophrenic Patients in the Community: Third Annual Report*, Royal South Hants Hospital, Southampton.

E. Goffman (1961), *Asylums*, Penguin, Harmondsworth.

E.M. Goldberg and R. Warburton (1979), *Ends and Means in Social Work*, Allen and Unwin, London.

Health Advisory Service (1982), *The Rising Tide: Developing Services for Mental Illness in Old Age*, NHS Health Advisory Service, London.

S. Henderson with D.G. Byrne and P. Duncan-Jones (1981), *Neurosis and the Social Environment*, Academic Press, Sydney.

House of Commons Committee of Public Accounts (1983), *Department of Health and Social Security: The Joint Funding of Care by the National Health Service and Local Government*, Eighth Report, Session 1982–83, HC 160, HMSO, London.

House of Commons Select Committee on the Social Services (1985), *Community Care: With special reference to adult mentally ill and mentally handicapped people*, House of Commons Paper 13–1, Session 1984–85, HMSO, London.

House of Commons Select Committee on the Social Services (1986), *Fourth Report: Public Expenditure on the Social Services*, HC 387, Session 1985–86, HMSO, London.

B. Hudson (1986), 'The nasty side of people's nature', *Health Service Journal*, 6 March, 319.

J. Humphreys, R. Blunden, C. Wilson, T. Newman and J. Pagler (1985), *Planning for Progress*, Research Report No. 18, Mental Handicap in Wales Applied Research Unit, University of Wales, Cardiff.

P. Huxley (1985), *Social Work Practice in Mental Health*, Gower, Aldershot.

J. Intagliata (1982), 'Improving the quality of community care for the chronically mentally disabled: the role of case management', *Schizophrenia Bulletin*, 8:4, 655–674.

P. Johnson and A. Rubin (1983), 'Case management in mental health: a social work domain?', *Social Work*, January/February, 49–55.

K. Jones (1984), *Ideas on Institutions: Analysing the Literature on Long-term Care and Custody*, Routledge and Kegan Paul, London.

K. Jones, J. Brown and J. Bradshaw (1978), *Issues in Social Policy*, Routledge and Kegan Paul, London.

B. Kenny and T. Whitehead (1973), *Insight: A Guide to Psychiatry and the Psychiatric Services*, Croom Helm, London.

M. Knapp (1984), *The Economics of Social Care*, Macmillan, London.

N. Korman (1984), 'Paying for community care', *Health and Social Services Journal*, 18 October, 1238–1240.

L. Kurtz, D. Bagarozzi and L. Pollane (1984), 'Case management in mental health', *Health and Social Work*, 9:3, 201–211.

A. Kushlick, R. Blunden and G. Cox (1973), 'A method for rating behaviour characteristics for use in large-scale surveys of mental handicap', *Psychological Medicine*, 3, 466–478.

N. Kyle and V. Roche (1983), 'Individual programme plans and behaviour modification', *Mental Handicap*, 11, 17–19.

H. Lamb (1980), 'Therapist case managers: more than brokers of services', *Hospital and Community Psychiatry*, 31, 762–764.

A. Lehman, S. Reed and S. Possidente (1983), 'Priorities for long-term care: comments from board-and-care residents', *Psychiatric Quarterly*, 54:3, 181–189.

A. LeUnes, L. Christiansen and D. Wilkerson (1975), 'Institutional tour effects on attitudes related to mental retardation', *American Journal of Mental Deficiency*, 79, 732–735.

J. Mansell, J. Jenkins, D. Felce and U. de Kock (1984), 'Measuring the activity of severely and profoundly mentally handicapped adults in ordinary housing', *Behaviour Research and Therapy*, 22:1, 23–29.

191

R. McConkey, B. McCormack and M. Naughton (1983a), 'A national survey of young people's perceptions of mentally handicapped adults', *Journal of Mental Deficiency Research*, 27:3, 171–185.

R. McConkey, B. McCormack and M. Naughton (1983b), 'Changing young people's perceptions of mentally handicapped adults', *Journal of Mental Deficiency Research*, 27, 279–290.

R. McConkey and B. McCormack (1984), 'Changing attitudes to people who are disabled', *Mental Handicap*, 12:3, 112–114.

F.W. Martin (1984), *Between the Acts: Community Mental Health Services 1959–1983*, Nuffield Provincial Hospitals Trust, London.

D. Mechanic (1969), *Mental Health and Social Policy*, Prentice Hall, Englewood Cliffs, NJ.

P. Morris (1969), *Put Away*, Routledge and Kegan Paul, London.

National Association for Social Work (1984), *Standards and Guidelines for Social Work Case Management for the Functionally Impaired*, NASW, Maryland.

National Development Team for Mentally Handicapped People (1982), *Third Report*, HMSO, London.

Office of Population Censuses and Surveys (1982), *General Household Survey, 1980*, HMSO, London.

Office of Population Censuses and Surveys (1983), *OPCS Monitor PP2*, 83/1, HMSO, London.

J. Pahl and L. Quine (1984), 'Families with mentally handicapped children: A study of stress and service response', Health Services Research Unit, University of Kent, Canterbury.

A. Pattie and C. Gilleard (1979), *Manual of the Clifton Assessment Procedures for the Elderly*, Hodder and Stoughton, Sevenoaks.

S. Pelletier (1983), 'Developmental disabilities programs', in L.C. Sanborn (ed.), *Case Management in Mental Health Services*, Haworth Press, New York.

I. Raafat (1986), 'From hospital care to hostel residency', *Health Services Journal*, 22 May, 701.

S. Ramon (1982), 'The logic of pragmatism in mental health policy', *Critical Social Policy*, 2:2, 38–54.

N. Raynes, M. Pratt and S. Roses (1979), *Organisational Structure and Care of the Mentally Retarded*, Croom Helm, London.

B. Robb (1967), *Sans Everything*, Nelson, London.

G. Room (1983), 'The politics of evaluation: the European Programme', *Journal of Social Policy*, 12:2, 145–164.

A. Scull (1977), *Decarceration: Community Treatment and the Deviant — A Radical View*, Prentice Hall, Englewood Cliffs, NJ.

G. Seltzer and M. Seltzer (1983), 'Satisfaction questionnaire', Paper presented at the American Association of Mental Deficiency annual meeting on Residential Satisfaction and Community Adjustment.

M. Seltzer (1984), 'Correlates of community opposition to community residences for mentally retarded persons', *American Journal of Mental Deficiency*, 89, 1–8.

C.K. Sigelman, C.J. Schoenrock, J.L. Winer, C.L. Spanhel, S.G. Hromas, P.W. Martin, E.C. Budd and G.J. Bensberg (1981), 'Issues in interviewing mentally retarded persons: an empirical study', in R.H. Bruininks, C.E. Meyers, B.B. Sigford and K.C. Lakin (eds), *Deinstitutionalization and Community Adjustment of Mentally Retarded People*, AAMD Monograph No. 4, American Association of Mental Deficiency, Washington DC.

J. Sinson (1985), *Attitudes to Downs Syndrome*, Mental Health Foundation, London.

R.P. Snaith, S.N. Ahmed, S. Melita and M. Hamilton (1971), 'Assessment of the severity of primary depressive illness', *Psychological Medicine*, 1, 143–149.

P. Solomon, B. Gordon and J. Davis (1984), 'Assessing the service needs of the discharged psychiatric patient', *Social Work in Health Care*, 10:1, 61–69.

R.M. Steinberg and G.W. Carter (1983), *Case Management and the Elderly*, Lexington, Mass.

L. Sterthous (1983), *Case Management: Variations on a Theme*, Technical Assistance Monograph, Mid-Atlantic Long-term Care Gerontology Center, Temple University, Philadelphia, Penn.

G.C. Tooth and E. Brooke (1961), 'Trends in the mental hospital population and their effect on future planning', *The Lancet*, 1, 710–713.

P. Townsend (1962), *The Last Refuge*, Routledge and Kegan Paul, London.

A. Tyne (1981), 'The principle of normalisation' (adapted from J. O'Brien), Campaign for Mentally Handicapped People, London.

A. Walker (1982), *Community Care: The Family, the State and Social Policy*, Blackwell/Robertson, Oxford.

A. Webb and G. Wistow (1982), 'The personal social services: Trends in expenditure and provision', Working Paper in Social Administration No. 5, Loughborough University.

A. Webb and G. Wistow (1985), *Planning, Need and Scarcity*, Allen and Unwin, London.

J.K. Wing and G.W. Brown (1970), *Institutionalisation and Schizophrenia: A Comparative Study of Three Mental Hospitals 1960–1968*, Cambridge University Press, Cambridge.

G. Wistow (1982), 'Collaboration between health and local authorities: why is it necessary?', *Social Policy and Administration*, 16, 44–62.

G. Wistow (1983), 'Joint finance and community care: have the incentives worked?', *Public Money*, 3, September, 33–37.

G. Wistow and B. Hardy (1986), 'Transferring care: can financial incentives work?', in A. Harrison and J. Gretton (eds), *Health Care UK 1986*, Policy Journals, London.

L. Wray and C. Wieck (1985), 'Moving persons with developmental disabilities toward less restrictive environments through case management', in K. Lakin and R. Bruinks (eds), *Strategies for Achieving Community Integration of Developmentally Disabled Citizens*, Brookes, Baltimore.

K. Wright and A. Haycox (1984), 'Public sector costs of caring for mentally handicapped persons in a large hospital', Centre for Health Economics, University of York, York.

T. Wykes (1982), 'A hostel-ward for "new" long-stay patients: an evaluative study of a "ward in a house"', in J.K. Wing (ed.), 'Long term community care: experience in a London Borough', *Psychological Medicine*, Monograph Supplement, 57–97.

M. Wyngaarden (1981), 'Interviewing mentally retarded clients: issues and strategies', in R.H. Bruininks, C.E. Meyers, B.B. Sigford and K.C. Lakin (eds), *Deinstitutionalization and Community Adjustment of Mentally Retarded People*, AAMD Monograph No. 4, American Association of Mental Deficiency, Washington DC.

Author index

195

Subject index

case review, 8-14, 90, 107, 127, 128, 155, 156, 158, 165, 169, 182
caseload, 102, 104, 108, 110, 169
catchment area, 56, 61
census, 54, 116
central initiatives, 29, 33, 44, 46
Chichester project, 5, 11, 42, 57, 59, 71, 119, 131, 135, 181
children, 10, 16, 22, 32, 33, 34, 37, 44, 49, 50, 87, 88, 135
chiropody, 127, 162
choice, 159, 183
chronic illness, 18, 57, 102
citizen, client as, 50, 51, 92, 128, 157, 176, 185
collaboration (*see also* joint working), 23, 24, 25, 27, 28, 64, 71, 172
college, 138, 184
community mental handicap team, 8-10, 50, 54
community psychiatric nurse, 59, 63, 124
conferences, 153, 154, 169
co-ordination of services, 30, 33, 57, 100, 102, 103, 105, 106, 107, 109, 111, 113, 114, 124, 125, 139, 169
core and cluster, 9, 10, 11, 52, 54, 176
cost-benefit, 27
cost-effectiveness, 21, 23, 32, 39, 64, 110, 140-52, 168, 171
costs, hidden, 134, 146, 166
counselling, 14, 33, 96, 103
Coventry project, 6, 13, 44, 66, 67, 68

Darlington project, 6, 13, 44, 65, 66, 67, 68, 116, 124, 127, 170
day care, 8-14, 37, 52, 54, 56, 112, 123, 127, 130, 137, 138, 146, 182, 184
day centre, 8, 9, 11, 12, 13, 14, 51, 54, 58, 61, 62, 68, 96, 184
death, 14, 164, 177
delay in getting project started, 41, 46, 66, 72, 75, 86, 131, 133, 134, 135, 173, 175, 177
dementia, 118
demonstration projects, 32, 33, 43, 46, 97, 114, 116, 122, 168, 173, 185
Department of Health and Social Security (DHSS), 2, 3, 32, 33, 34, 36, 38, 39, 41, 43, 44, 45, 46, 48, 54, 56, 61, 64, 65, 77, 132, 133, 134, 135, 141, 144, 153, 157, 168
dependency level, 14, 83, 115, 148, 149

Derby project, 4, 8, 42, 74, 78, 115, 122, 124, 126, 127, 135, 136, 137, 144, 170
dowry payments, 83, 142, 144, 147, 148, 151
drugs, 21, 168

education, 8, 9, 10, 12, 22, 27, 37, 44, 50, 51, 77, 87, 94, 96, 107, 127, 137, 138, 165, 166, 182, 184
efficiency, 98, 99, 100, 101, 106, 108, 141
elderly, 13, 14, 16, 22, 23, 28, 30, 34, 38, 42, 44, 46, 63-8, 76, 79-80, 90, 92, 95, 99, 105, 107, 108, 116, 119, 121, 129, 132, 137, 141, 145, 146, 160, 161, 176, 177, 186
elderly mentally infirm, 14, 27, 42, 44, 56, 63-8, 130
eligibility criteria for clients, 97, 114
eligibility criteria for projects, 46
employment, 9, 51, 57, 58, 96, 112, 133, 135
environment questionnaire, 164
evaluation of projects by PSSRU, 15, 32, 33, 34, 36, 38, 40, 41, 43, 45, 81, 141, 143, 145, 153-71, 172
experimentation, 32-3, 170, 185

families, 11, 16, 22, 27, 37, 49, 51, 55, 87-90, 106, 121, 129
fire precautions, 131, 175, 176
flats, 8, 10, 11, 12, 55, 74, 132
follow-up, 106, 167
foster parents, 10, 135
friendship, 92, 121, 131, 162
furniture, 10, 88, 133
further education, 8, 9, 127, 137, 138, 184

general management, 32-3, 177
general practitioner (GP), 65, 93, 182
geographical criteria for selection of clients, 100, 117, 119
geographical spread of projects, 37, 46-7
Glossop project, 4, 10, 44, 135
Greenwich project, 6, 11, 44, 55, 59, 118, 120, 121
group home, 11, 12, 57, 74, 91, 119, 134, 180

Health Advisory Service, 64
Health Service Commission, 91
Hillingdon project, 7, 14, 30, 44, 66, 67

nursing home, 30, 65, 144, 176

occupational therapy, 8, 58, 62-3, 81, 120, 162
Ombudsman, 91
opposition to project, 69, 72, 89-90, 91, 93
ordinary housing, 6, 8, 10, 11, 13, 30, 37, 58, 130, 146, 176, 183
outcomes, 155, 156, 157-64, 167, 170
output efficiency, 100

paramedical, 59
partnership, 28, 74, 78
peer supervision, 110, 180
pensions, 179
Personal Social Services Research Unit (PSSRU), 1, 2, 7, 32, 34, 35, 36, 38, 40, 41, 43, 44, 45, 48, 67, 77, 80, 81, 143, 145, 153, 154, 156, 157, 165
philosophy of care, 17, 23, 55, 60, 81, 135, 169, 183
physiotherapy/physiotherapist, 59, 75, 127
planning permission, 90, 91, 175, 176
political commitment, 79
prevention of hospital admission, 64
prevention of mental illness, 22
priority groups, 25-6, 27, 28, 68-9, 173, 185
privacy, 58, 98, 131, 159, 160, 183
private sector, 64, 65, 130
production of welfare, 15, 34, 36, 40, 156-7
project co-ordinator/co-ordination, 35, 38, 77-8, 123, 179, 181
promotion by PSSRU, 36, 43, 45, 153
property market, 91
protocol, 168
psychiatry, 21, 65, 161
psychogeriatric, 6, 65
psychology, 63, 104, 105, 113
psychotropic drugs, 19
public relations, 15, 61, 62, 82-94, 118, 122, 182
publicity, 121, 153
pump-priming money, 26, 66, 72
purpose-built accommodation, 7, 10, 130

qualifications of staff, 88, 102, 126, 178, 180

radio, 62, 94, 163

reality orientation, 7, 14, 136
recreation, 9, 12, 51, 56, 58, 138
recruitment of helpers, 108
recruitment of staff, 60, 86, 174, 176
referral of clients, 67, 99, 101, 107, 115, 116, 117, 118, 119, 136
Registered Homes Act, 90, 132
rehabilitation, 5, 6, 12, 53, 57, 58, 60, 63, 64, 71, 72, 73, 84, 85, 96, 116, 118, 119, 120, 121, 122-3, 124, 131, 135, 148, 161, 174, 177, 183
relatives, 4, 14, 67, 68, 78, 87-90, 96, 120, 121, 122, 141, 145, 146, 157, 162, 166, 169, 178, 185
reminiscence therapy, 7, 14, 137
resettlement worker, 9, 60, 119, 124
residential care, 4, 30, 37, 41, 52, 64, 65, 66, 99, 108, 109, 114, 137, 144, 176
resource centre, 4, 5, 6, 8, 9, 138
revenue, 4, 26, 28, 69, 83, 132-4
review meetings, 184
rights, 4, 40, 49, 51, 93, 98, 120, 132, 183, 185
risk, 28, 98, 131, 183
rural training, 8, 50, 77, 127, 137

salary scale, 84
savings, 26, 28, 56, 66, 73, 74, 99, 142, 144, 145, 146-7, 149
scandals, 21
schizophrenia, 11, 12, 19, 58, 112, 118, 161
segregation, 19, 49, 182
selection of carers, 132
selection of clients, 58, 59, 60, 67, 72, 100, 114, 115, 118, 119-23, 124, 168
selection of projects, 7, 35, 38, 41, 45, 46, 70, 71
self-advocacy, 5, 9
seminar organised by PSSRU, 36, 38, 41, 43, 153
sheltered housing, 6, 8, 12, 13, 37, 65-6
shortlist of projects, 35, 38
skills and behaviour, 161, 164, 167
slippage, 173
social change, 19, 22
social contacts, 160, 162, 164
social security, 28, 29, 30, 71, 132-4, 142, 144, 146, 155, 166, 174-5
Social Services Committee, 28, 33, 141, 173
social work/workers, 8, 11, 12, 16, 22, 54, 59, 60, 62-3, 65, 84, 98, 105, 106,